ECONOMIC DEVELOPMENT AND INTERNATIONAL TRADE

Economic Development and International Trade

Edited by
David Greenaway

St. Martin's Press New York

First published in the United States of America in 1988

Printed in Hong Kong

ISBN 0–312–01588–7

Library of Congress Cataloging-in-Publication Data
Economic development and international trade/edited by David
Greenaway.
p.   cm.
Bibliography: p.
Includes index.
ISBN 0–312–01588–7: $30.00 (est.)
1. Commerce.   2. Economic development.   3. Developing
countries–Economic policy.   I. Greenaway, David.
HF1008.E27 1988
382—dc19
87–25629   CIP

Contents

LIST OF TABLES   vii

LIST OF FIGURES   ix

EDITOR'S PREFACE   x

NOTES ON THE CONTRIBUTORS   xi

1   ECONOMIC DEVELOPMENT AND INTERNATIONAL TRADE: AN INTRODUCTION
    David Greenaway   1

2   TRADE PERFORMANCE AS AN INDICATOR OF COMPARATIVE ADVANTAGE
    Robert H. Ballance   6

3   TRADE AS AN ENGINE OF GROWTH: THEORY AND EVIDENCE
    James Riedel   25

4   TRADE STRATEGIES AND ECONOMIC DEVELOPMENT: THEORY AND EVIDENCE
    Chris Milner   55

5   EVALUATING THE STRUCTURE OF PROTECTION IN LESS DEVELOPED COUNTRIES
    David Greenaway   77

6   EXPORT INSTABILITY AND GROWTH PERFORMANCE
    A. I. MacBean and D. T. Nguyen   95

7   THE DEBATE OVER TRENDS IN THE TERMS OF TRADE
    David Sapsford   117

8   INTRA-FIRM TRADE AND THE DEVELOPING COUNTRIES
    Mark Casson and Robert D. Pearce   132

9   EXPORT PROCESSING ZONES IN DEVELOPING COUNTRIES: THEORY AND EMPIRICAL EVIDENCE
    V. N. Balasubramanyam   157

v

10 TRADE AND AID
    Paul Mosley   166

11 REVENUE IMPLICATIONS OF TRADE TAXES
    G. K. Shaw   174

    END-NOTES   188

    REFERENCES   195

    AUTHOR INDEX   206

    SUBJECT INDEX   209

List of Tables

1.1   The growth of trade and output   2

2.1   Comparative performance in Brazilian and South Korean steel industries, 1979–80   11

2.2   Comparative advantage by stage of processing: textiles and apparel, 1979–80   17

2.3   Exports with a marked *RCA* in selected groups of countries   22

3.1   Average annual rates of growth of real GDP by industrial origin in developing countries, 1950–80   36

3.2   Composition of imports by end use, developed and developing countries, 1970 and 1980   39

3.3   Structure of developing-country exports, selected years, 1955–82   41

3.4   Shares of broadly non-competing and directly competing developing-country exports of non-fuel primary commodities to developed countries   47

3.5   Shares of developing countries in apparent consumption of manufactured goods in industrialised countries   48

3.6   *Ex post* elasticities of export volume of developing countries with respect to real income in developing countries   49

3.7   *Ex post* elasticities for food exports of developing countries with respect to real income in developed countries   50

3.8   Variance and covariance of price and quantity of selected food exports from developing countries, 1960   51

4.1   A cross-country comparison of trade regime bias   58

4.2   Incentives to sales in domestic and export markets   58

4.3   'Measured' import substitution for selected countries, 1948–65   60

4.4   Growth of manufactured exports for a sample of semi-industrial countries   61

5.1   Evidence on effective protection in LDCs and NICs   83

5.2   Estimates of the incidence of protection   92

6.1 Manufactures as a percentage of merchandise exports 97
6.2 Effects of export instability on economic growth: a
    summary of cross-country results 115
7.1 Estimated long-run trend growth rates in NBTT 122
7.2 Further estimates of long-run trend growth rates in NBTT 124
7.3 Sub-period estimates 127
7.4 Some new evidence on NBTT 129
8.1 Factors affecting the propensity to internalise intermediate
    product trade 137
8.2 Comparative growth rates for the dollar value of OECD
    exports of fully assembled products and their components
    to the world 140
8.3 An assessment of the importance of trade in parts and
    components in the motor vehicle and office machinery
    industries 141
8.4 Average annual percentage growth of US imports under
    tariff provisions 806.30/807.00, 1969–81 143
8.5 Value and structure of US imports under tariff provisions
    806.30/807.00, 1969–81 144
8.6 US imports under tariff provisions 806.30/807.00, 1969–83,
    analysed by country of export 145
8.7 Structure of sales of US foreign affiliates by industry,
    1977–82 147
8.8 Structure of purchases by US foreign affiliates from the
    US, by industry, 1977–82 148
8.9 Structure of sales of US foreign affiliates by country,
    1977–82 154
11.1 Trade taxes, openness and income per capita 175

List of Figures

3.1	The trade engine	29
3.2	Average annual rates of growth of real GDP and real per capita GDP in developed and developing countries, 1950–80	35
3.3	Index of manufacturing production (average annual rate of growth)	37
3.4	Share of manufacturing in GDP in developed and developing countries, 1950–80	38
3.5	Average export structure for total sample of LDCs (54 countries)	42
3.6	Average export structure for balanced exporters (11 countries)	43
3.7	Average export structure for African primary exporters (20 countries)	44
3.8	Average export structure for non-African primary exporters (23 countries)	45
4.1	Static gains from trade	66
5.1	The incidence of protection	88
7.1	Long-run trend in NBTT	131
10.1	Approximate combinations of r and g, for given c, which will make exports worth more/less than the aid component of an equal amount of foreign assistance	169
11.1	Maximising tariff revenue and maximising real income	180
11.2	Tariff revenue yields and non-trade tax yields as a function of tariff rates	182
11.3	Tariff rates with equal yields	184
11.4	The maximisation of total revenue	185
11.5	Yield-maximising tariff rates and the degree of evasion	186

Editor's Preface

The relationship between economic development and international trade has been a source of controversy for many years. A large number of issues have preoccupied both academic and professional commentators – issues such as the alleged instability of primary commodity prices, the declining terms of trade of primary producers, and the relative merits of export-promotion and import-substitution programmes. This book is concerned with these and other issues. It comprises a collection of essays which aims to illuminate a number of controversial issues in economic development and international trade. The essays have been specifically written for this volume and have been prepared with a student audience in mind. Thus, although one would hope that the contents are of interest to fellow professionals, the manner of presentation is geared towards undergraduate and postgraduate students following courses in development economics, international trade, and international trade and economic development. The volume is intended to be a complement to a main text, a means whereby topics which are of necessity covered only briefly in a text can be explored more fully.

As editor I would like to thank my contributors for their co-operation, and their participation in preparing this volume. I hope that like my they feel this to have been in a worthwhile exercise.

June 1987   DAVID GREENAWAY

Notes on the Contributors

V. N. Balasubramanyam is Professor of Development Economics at the University of Lancaster.

Robert H. Ballance is Chief, Statistics and Survey Unit in the Division for Industrial Studies at UNIDO, Vienna.

Mark Casson is Professor of Economics at the University of Reading.

David Greenaway is Professor of Economics at the University of Nottingham.

A. I. MacBean is Professor of Economics at the University of Lancaster.

Chris Milner is Senior Lecturer in Economics at Loughborough University.

Paul Mosley is Professor of Overseas Administrative Studies at Manchester University.

D. T. Nguyen is Senior Lecturer in Economics at the University of Lancaster.

Robert D. Pearce is Senior Research Fellow in Economics at the University of Reading.

James Riedel is Professor of International Economics at the School of Advanced International Studies, Johns Hopkins University, Washington.

David Sapsford is Lecturer in Economics at the University of East Anglia.

G. K. Shaw is Rank Foundation Professor of Economics at the University of Buckingham.

1 Economic Development and International Trade: An Introduction

DAVID GREENAWAY

Over the post-war period an extraordinary expansion of world trade has occurred. Between 1950 and 1985 world exports increased thirtyfold in value terms and ninefold in volume terms. The factors behind this growth are well explained elsewhere (see, for instance, Blackhurst *et al.*, 1977, 1978) and need not concern us here. From our present standpoint the simple fact that world trade has increased over the post-war period is important, all the more so because the growth of trade which has occurred has consistently outstripped the growth of output. Table 1.1 illustrates this point. This means that, on average, countries have been becoming more open in the sense that exports have accounted for an increasing proportion of national income. As a result, countries have increasingly found their welfare to be susceptible to shocks transmitted through the traded goods sector.

Clearly, openness varies from one economy to another. It is also true that the most important contributors to the growth in world trade have been the industrialised economies. Nevertheless, less developed countries account for about one-quarter of total trade by value, and as Table 11.1 shows, LDCs are among the most open of economies. Of the countries listed, none has a ratio of exports plus imports to GNP of less than 10 per cent, more than 56 per cent have ratios in excess of 50 per cent, and some 12 per cent, have ratios which exceed 100 per cent. The economic well-being of many LDCs is extremely sensitive to changes originating in the foreign trade sector.

The role which international trade may play in the development process has been a source of some controversy and has long been debated both in academic and policy circles. At the strategy level debate has focused upon the relative merits of inward-oriented and outward-oriented trade strategies. Proponents of the former have typically emphasised the rigidities and inflexibilities of markets in LDCs which, it is contended, provide arguments for inward orientation supported by instruments designed to encourage

1

2 *An Introduction*

TABLE 1.1   The growth of trade and output

	1947–73	1973–78	1979–83	1984	1985
Annual average change in real exports (%)	7.5	4.0	2.0	9.0	3.0
Annual average change in real output (%)	5.0	3.0	1.5	5.5	3.0

Source: adapted from various GATT publications.

import substitution. Proponents of outward-oriented strategies have generally emphasised the alleged virtues of competition and the benefits of resource allocation being guided by the invisible hand of the market mechanism rather than the visible hand of bureaucracy. At the more specific level, discussion and analysis have hinged upon more specific issues that have fed in to this wider debate. For example, are the prices of primary commodities inherently more unstable than those of manufactures? Is there a tendency for the prices of primary commodities to decline through time relative to manufactures? How protected are the economies of LDCs? Do export processing zones provide a vehicle whereby outward orientation can be achieved? These and other questions are the subject matter of this book.

The book opens with an essay by Robert Ballance which examines trade performance as an indicator of comparative advantage. The concept of comparative advantage is central to the neoclassical analysis of international trade (and indeed to the neoclassical paradigm in a more general sense). Ballance is concerned with recent efforts to operationalise the concept. He discusses the conceptual framework for measuring comparative advantage, as well as practical problems of measuring various indicators. The properties of a variety of measures are discussed and the results of recent studies evaluated. The results of this work appear to confirm the suspicions of the majority of analysts, namely that most LDCs enjoy a comparative advantage in simple processed manufactures which tend to be resource-based or linked to agricultural production. These patterns are not immutably fixed, however, as work on the 'stages' approach to comparative advantage has demonstrated.

The issue of comparative advantage and the role of the export sector in the growth process is the focus of James Riedel's essay in Chapter 3. In the early post-war years, the notion of trade as an engine of growth was an influential one. Recently it has been argued that there are grounds for pessimism where LDCs are concerned. The slowdown in growth which has been observed in the industrialised economies implies that the trade engine is running out of fuel. In the absence of an offsetting growth of trade between LDCs, their growth prospects appear to be somewhat bleak. Riedel looks closely at the links between export performance and growth, and carefully evaluates the empirical evidence on trade as an engine of growth. From his appraisal of the evidence he concludes that the pessimism of the trade-as-an-engine-of-growth perspective is unfounded and cannot be supported by the evidence.

Export pessimism associated with the trade engine scenario is but one element in a wider issue, the role of trade strategy in general. This forms the subject matter of Chapter 4 by Chris Milner. As we noted earlier, trade strategies are often simplified to descriptions of import-substitution and export-promotion strategies. As Milner shows, there are very real difficulties in identifying specific strategies – there is no unique index of inward or outward orientation. Nevertheless, it is possible to ascribe alternative strategies to different countries by reference to a variety of criteria. In doing so Milner discusses the performance of countries following different strategies as well as the rationale underlying inward and outward orientation.

An important input in discriminating between alternative trade strategies is information on the structure of protection. This is the subject of Chapter 5 by David Greenaway. There are several methodologies which have been used in evaluating protective structures. Chapter 5 focuses on the most widely used technique, effective protection analysis, and a less widely used approach, incidence analysis. For both techniques measurement problems are examined and the results from a range of studies are reported. The work on effective protection suggests that highly complex tariff structures can result in average effective tariffs which are very high, and which have a very wide range. The most important point that emerges from the work on incidence analysis is that endeavours to protect the import substitute sector inevitably disprotect the export sector.

The question of export instability and its consequences for growth and savings has been a source of lasting concern over the post-war period. Some theoretical support exists for the proposition that export instability will reduce growth below what it would have been with a more stable set of prices. The concern of Alastair MacBean and D. T. Nguyen in Chapter 6 is with the empirical evidence relating to the existence of export instability, and its impact on growth. The authors carefully and thoroughly evaluate evidence from cross-section and cross-country analysis, from case studies of individual countries, and from large-scale econometric models. Evidence relating to a variety of hypotheses is reported. The authors find evidence to support the view that export instability can have an adverse effect on growth from cross-section studies, although these results are sensitive to the samples used. In view of this the authors deliver a 'not proven' verdict on the issue.

The debate over whether there is a secular tendency for the terms of trade of primary producers to deteriorate *vis-à-vis* manufacturers has been discussed for at least as long as the export instability issue. This alleged tendency is the core of the Prebisch–Singer hypothesis. In Chapter 7

David Sapsford evaluates the factors which might contribute to a secular deterioration in the net barter terms of trade of primary producers. These have recently been reiterated by Singer (1986) and relate to differing price and income elasticities of primary products and manufacturers as well as differences in market structure. The existing evidence on the subject is reviewed by Sapsford. Some recent influential work, in particular Spraos (1980) has challenged the existence of a long-run declining trend. Sapsford reports recent work which suggests that if the possibility of a structural break in the series around 1950 is recognised, support for the Prebisch–Singer hypothesis can be found.

There is now a great deal of documentary evidence relating to the presence of multinational enterprises (MNEs) in less developed countries. The presence of MNEs has been a source of some controversy, with extensive discussion focusing on, *inter alia*, transfer pricing and inappropriate technology. Mark Casson and Robert Pearce in Chapter 8 examine the factors which underlie intra-firm trade, and its role in the trade of less developed countries. The authors examine the determinants of intra-firm trade in some detail, namely the number of circulating intermediate products in a production process, the relative importance of intermediate and final output trade, the ability or otherwise of the firm to internalise trade, and the composition of final output. The manner in which each of these factors encourages intra-firm trade which involves less developed countries is explored, together with the impact of host country factors.

Over the last fifteen years or so many less developed countries have invested significant resources in the development of export processing zones (EPZs). These are free zones which are designed to encourage export activity. In Chapter 9, V. N. Balasubramanyam evaluates the basic theory which underpins the EPZ phenomenon and reviews the experience of a number of countries. The exact welfare effects of an EPZ depend upon the interaction between the zone and other sectors of the economy, as well as the wider policy environment. The latter is especially important. Balasubramanyam argues that in many instances EPZs are introduced to do little more than alleviate the disprotection inflicted upon the export sector by a highly protected import substitute sector. In this respect the EPZ can be regarded as a classic second best policy.

A major and widely publicised platform of the United Nations Conference on Trade and Development (UNCTAD) has been 'trade not aid'. Essentially this argument has been articulated on the grounds that for political and economic reasons, a pound's worth of trade was worth more to the recipient economy than a pound's worth of aid. In Chapter 10 Paul Mosley offers a careful appraisal of the factors which impact upon the relative worth of trade and aid. In turn the direct economic effects, and the indirect effects on savings, relative prices and public expenditure patterns, are discussed. The problem turns out to be rather more complicated than simple comparisons suggest. It is shown to be the case that, in terms of direct effects, gains from aid will exceed gains from trade on the basis of any plausible assumptions regarding the relevant parameters. However, once indirect effects are taken into account, the comparison is not as straightforward, and this simple result no longer holds. Moreover, non-economic considerations, and in particular the objective of greater self-sufficiency, need also to be taken into account. Once this is done the economist has problems in making any cost-benefit appraisal.

A neglected aspect of the analysis of trade and development relates to the role of trade taxes. Empirical evidence suggests that the fiscal importance of trade taxes in less developed countries can be very significant. G. K. Shaw explores this issue in Chapter 11. The factors which contribute to a heavy dependence on trade taxes are examined in some detail. An obvious concern of the economist is with the 'optimal' rate of revenue tariff, and this too is considered. Shaw demonstrates how conventional wisdom on the maximum revenue tariff needs to be qualified according to the way in which any tariff revenue is invested. In addition, the yield interdependency of trade taxes with other taxes needs to be explicitly recognised. Shaw concludes that the 'optimal' revenue tariff will generally lie below the revenue-maximising tariff due to this interdependence and associated problems of non-compliance.

2 Trade Performance as an Indicator of Comparative Advantage

ROBERT H. BALLANCE*

INTRODUCTION

The concept of comparative advantage is rightly regarded as one of the triumphs of economic thought. It has long served as a guide for principles of action, not only for countries but also for any economic organisation which aspires to a rational allocation of resources. Although widely accepted, the concept remains a product of *abstract* economic thought, and the quantification of comparative advantage has proven to be elusive. This chapter focuses on this particular aspect, which is only part of a much larger literature on the subject of comparative advantage.

Efforts to quantify international differences in comparative advantage (Balassa, 1965) were first prompted by interest in the consequences of tariff reductions negotiated during the course of the Dillon and Kennedy Rounds. A series of more recent events led economists to renew their attempts to measure international differences in comparative advantage. Paramount among these events has been the emergence of certain LDCs as major exporters of manufactures, a trend which has resulted in additional competitive pressures in world markets. The growth of foreign private investment and the movement of labour-intensive industries to low-wage countries have focused attention on relative differences in international cost structures of competing firms. Abrupt movements in energy prices have altered traditional patterns of factor usage in some industries and created uncertainty regarding international patterns of comparative advantage. Finally, the growing popularity of export-oriented strategies in many LDCs has generated additional interest in measuring existing (or potential) comparative advantages.

Spurred on by such events, economists have persisted in their attempts to apply the concept of comparative advantage to real-world circumstances. The chapter begins with an examination of the theoretical and empirical

6

problems encountered in this work. The next section examines alternative methods used in constructing estimates of comparative advantage. The chapter concludes with a survey of recent evidence from the LDCs.

A CONCEPTUAL FRAMEWORK FOR MEASURING COMPARATIVE ADVANTAGE

Any attempt to identify comparative advantage must begin by considering whether such an exercise is really possible. The most fundamental problem is that the concept is expressed in abstract terms based on relative prices which would prevail in the complete absence of trade (in other words, autarkic prices). Because all countries engage in some amount of international trade, the empiricist has no information on autarkic prices from which to construct estimates of comparative advantage. Indirect methods of measurement which use information derived from post-trade equilibrium events must be employed. The derivation of such methods will depend, in turn, on the assumed relationship between the observable and non-observable variables which give rise to the concept of comparative advantage.

The basis for theory is that comparative advantage (CA) is governed by economic conditions in various trading countries. The precise conditions, or determinants (D), will vary depending upon the user's choice of a theory to explain CA. Regardless of the preferred conceptual basis, the resultant impressions of comparative advantage will give rise to observable events involving trade (T), production (P) and consumption (C). The relationships can be represented schematically as follows:

$$D \longrightarrow CA \longrightarrow T, P, C$$

Tests of trade theories do not require a direct measure of comparative advantage. The theories explain comparative advantage by explaining trade or other phenomena in terms of determinants which are themselves observable. While each theory will specify the relationship between observable determinants and CA, it will also imply similar, or at least derivable, relationships between D and T, P, C (Deardorff, 1984). For example, an application of the popular Heckscher–Ohlin theorem requires data on trade, factor intensities and factor endowments, but a direct measure of CA is not necessary.

The researcher's needs are different if an explicit assessment of comparative advantage, rather than an explanation of patterns of trade or production, is the objective. In this case, analysts have assumed that post-trade measures such as T, P, C and perhaps other statistics can be used to construct an index of 'revealed comparative advantage' (RCA) which will approximate the true pattern of comparative advantage. The relationship implied by such an approach might be depicted as:

$$CA \longrightarrow T, P, C \longrightarrow RCA$$

In the simplest case – one involving only two countries, two products and two factors – a straightforward application of the *RCA* model can be expected to yield deterministic relationships between *CA* and *T*, *P* and *C*. But in a world populated by many countries, products and factors, deterministic links between the two sets of variables no longer hold (Drabicki and Takayama, 1979).

The fundamental problem is that the theory of comparative advantage gives no reason to assume a clearly identifiable relationship between observable variables and autarkic prices. This fact has been demonstrated by Hillman (1980), who shows that use of the *RCA* statistic as a basis for cross-industry comparisons of a given country will not necessarily yield a consistent measure of comparative advantage. Nevertheless, Hillman notes that when the approach is used in cross-country comparisons of specific commodities, *RCA* estimates may provide consistent results in certain circumstances. Forstner (1984), in restating Hillman's arguments, found qualified support for the approach in a world with only two factors (labour and capital) but with many countries and commodities. Under these conditions the probability of a positive correlation between *RCA* and relative capital endowments of trading countries is positively related to the relative capital intensity of the product or industry under study.

Modest support for the *RCA* approach has also come from other theoretical work. Using a general model of comparative advantage, Deardorff (1980) has shown that, on average, a negative correlation between net exports (defined as exports minus imports) and autarkic prices can be expected. The result implies that there would be definite limits on the extent to which the pattern of trade may depart from that identified in the deterministic specification of the model sketched here. This fact would seem to suggest that, while comparative advantage may not be directly measurable, inferences may still be feasible.

ISSUES OF MEASUREMENT AND ESTIMATION

In addition to the theoretical issues which surround the *RCA* methodology, empiricists must also take account of problems relating to questions of measurement and bias. One concerns the fact that countries are of widely different sizes. A large country with only a minor cost advantage (i.e. a small degree of comparative advantage) can still be a relatively important exporter in comparison to a smaller country that enjoys a significant cost advantage. Ideally, indicators of cost advantage or disadvantage would be needed in order to distinguish between the two countries. But such indicators require data on the domestic costs that would prevail in the absence of trade. Since actual costs are incurred in the presence of trade, this line of reasoning – like the search for autarkic prices – is not promising. A way out of the dilemma would be to construct measures that 'adjust for country size'. Two obvious alternatives are (a) to relate exports to domestic production or (b) to relate imports to domestic consumption.

A second problem arises from the fact that trade statistics are not available for each and every traded item. The available data generally refer to categories of products. As a result, most countries are shown as importers and exporters of the same product category. In such cases crude indices of comparative advantage might reveal that a country would have a comparative advantage and a comparative disadvantage in the same product category. Thus, in addition to standardising for country size, it may be appropriate to account for 'two-way' or intra-industry trade. The most common method of adjustment is to express the *RCA* indices in terms of net exports. If a country's comparative advantage in one product exceeds its comparative disadvantage in another, exports of the first should exceed imports of the second, and net exports would be positive. Similarly, a negative value for net exports would imply a greater degree of comparative disadvantage.

Once account has been taken of differing country sizes and the existence of intra-industry trade, attention has turned to potential sources of distortion in the estimates of comparative advantage. One possibility is that the level of data aggregation can be so great as to obscure the true pattern of comparative advantage. For example, a country may specialise in the production of high-quality steel products and satisfy its raw material requirements by importing semi-processed items such as pig iron and crude steel. Measures of comparative advantage using data for the entire steel industry may not reflect the fact that the country enjoys a comparative advantage only at higher stages of processing. Researchers have attempted to minimise the aggregation problem by using data for more narrowly defined product categories. Their efforts are complicated by the fact that most countries employ different classification systems for production and trade. For each country the researcher is required to match, or concord, two sets of data which are not compatible. Often, consistent figures for production, imports and exports can be obtained only by combining products into highly aggregated categories. In order to study comparative advantage for narrowly defined products, it is usually necessary to construct measures of *RCA* which rely solely on trade data.

A second potential source of distortion results from industry-specific policies – for example, various forms of tariff protection, non-tariff barriers, subsidies to stimulate production, etc. When the extent of public intervention is great, actual trade performance may not reflect the pattern of comparative advantage that would prevail in a world of completely free trade. In recognition of this possibility some analysts have chosen to exclude imports from their calculations. They argue that because governments commonly resort to tariff and non-tariff measures to limit imports, estimates which use import data may be prone to bias (Balassa, 1977a). Other researchers contend that governments which support a particular industry through import restrictions will also intervene to alter domestic patterns of production or consumption. Examples of such policies would include the provision of funds for research and development or plant construction, public procurement practices which favour domestic producers, generous terms for credit, tax rebates, etc. Analysts who adopt this line of argument (e.g. Donges and Riedel, 1977) prefer indices based on net trade flows.

Some of these problems can be illustrated using data for the steel industry in Brazil and South Korea. Table 2.1 provides figures on trade, production and consumption along with several crude measures of *RCA* which can be constructed from the data. Heuristically, a country's comparative advantage could be expected to vary proportionately with the share of exports in production (X/P) or the share of net exports in production (N/P). The same type of relationship would be expected for a measure showing the share of production (P) in consumption (C) where the latter is defined as production plus imports less exports. Finally, comparative advantage could vary inversely with the share of imports in consumption (M/C). Three of these expressions indicate that South Korea has a comparative advantage greater than Brazil. When *RCA* is measured by the share of exports in production, the difference between Korean and Brazilian steel producers is significant. The distinction between the two countries is less pronounced when the share of net exports in production is the basis for comparison, and is further reduced if *RCA* is expressed as the share of production in total consumption of steel. The situation becomes even more ambiguous when the fourth expression, imports as a share of total consumption (M/C), is considered. In that case Brazil, rather than South Korea, is shown to have the greater comparative advantage.

There are several plausible reasons for the lack of agreement (concerning both relative and absolute differences) in the estimates for the two countries. First, the comparability of industry-wide estimates such as these may be limited when the respective industries have distinctly different product ranges and patterns of product specialisation. Related factors concern the size of the two markets and access to raw materials. Brazil has the larger steel market, and demand for steel products is more diverse. Similarly, Brazilian producers have ample supplies of raw materials: the country's state-owned Carajás mine is the world's largest supplier of iron ore. Because South Korean producers import iron ore and serve a smaller domestic market, they may be more specialised and more inclined to produce for

TABLE 2.1 Comparative performance in Brazilian and South Korean steel industries, 1979–80[a]

	Brazil	South Korea (in millions of $US)		Brazil	South Korea (in percentages)
Production	7144	4403	Exports ÷ production (*X/P*)	11.7	33.4
+ Imports	551	1073	Imports ÷ consumption (*M/C*)	8.0	26.8
= New supply	7695	5476	Net exports ÷ production (*N/P*)	4.0	9.1
− Exports	834	1473	Production ÷ consumption (*P/C*)	104.1	110.0
= Consumption	*6861*	*4003*			

[a] Figures refer to two-year averages.
Source: UNIDO (1985), p. 83.

export. Korean steel-makers have, in fact, long worked to put together their own export strategy in order to penetrate markets in Japan and other Asian countries. These differences are probably accentuated by the policy choices in the two countries. Brazil, for example, has employed measures designed to restrict imports, while South Korean policy-makers have favoured measures to boost exports and to limit the degree of import competition.

The comparisons in Table 2.1 not only illustrate some of the ambiguities faced by users of the *RCA* approach but also suggest the need to consider more closely the manner in which the results are to be interpreted. Theories of comparative advantage imply that any set of estimates for a particular product or industry should provide an indication of the absolute differences in the comparative advantage between each country. Such indicators would be described as 'cardinal' measures of comparative advantage. But in view of the theoretical and empirical problems associated with *RCA*, a less stringent interpretation of the results may be desirable. One alternative is to treat the measures as indicators of the degree of comparative advantage enjoyed by one country relative to another without drawing inferences about absolute differences in the magnitudes of the two measures (e.g. Balassa, 1979; UNCTAD, 1983). This interpretation would result in a ranking of countries according to their degree of comparative advantage, and is referred to as an 'ordinal' measure. Still another possibility, suggested by Yeats (1985), is to regard the estimates as dichotomous indicators that merely distinguish between those countries which have a comparative advantage in a particular commodity or industry and those which do not.

Methods of measurement

In view of all these considerations, it is not surprising that the literature offers a variety of definitions for *RCA*. Based on the choice of observable variables which they employ, three approaches can be identified. First, some analysts have chosen to make use of both production and trade statistics in constructing their estimates. A second, and more common, method of measurement depends solely on trade statistics, while the third approach is based on deviations between actual and expected values of production and consumption. The first of these classes of estimators is encapsulated by the examples shown in Table 2.1, but the other methods require further description.

Among the 'trade-only' measures of *RCA*, several versions can be identified. The original formulation put forward by Balassa (1965) and retained in his subsequent work (Balassa, 1977a, 1977b, 1979) expresses *RCA* as the share of country *i*'s exports in world trade of product *j* divided by that country's share of world trade in manufactures. An alternative, employed by Donges and Riedel (1977), defines *RCA* as the ratio between the share of a country *i*'s net exports of product *j* in its total trade (exports plus imports) of product *j* divided by the corresponding share for all manufactured products. A third version, the net export ratio, is equivalent to the numerator in the Donges–Riedel index and has been examined by UNIDO (1982). More recently, UNIDO (1986) carried out a study of *RCA* using a slightly different expression which reflects the apparent theoretical preference to focus on net exports. This formulation serves to normalise net exports with respect to the value of the country's total trade in manufactures and the weight of the product in world trade in manufactures. Each of these versions is shown by the following equations:

$$\text{Balassa measure (BAL)} = \frac{X_{ij}}{X_{wj}} \bigg| \frac{X_{im}}{X_{wm}} \tag{2.1}$$

$$\text{Donges–Riedel measure (DR)} = \left[\frac{X_{ij} - M_{ij}}{X_{ij} + M_{ij}} \bigg| \frac{X_{im} - M_{im}}{X_{im} + M_{im}} - 1 \right] \cdot \text{sign } (X_{im} - M_{im}) \tag{2.2}$$

$$\text{Net-export ratio (RNX)} = \frac{X_{ij} - M_{ij}}{X_{ij} + M_{ij}} \tag{2.3}$$

$$\text{Normalised net-export ratio (NNR)} = \frac{X_{ij} - M_{ij}}{T_{im} \, (T_{wj}/T_{wm})} \tag{2.4}$$

where X = exports, M = imports, i = country, j = commodity, m = total manufactures, w = world and $T = (X + M)/2$.

The final class of estimators adopts a probabilistic framework where *RCA* is expressed in terms of the deviations between actual and expected levels of trade, production and consumption. In order to measure deviations from expected levels, a 'norm' is required to represent economic conditions in a hypothetical world without trade. One approach, following the work of Kunimoto (1977), is to construct a world in which relative autarkic prices would be equal everywhere. Countries are assumed to be identical with regard to their consumer preferences, their relative factor supplies and technologies. Although they may differ in terms of the absolute amount of available domestic resources, relative autarkic prices would still be equal. Under these conditions the pre-trade norm for determining expected values is a world in which no country has a comparative advantage relative to another. The approach gives rise to ambiguities, since alternative versions of a world with 'neutral' comparative advantage can be hypothesised. Furthermore, the ability of such a norm to approximate the 'true' comparative advantage in an autarkic world has been questioned (Ballance, Forstner and Murray, 1985, 1986).

Whatever the chosen norm, derivation of the expected values can be illustrated by making use of the net trade identity:

$$N_{ij} = Q_{ij} - C_{ij} \tag{2.5}$$

where Q and C are production and consumption of commodity j in country i respectively. When expressed in terms of the deviations between actual and expected levels of trade, production and consumption, equation (2.5) becomes:

$$(N_{ij} - EN_{ij}) = (Q_{ij} - EQ_{ij}) - (C_{ij} - EC_{ij}) \tag{2.6}$$

where expected values are denoted by EN, EQ and EC. In a world where relative autarkic prices are everywhere identical, $EN_{ij} = 0$, meaning that equation (2.6) can be written in terms of deviations as:

$$N_{ij} = D(Q_{ij}) - D(C_{ij}) \tag{2.7}$$

In order to relate the concept of expected value to observable variables, Bowen (1983) assumes a hypothetical world where the consumer preferences of countries are not only identical but also homothetic. Each country's consumption of j would then be proportional to world consumption (production) and can be stated as follows:

$$C_j = S_i \cdot Q_{wj} \tag{2.8}$$

where S_i is a proportionality coefficient for country i. In line with the foregoing assumptions, this coefficients can be expressed as:

$$S_i = Y_i / Y_w \tag{2.9}$$

where Y_i is income of country i and Y_w is world income. With neutral comparative advantage and no trade, $EQ_{ij} = EC_{ij} = S_i \cdot Q_{wj}$. After substituting for S_i in (2.8), (2.7) provides the basis for three interrelated indices which represent scaled deviations of actual from expected values of trade, production or consumption, where the scaling factor is expected production (consumption):

$$D_{ij}^N = \frac{N_{ij}}{(Y_i/Y_w) \, Q_{wj}} \tag{2.10a}$$

$$D_{ij}^Q = \frac{D\,(Q_{ij})}{(Y_i/Y_w) \, Q_{wj}} = \frac{Q_{ij}}{(Y_i/Y_w) \, Q_{wj}} - 1 \tag{2.10b}$$

$$D_{ij}^C = \frac{D\,(C_{ij})}{(Y_i/Y_w) \, Q_{wj}} = \frac{C_{ij}}{(Y_i/Y_w) \, Q_{wj}} - 1 \tag{2.10c}$$

The three indices, which are related to each other in the way shown by (2.6), may be either positive or negative, and would be zero in the absence of any comparative advantage or disadvantage. While the trade intensity index (2.10a) and the production intensity index (2.10b) have a positive relationship with comparative advantage, the consumption intensity index (2.10c) is expected to be negatively related.

An appealing feature of this line of reasoning is that it highlights the fact that comparative advantage depends on the interaction between consumption and production. The assumption that preferences are identical and homothetic is in line with the popular Heckscher–Ohlin theorem of comparative advantage, and provides one way of characterising the hypothetical world of no relative advantages. Its extension to the real trading world, however, has been questioned as a result of empirical studies involving actual patterns of trade, production and consumption (Ballance, Forstner and Murray, 1985).

Given the wide range of methods and indicators employed to measure comparative advantage, it is not surprising that users have turned to the question of whether these many versions can yield consistent results. The identification of a single index or class of estimators that can be regarded as an accurate measure of 'true' comparative advantage is not possible. However, there is evidence to suggest that the results of empirical studies to estimate comparative advantage are sensitive to the choice of measure being used (Ballance, Forstner and Murray, 1986). The degree of inconsistency is greatest when a cardinal interpretation of the indices is adopted. It is less so when an ordinal or a dichotomous viewpoint is employed. Finally, consistency studies support the theoretical preference for use of net exports as a choice for an *RCA* index. Other expressions which are generally more demanding in terms of data requirements are inconsistent, both between each other and with *RCA* measures using net exports.

INTERNATIONAL PATTERNS OF COMPARATIVE ADVANTAGE

Although conceptual and theoretical considerations limit the economist's ability to employ comparative advantage in an operational context, empirical studies have nevertheless proven valuable in gaining a better understanding of global trends. Much of this empirical work has consisted of straightforward estimates of *RCA* which are then used as a basis for gauging changes in comparative advantage. More recently, the *RCA* approach has also been employed as a means for assessing the role of factor endowments and/or factor intensities. The results of some of these studies, along with their implications for changes in international competitive ability, are summarised in this section.

Among the studies attempting to measure comparative advantage through the use of *RCA*, one of the most wide-ranging investigations employed three different indicators and dealt with 129 industries and 47 countries (UNIDO, 1982). The results showed that in the majority of developing countries (LDCs) comparative advantage was limited to the production of simply processed manufactures, most of which were closely linked to agriculture or were otherwise resource-based. LDCs at higher levels of development were found to be less dependent on the availability of natural resources; some of the industries in which they excelled were clearly labour-intensive, while others were either labour-intensive or used fairly standard, mature technologies.

These findings are not surprising in view of the large amounts of unskilled labour and limited technological expertise available in LDCs relative to Western countries. Other, more narrowly focused studies have provided additional insights. The evidence compiled from the latter type of studies suggests a two-way classification of countries, depending on the industry involved and whether or not the country enjoys a comparative advantage. In the case of some industries (for example, textiles, apparel and wood and wood products), countries with a comparative advantage have developed their industries primarily by supplying foreign markets; domestic consumption is not of paramount importance. Countries lacking a comparative advantage in these industries have still met the bulk of their needs through domestic production while satisfying the remainder through imports. In the second group are industries such as steel and electronics, where the tendency has been to exploit a comparative advantage only as an extension of the domestic market. The situation is illustrated by the case of Japan. Although the country is regarded as having a comparative advantage in a wide range of both steel products and consumer electronics, as much as three-quarters of domestic production is still consumed at home (UNIDO, 1985). Again, countries with a comparative disadvantage have satisfied most of their needs through domestic industries.

International trade, however, can be pictured as more than the result of a simple pattern of comparative advantage by which countries export the products produced in one or more industries while their trading partners export products of other industries. Patterns of trade and product specialisation entail much more than the processing of indigenous raw materials into final goods which are either consumed at home or exported. Instead, they are highly interdependent processes whereby some countries produce and export raw materials to others which process the materials into intermediate products for export to third countries for yet further processing. The degree of interdependence, the number of processing stages and the international location of these stages will vary among industries. In some cases more than one stage of processing will occur in the same country; production efficiencies may dictate that subsequent processing occurs in the same plant. When patterns of trade are analysed in this fashion, a more elaborate picture of comparative advantage emerges. Instead of using indigenous raw materials to make final goods, countries that are endowed with raw materials may excel in the extraction and simple processing of these materials into intermediate products which are then exported. Other countries import these products for processing into higher-staged intermediate products which, in turn, are exported. Eventually, a final good emerges from this chain of processing.

The degree to which all these activities have become integrated into the international economy results in a highly complex picture of trade and production. This situation is illustrated in Table 2.2, which provides summary statistics for several major producers of textiles and apparel. Because of its advantages in the production of man-made fibres from petrochemicals, the United States is one of the dominant countries in the first stage of processing. It does not engage in much trade at the second stage. Instead, American firms process the fibres into yarn and then turn the yarn into fabrics (probably in multi-stage plants). Thus, the United States has a favourable competitive position in the production of fibres and fabrics. At the final stage, however, the USA is very definitely at a comparative disadvantage. Unlike the United States, Japan is a relatively large importer of fibres (mainly cotton). Japanese firms have a modest comparative advantage in the production and export of yarns and a significant advantage in cotton and man-made fabrics, but they, too, are at a considerable disadvantage at the fourth stage, the production of apparel.

Patterns of comparative advantage are again different in the LDCs. Table 2.2 shows the trade performance of all LDCs as well as of a subset of this group known as the newly industrialising countries (NICs), several of which are important suppliers of textiles and clothing. As a group, the LDCs are

TABLE 2.2 Comparative advantage by stage of processing: textiles and apparel, 1979–80[a]

Processing stage	Exports	Imports	Net exports as a share of total trade[b]
	(in million $US)		
United States			
1. Cotton and man-made fibres	3281	65	0.96
2. Cotton and man-made yarns	616	138	0.63
3. Cotton and man-made fabrics	1328	852	0.22
4. Cotton and man-made apparel	874	5846	−0.74
Japan			
1. Cotton and man-made fibres	592	1369	−0.40
2. Cotton and man-made yarns	778	372	0.35
3. Cotton and man-made fabrics	2665	399	0.74
4. Cotton and man-made apparel	393	1425	−0.57
All LDCs			
1. Cotton and man-made fibres	2153	3255	−0.20
2. Cotton and man-made yarns	2363	1124	0.36
3. Cotton and man-made fabrics	4229	2466	0.26
4. Cotton and man-made apparel	8672	1598	0.69
NICs[c]			
1. Cotton and man-made fibres	259	1097	−0.62
2. Cotton and man-made yarns	1242	272	0.64
3. Cotton and man-made fabrics	1865	930	0.33
4. Cotton and man-made apparel	5075	234	0.91

[a] Figures are based on two-year averages.
[b] Net exports divided by exports plus imports.
[c] NICs include Argentina, Brazil, Hong Kong, Mexico, Singapore, South Korea and Taiwan.
Source: UNIDO (1985), p. 95.

net importers of textile fibres, although their competitive position is somewhat stronger at intermediate processing stages and they enjoy a comparative advantage in markets for apparel. In the case of the NICs, the pattern is more accentuated. Several of the NICs are highly specialised in specific processing operations, and import cotton and man-made fibres from other countries. Apparel, the final stage of production, is acknowledged to be the most labour-intensive of the four stages, and the competitive superiority of the NICs is most pronounced at that stage. An extreme example is found in the case of Hong Kong which, in 1980, accounted for 17 per cent of all exports of apparel by non-communist countries. The city-state achieved a leading position as a world supplier despite the fact that it was simultaneously a large net importer of textiles (UNIDO, 1985).

Such variations in competitive ability at different stages of processing are not unique to producers of textiles and apparel. Similar patterns can be observed in other industries ranging from consumer electronics to petrochemicals.

For countries which have chosen to enter an industry at an intermediate stage, an important implication is that success depends on a close integration of their processing operations with both foreign suppliers and export markets. Producers in these countries are definitely not simply importers of raw materials and exporters of final goods: they have established themselves as processors of imported materials into higher staged goods and have rationalised their industrial structures to suit the prevailing pattern of industrial interdependence.

Studies of the above type provide at least a partial picture of international patterns of comparative advantage in specific industries. The results are less useful in gaining an impression of the likely directions of change in this measure. In order to consider dynamic aspects of comparative advantage, researchers have explicitly linked their estimates of *RCA* with other information on factor endowments and/or factor intensities. An underlying assumption is that the relative abundance of a particular factor, in conjunction with the intensity of the factor's use in production processes, will have an impact on comparative advantage. Such studies are based on intuitive hypotheses rather than rigorously derived propositions. Instead, they attempt to provide some means for anticipating future changes in *RCA* (and, by implication, comparative advantage) on the basis of additional knowledge regarding patterns of factor endowments and inter-industry differences in factor intensity.

One interpretation (Balassa, 1977a, 1976b and 1979) adopts the existing commodity composition of trade as a frame of reference and relates changes in comparative advantage to changes in countries' factor endowments. Known as a 'stages' approach to comparative advantage, the argument suggests that competitive abilities will change as a result of the steady accumulation of physical capital, the formation of human capital (or labour skills) and growing technological sophistication. As time passes, the cost advantages of manufacturers in the more advanced LDCs will shift away from products/industries in which cheap, unskilled labour is the dominant input in favour of others which are more capital-intensive, more skill-intensive and more technologically sophisticated. Thus LDCs can be expected to move along a scale of comparative advantage as development proceeds. Asian countries are often used as an example. A case in point is Japan, where comparative advantage gradually shifted towards capital-intensive exports and away from exports which are relatively intensive users of unskilled labour. In turn, other countries with adequate supplies of labour and skills (e.g. South Korea) may replace Japan in exporting the original product. Finally, LDCs at lower levels of industrialisation supplant the previous suppliers in the export of products that are intensive in the use of unskilled labour.

From the standpoint of changing factor endowments, a stages interpretation holds considerable appeal. The limited empirical evidence, however, casts some doubt on the existence of such a smooth transition in national patterns of comparative advantage. Using data for seventy-nine industries, *RCA*s for twenty-eight countries were calculated during the mid-1960s and mid-1970s (Ballance, Ansari and Singer, 1982). In order to test the possibility of a stage-like change in comparative advantage, the countries were arranged in four groups according to their level of development – LDCs, NICs, recently developed countries, and industrialised countries. When each group's pattern of *RCA*s was compared, the results did not conform to a sequential interpretation. *RCA*s for recently developed countries, NICs and other LDCs were found to converge over time. Moreover, comparisons of these figures with *RCA* estimates for industrialised countries revealed a growing divergence in each case. The lack of support for a stage-like development may be due to any of several statistical or conceptual problems discussed in preceding sections. Or it may reflect the fact that the evolution of comparative advantage often appears to be discontinuous – at least when only a limited number of countries and development stages are considered.

Other researchers have made use of the product cycle model when attempting to assess patterns of change – at least two versions of which have been tested in conjunction with *RCA*. The original view, while accepting the factor proportions explanation for trade in 'old' products, introduced the idea that some products pass through a 'cycle' from new to old. The production of new products requires large amounts of skilled labour in the form of scientists, engineers, professional managers and skilled craftsmen. Once these new products enter the market, they experience a phase of rapid growth and the reliance on skilled labour gives way to more capital-intensive techniques of production. Production techniques eventually mature and products are standardised. At that point, inputs of unskilled labour play a greater role in the production of mature products. Such systematic changes in the input requirements are thought to affect the location of production facilities. LDCs may enjoy a comparative advantage in products produced with standardised techniques and comparatively large amounts of unskilled labour.

The alternative interpretation of the product cycle (Finger, 1975) distinguishes between standardised and non-standardised products. It associates export performance with producers' abilities (and inclinations) to alter their products' characteristics either in response to demand or in order to achieve some degree of product differentiation. Standardised products are indicated by a low rate of product development, while unstandardised products are associated with a high rate of product development. Thus product development is seen as a form of competition intended to retain old markets or to gain new ones by offering for sale at established prices products which buyers regard as different from the existing list of available products. LDCs are thought to have the best prospects for attaining a comparative advantage in standardised products.

The two interpretations focus on somewhat different sets of products. Unstandardised products are not necessarily the same as new products. Manufacturers of office machines and scientific instruments, for example, incur large R & D expenditures, require large numbers of skilled workers, and have high rates of product development. However, producers of plastic and rubber articles, soaps and cleansers also have high rates of product development but require little skilled labour. Both types of products would be described as 'unstandardised', although only the former would be 'new products'.

In order to test these two views, industries must first be distinguished according to their factor intensities and rates of product development. Based on the work of others, Ballance, Ansari and Singer (1982) assembled such a classification. *RCA* indices were calculated for each industry and averages were then derived for each product category for a large number of industries and countries. In order to gain some impression of patterns of change, *RCA*s were calculated for two periods, the mid-1960s and mid-1970s. An additional step was to arrange countries according to their level of development. This distinction resulted in three groups, described as recently developed countries, newly industrialising countries (NICs) and other LDCs.

Table 2.3 summarises the results of this exercise. When industries are arranged according to the original interpretation of the product cycle, exports of mature products account for 25–34 per cent of all manufactured exports from each of the three groups. The factor orientation of most mature industries favours labour-intensive processes utilising relatively large amounts of unskilled workers. Although mature products produced with relatively capital-intensive inputs are a minor portion of total exports, trends in the three country groups provide some support for a stylised view of the product cycle. For example, countries at the more advanced end of the development spectrum lead in the export of mature, capital-intensive products, while these goods are of lesser importance for NICs and other LDCs. With regard to new products associated with this interpretation, exports of all groups were of little importance. No more than 5 per cent of total exports were accounted for by this product category, presumably because most industries required comparatively large amounts of skilled labour.

The second half of Table 2.3 provides comparable data for the product development version of the model. As expected, exports of standardised products far exceed those of unstandardised items. In terms of factor orientation, standardised industries in all the countries considered depend mainly on labour-intensive products for their exports. Recently developed countries also lead in the export of unstandardised products, although the NICs accounted for a comparable portion of those exports which are relatively labour-intensive.

In conclusion, mature and manufactured or standardised products account for a large portion of the manufactured exports from countries with a modest or limited industrial base. Moreover, several countries – whether recently developed, NICs or other LDCs – made significant gains in their ability to compete in world markets for such products during the 1960s and 1970s. However, any distinction between the performance of exporters at different levels of development is more difficult. The classification of countries is too crude to test the possibility that comparative advantage will systematically shift down this scale. All that can be said is that, with few exceptions, trends in *RCA* values suggest that the more advanced of the countries considered (the recently developed and the NICs) made the greatest strides in exporting relatively sophisticated products. This impression must be a qualified one in view of the small number of countries considered and the difficulties encountered in measuring factor intensity and comparative advantage. It nevertheless underlines the links between development of a skilled labour force and degree of technological sophistication for export performance.

RCA IN PRACTICE – IMPLICATIONS AND APPLICABILITY

The foregoing discussion has considered the extent to which estimates of *RCA* can introduce an 'operational element' into the law of comparative advantage. Based on available evidence, use of the concept can clearly add to our understanding of international differences in competitive abilities and the ways in which these may change over time. But the gap between theory and empirical application remains a large one, and it is relevant to conclude this chapter by reconsidering some of the ways in which this disparity can limit the usefulness of *RCA*.

First, most theories of comparative advantage entail predictions about trade performance within *classes* of industries, and the same broad applicability would apply to estimates of *RCA*. The relationship between *RCA*, comparative advantage and its determinants can be substantiated in general ways by drawing upon evidence for a large number of countries and industries. But when issues or policy decisions relating to specific industries in particular countries must be decided, such broad trends can only provide a basis for inference and can not serve as a guide. Even circumstances that would be judged paradoxical from the viewpoint of orthodox trade theories cannot be discounted, provided such events were outweighed, on average, by normal trade performance.

Second, the evidence regarding international differences in comparative advantage must necessarily be expressed in tentative terms. One source of indeterminancy concerns the appropriate interpretation which must be attached to measures of comparative advantage. Ordinal or dichotomous evaluations must be employed, although more precise measures which

TABLE 2.3 Exports with a marked *RCA*[a] in selected groups of countries[b] (percentages and number of industries)

Product category[c]	Factor Orientation	Recently developed countries		NICs		Other LDCs	
		Average increase in *RCA*, mid-1960s to mid-1970s	As a share in total manufactured exports (number of industries), mid-1970s	Average increase in *RCA*, mid-1960s to mid-1970s	As a share in total manufactured exports (number of industries), mid-1970s	Average increase in *RCA*, mid-1960s to mid-1970s	As a share in total manufactured exports (number of industries), mid-1970s
Mature products (using relatively large amounts of unskilled labour)	labour-intensive	25.7	21.0 (19)	103.2	32.5 (19)	292.5	22.6 (17)
	capital-intensive	265.3	7.7 (5)	177.4	1.8 (3)	94.6	1.7 (2)
	total[d]	101.0	28.7 (24)	117.5	34.3 (22)	258.6	24.6 (20)
New products (using relatively large amounts of skilled labour)	labour-intensive	58.5	4.3 (5)	156.0	5.3 (6)	209.9	0.6 (2)
	capital-intensive	63.1	0.6 (2)	91.5	0.1 (1)	268.5	0.4 (1)
	total[d]	70.6	6.8 (9)	152.1	5.4 (7)	220.9	1.0 (3)

Standardized products (low rates of product development)	labour-intensive	30.4	22.3 (20)	115.9	34.6 (19)	311.9	20.3 (16)
	capital-intensive	129.0	3.1 (4)	140.0	0.7 (2)	216.8	1.5 (2)
	total[d]	53.1	25.8 (25)	121.2	35.3 (21)	298.7	21.8 (18)
Unstandardized products (high rates of product development)	labour-intensive	44.8	2.9 (4)	161.8	3.2 (6)	59.2	2.9 (3)
	capital-intensive	297.7	5.2 (3)	169.2	1.2 (2)	50.6	0.6 (1)
	total[d]	172.3	8.1 (7)	167.7	4.4 (8)	91.4	3.8 (5)

[a] RCA indices were defined as in equation (1) above. A 'marked' comparative advantage was assumed to exist if: (a) an RCA exceeded a normalised level of 100 by at least 50 per cent, and (b) the industry's ratio of net exports to total trade (exports plus imports) was not less than the corresponding ratio for all manufactures. Finally, expressions for each country group were obtained as a weighted average of individual country estimates where the value of exports plus imports, i.e. total trade, were taken as weights.

[b] Recently developed countries were defined to be Greece, Israel, Portugal, Spain, Yugoslavia. NICs include Argentina, Brazil, Hong Kong, Mexico, Singapore, South Korea, Turkey. Ten additional countries make up the group of other LDCs.

[c] For a detailed listing of the industries included, see UNIDO (1981), pp. 103–8.

[d] The total share may include industries for which the classification by factor intensity was not applicable.

Source: Ballance, Ansari and Singer (1982), pp. 146 and 151.

specify absolute differences in comparative advantage (i.e. a cardinal evaluation) would be of most use to the policy-maker. A more serious limitation results from the fact that actual patterns of comparative advantage are highly intricate. The extent of specialisation can be so great that an industry-wide study would have to take account of numerous products and production stages. Because the concept is a relative one, a systematic search for comparative advantage cannot be conducted merely in terms of one industry to the exclusion of others. For these reasons, the volume of information required in order to construct a truly complete picture of comparative advantage is beyond the capabilities of analysts.

In conclusion, the law of comparative advantage represents a universally applicable conceptual framework for interpreting international patterns of specialisation. The principle that relative rather than absolute efficiency largely determines the competitive abilities of various industries is logically incontestable and enjoys considerable empirical support. Thus, governments would be ill-advised to ignore the principle. However, to assume that empirical evidence of comparative advantage can serve as a basis for specific policy decisions would go too far. Ultimately, firms, managers and workers will themselves determine their competitive abilities, and policy-makers can only pay tribute to the law of comparative advantage by preserving an environment in which such decisions can be made.

3 Trade as an Engine of Growth: Theory and Evidence

JAMES RIEDEL*

INTRODUCTION

There are two fundamentally different perspectives on the relationship between trade and growth in developing countries. Both perspectives agree on the importance of trade. Where they differ is on the mechanism which makes trade important. Orthodox theory assumes that changes in prices bring about substitution in production and consumption, both at home and abroad. Trade is important because it permits a more efficient allocation of national resources, but the optimal extent of trade is to be determined by decisions about costs and benefits of production and consumption at the margin. The perspective of development theory, by contrast, assumes little substitutability in production or consumption at home and abroad. In consequence, changes in relative prices have negligible consequences for the allocation of resources. What matters, instead, is the level of external demand. Trade is important, according to this perspective, because resources would otherwise not so much be inefficiently used as not be used at all. A logical consequence of the perspective of development theory is the attempt to earn or save foreign exchange regardless of the cost.

In this chapter the main competing theories about the role of trade in the economic growth of developing countries are evaluated. The key assumptions of the competing theories are identified and their plausibility is assessed on the basis of the evidence. By focusing on the empirical relevance of the key assumptions of competing theories, we go to the heart of the policy debate about the role of trade in developing countries. The main disagreement between the competing theories is not over *whether* trade is important, it is rather over *how* the trade link works. More precisely, it is over whether the external environment, working through international trade, determines the performance of the domestic economies of developing countries. To analyse this issue it is necessary to consider the nature of the trade link, or,

25

in other words, to examine the alternative assumptions about the relationship between the external environment and the economic performance of
developing countries.

THEORETICAL PERSPECTIVES ON TRADE AND GROWTH IN DEVELOPING COUNTRIES

The perspective of orthodox theory

External economic relations have long been considered important for economic growth. Adam Smith in his classic work, *An Inquiry into the Nature
and Causes of the Wealth of Nations*, argued that international trade was
essential for achieving economic efficiency, the gains from which are a
principal source of wealth. Economic efficiency, Smith explained, derives
from a 'division of labour', the limit to which is set by the 'extent of the
market'. International trade is the principal means by which a nation can
extend the market beyond its borders, thereby allowing greater specialisation in production, enhanced efficiency in the use of scarce resources, and
greater national income. Growth results from the accumulation of capital
and other productive resources, and such accumulation is limited by the size
of the national income. To the extent that trade allows for greater national
income, it expands the capacity to accumulate and hence to grow.

The relationship between trade and growth described by Adam Smith,
mainly working via the links between trade and efficiency, efficiency and
income, income and investment, and investment and growth, still remains
the orthodox theoretical view. The advances in theory in the intervening 200
years have been mainly to elaborate and extend the relationship between
trade and efficiency. David Ricardo, the father of international trade theory,
made his contribution by introducing the concept of comparative advantage,
thereby showing that trade allows for gains in static efficiency in addition to
the gains associated with economies of scale that were the main focus of
Adam Smith's work.

Neoclassical theory, the orthodoxy of modern economics, has gone no
further in elaborating the inter-connection between trade and growth than
to expand upon the sources of static gains in efficiency. Classical economists
like Ricardo, wed as they were to the labour theory of value, pointed to
international differences in the productivity of labour as the main determinant of the differences in relative prices that provide the motive for trade
and are the source of the gains in efficiency. By contrast, neoclassical
economists explain international differences in relative prices, and hence the
basis of trade, in terms of influences on both supply and demand. In addition
to technologically related differences in relative labour productivity, variations among countries in tastes and preferences are also potential sources of

gains from trade. Most important, however, by introducing capital as a separate factor of production, relative endowments of capital and labour become important determinants of the nature and characteristics of trade in neoclassical theory.

The neoclassical theory of international trade has proved to be particularly useful for explaining the trade patterns of developing countries and for analysing the potential gains from trade or, put differently, the potential cost of autarky to developing countries. Whatever the differences between developed and developing countries in terms of technology and tastes, both of which are difficult – if not impossible – to identify, there is no doubt that enormous discrepancies exist in terms of relative factor endowments. Relative abundance of labour and scarcity of capital (broadly defined to include human capital) is virtually what defines a developing country. Given these differences, the gains from trade are potentially considerable. Furthermore, being poor and in many cases small, developing countries have limited domestic markets, which may preclude the attainment of an efficient scale of production in the absence of international trade.

To summarise, the connection between trade and growth is indirect according to orthodox theory, operating principally through the effect of trade on economic efficiency which, in turn, is a key determinant of the capacity to save, invest and hence to grow.[1] Trade is important for developing countries because they are likely to find that, without it, income is too low to afford savings and investment at levels that allow a satisfactory rate of growth.

Perspective of development theory

However important external factors may be for economic growth according to orthodox theory, they play a starring role, either as hero or villain, in much of the literature on economic development. Whereas the link between trade and growth is indirect in orthodox theory, in much of the literature on economic development the rate of growth of developing countries is alleged to depend indirectly on their ability to export and import. In the literature on development, trade is portrayed either as an autonomous 'engine of growth' or, according to its radical critics, as the single most important obstacle to it.

Trade as an 'engine of growth'

The notion of trade as an autonomous 'engine of growth' in developing countries is, ironically, more often (if not exclusively) appealed to by those who would have developing countries reduce their reliance on trade. The intellectual foundations of the import-substitution strategy of development laid in the 1950s by Raul Prebisch, Gunnar Myrdal and, most importantly,

Ragnar Nurkse were that, while trade served as the engine of growth in the nineteenth century, it could no longer be relied upon to play that role in the twentieth, because of a slowdown in the growth of demand in developed countries for the exports of developing countries.[2] Subsequently Lewis (1980) declared trade to have been the 'engine of growth' after the Second World War in developing countries, only to argue that the 'engine' is running out of fuel as the industrial countries enter a prolonged period of economic slowdown. The solution, according to Lewis, is to turn to an alternative source of fuel – trade among developing countries – which he asserts can 'take up the slack left by MDCs [more developed countries] as MDCs slow down' (Lewis, 1980, p. 560).

As the name implies, the theory of trade as an 'engine of growth' is mechanistic. The moving parts are, like a machine, connected by 'gears' whose tightness of fit determines the mechanical efficiency of the engine. As is illustrated in Figure 3.1, in the trade engine there are two critical 'gears', one linking growth of developing countries to trade, the other linking the trade of developing countries to economic prosperity and growth in developed countries (or to other exogenous non-price determinants of the external demand for exports from developing countries). It must be assumed further that alternative sources of foreign exchange – aid and foreign capital – are determined exogenously. The validity of the theory of the 'trade engine' rests on the tightness of fit of the two principal 'gears' and on the validity of the accompanying assumption that aid and foreign capital to developing countries are strictly rationed. At this point it is useful to consider the underlying assumptions of the theory, the relevance of which will later be assessed empirically.

Link between trade and growth

Consider first the 'gear' linking the growth of developing countries to trade. There are two main versions of this link in the literature, the mechanism differing according to whether the constraint on growth is seen principally to be one of supply or demand. The supply-oriented version builds on the orthodox theory of growth which relates growth of output to an expanding supply of labour and capital and to technological advances, which raise the productivity of labour and capital. The extension of this model in the development literature, which establishes trade as the direct determinant of growth, follows from the introduction of foreign investment goods (or foreign intermediate inputs) as separate, non-substitutable factors of production. As a consequence of technological ignorance, structural imbalances or economic rigidity, it is hypothesised that developing countries are incapable of producing certain non-substitutable investment goods. The ability to expand productive capacity hinges, therefore, on the ability to import such goods. The ability to import depends directly on the ability to export,

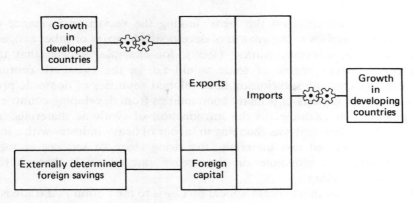

Figure 3.1 The trade engine

given the assumption that more foreign exchange cannot be obtained from foreign borrowing or redirected from the import of consumption goods. Limited substitutability of imported for domestic goods in consumption and production is the essential ingredient of the supply-oriented model of the direct link between exports and economic growth.

The demand-oriented model of the link between exports and growth is offered by those who view the structure of developing economies as dualistic, there being two independent sectors: a traditional, subsistence sector in which productive resources, mainly labour, are largely under- or unemployed, and a small enclave export sector with minimal links to the traditional sector. The traditional sector is caught in the vicious circle of poverty – poor because it cannot invest, and unable to invest because it is poor. Growth occurs only to the extent that the enclave export sector expands to absorb the labour that is readily available in perfectly elastic supply from the traditional sector.[3] Thus exports are the key to growth, but they can expand no faster than is permitted by the first 'gear' in the 'trade engine', that linking exports of developing countries to the growth of developed countries or other exogenous determinants of demand.

Link between export performance and growth of developed countries

The proposition that the export performance of developing countries is determined by forces outside the developing countries themselves is just as crucial to the theory of trade as an engine of growth as the proposition that growth in developing countries depends on trade. The metaphor of an engine is valid only if one can distinguish what goes into the engine from what comes out. Without the proposition that exports are driven externally, the link between trade and growth is intermediate.

Those who have appealed to the theory of the 'trade engine' have, in fact, focused their attention on the 'gear' linking the export performance of developing countries to the growth of developed countries or other exogenous sources of demand. Nurkse (1959), for example, alleged that the nineteenth-century engine of trade would fail in the twentieth century because of increasing substitution in developed countries of domestic production for the exports of primary commodities from developing countries. He pointed, for example, to the introduction of synthetic materials, an industrial structure that was changing in favour of heavy industry with a low content of imported raw materials, the rising share of services in total expenditures, and economies in the use of raw materials through the reprocessing of scrap.

By contrast, the more recent appeal by Lewis to the notion that trade is a faltering engine of growth attributes the problem to a general reduction in the rate of growth of income and expenditure in developed countries, his view being that 'As MDCs [more developed countries] grow faster, the rate of growth of their imports accelerates and LDCs export more'. Moreover, Lewis believes that the link between the growth of developed countries and the exports of developing countries has remained virtually constant for 100 years: 'The growth rate of world trade in primary products over the period 1873 to 1913 was 0.87 times the growth rate of industrial production; and just about the same relationship, about 0.87, also ruled in the two decades to 1973' (Lewis, 1980, p. 556). The justification of demand pessimism given by Nurkse applies to the exports of primary commodities from developing countries, which have declined as a share of the exports of developing countries (excluding fuel) from about 90 per cent in 1955 to less than 54 per cent in 1980. The empirical analysis by Lewis of the 'gear' linking the trade of developing countries to industrial expansion in developed countries is also based exclusively on exports of primary commodities, an assumption justified by the assertion that, while 'world trade in primary products is a wider concept than exports from developing countries . . . the two are sufficiently closely related for it to serve as a proxy'.

In fact, developing countries account for only about 40 per cent of world trade in primary products (excluding fuel). Since primary products also constitute little more than half of exports from developing countries (excluding fuel), there are obvious objections to any theory that begins by dividing the world into an industrialised North and a primary-commodity producing South. Nevertheless, those who appeal to the theory of the trade engine generally do not admit the limitations of their analysis; its applicability, however, depends on the extent to which developing countries, either individually or collectively, rely on exports of primary products. The popular view is, therefore, that exports from developing countries in general (and not just of primary commodities) depend on economic prosperity in developed countries.[4] Accordingly, it is important to consider the applicability of the thesis of the trade engine to exports of developing countries as a whole in assessing its validity.

Role of prices

On closer examination of the disagreement between neoclassical economics on the one hand, and development economics on the other hand, it emerges that the peripheral issue is the role of prices in determining the export performance of developing countries. Nurkse's analysis of the substitution of developed-country products for the exports of primary commodities of developing countries ignored the effects of prices.[5] Lewis, on the other hand, rules them out by asserting that, 'The main link between MDC and LDC economies has been MDC demand for LDC primary commodities. This has been a link in terms of physical volume not much affected by price' (Lewis, 1980, p. 559).

The exclusion of a role for price competition in the markets for exports from developing countries is not accidental. It is the principal means by which the economic relationship between developed and developing countries is reduced to one of simple mechanical links. For if developing countries are capable of expanding exports by claiming a larger share of the market of developed countries through price competition, no stable mechanical link will be maintained between economic expansion in developed countries and the growth of export volume of developing countries.

The extent to which developing countries can engage in price competition depends on the price elasticity of demand in their market for exports and the price elasticity of domestic supply of exports. Attempts to model trade as an 'engine of growth', therefore, start by assuming that developing countries specialise completely in 'tropical' primary products for which no close substitute is produced in 'temperate' developed countries (see, for example, Findlay, 1980). Under this assumption, demand for exports of developing countries is inelastic with respect to price and hence is primarily constrained by the level of expenditure in the markets of developed countries. The first 'gear' of the trade engine is established thereby. The second 'gear', that linking the growth of the national income of developing countries to the growth of their exports, is then established by assuming either that investment is dependent on the ability to import, or that growth occurs exclusively in export enclaves which can readily expand supply (being able to draw on a virtually inexhaustible supply of labour) but face inelastic demand in world markets.

Terms of trade

Although price competition is largely absent from the mechanics of the trade engine, the terms of trade for developing countries are a matter of great concern both to structuralists, who appeal to the notion of trade as an engine of growth, and to their more radical cousins, the neo-Marxists, who view trade as nothing more than a 'strategy for underdevelopment'.

There is no reason to dwell on the latter concept, since the issues are neither empirical nor theoretical, but theological. Trade is considered by the neo-Marxists to be exploitative because more current labour is embodied in the goods exported by developing countries than in those they import with equal value (Frank, 1967). This is nothing other than a tautological restatement of the fact that developing countries have a comparative advantage in relatively labour-intensive products (see Samuelson, 1976). Trade between developing and developed countries is then exploitative by definition.[6]

The pessimism about the terms of trade of those who advocate the theory of the trade engine, by contrast, derives logically from the underlying assumptions of their model.[7] Assume a world in which developing countries specialise completely in 'tropical' products which they can supply in virtually unlimited quantity, but for which demand is inelastic. Assume further that developing countries are dependent on developed countries for the supply of the investment goods needed to expand their productive capacity. From these assumptions it is easily deduced that growth in developing countries depends on their ability to export which depends, in turn, on growth in developed countries. The terms of trade reinforce the inexorable mechanics of the trade engine because the prices of exports from developing countries tend to decline and so their terms of trade deteriorate whenever any internal impulse might give rise to domestic growth (see Lewis, 1980; Findlay, 1980).

IMPLICATIONS OF ALTERNATIVE PERSPECTIVES FOR POLICY

If all that were at issue were the quantitative importance of trade for growth in developing countries, there would be little ground for debate between neoclassical economists and the structuralists who dominate the literature on economic development. Both recognise that trade is and always has been important for growth in developing countries. The correspondence between growth rates and export expansion in developing countries is well documented. Cross-country analysis has established the fact for the period since the Second World War (see Michaely, 1977; Balassa, 1978; Tyler, 1981). Moreover, the painstaking review by Lloyd Reynolds of contemporary developing countries in the nineteenth century reveals that, then too, 'the turning point [in a nation's experience of growth] is usually associated with a marked rise in exports' (Reynolds, 1983, p. 963).

This evidence does not warrant the conclusion that trade served as the engine of growth, although this is the usual interpretation. Even Reynolds, who concludes that 'political organization and the administrative competence of government' are the 'single most important explanatory variable' for the experience of developing countries with economic growth, payslip service to the theory advanced by Lewis of trade as an engine of growth. As the foregoing review of the theory reveals, however, the idea of trade as an engine of growth implies far more than that trade is important. It implies, in addition, that export success and hence the capacity to grow are determined outside developing countries themselves. This view is inconsistent with Reynolds's hypothesis that political organisation and administrative competence are what count and his historical finding that 'the turning point is almost always associated with some significant political event' (Reynolds, 1983, p. 963).

The premise that export performance and growth are externally determined is the basis for the policy recommended by those who advance the theory of the trade engine. This policy invariably involves a rejection of free trade. The rejection of free trade is advocated as the only way of lifting the siege on the economies of developing countries that is imposed by the developed world. No less important, the premise that exports are externally driven provides a convenient justification for dismissing the past success of some countries in world markets and for denying that such success might continue under the less favourable circumstances that many now foresee for the developed countries.

The orthodox view of the connection between trade and growth certainly does not deny that slower growth in developed countries probably spells slower rates of export expansion and growth for developing countries. Where it differs is in what is implied for policy. The aim of policy from the orthodox viewpoint is to ensure that resources are employed efficiently. If that is accomplished, growth follows and so do exports, the latter accounting perhaps for a relatively large part of the growth of income in countries with small domestic markets or an unbalanced endowment of resources by world standards. A close association between expansion of exports and growth of income should not be construed, however, as implying that one drives the other, but rather that both are propelled simultaneously by other forces. As Reynolds hypothesises, government plays an important part, in some cases stimulating but in others retarding efficient accumulation. What is appropriate policy, however, mainly depends on internal circumstances, which are, for the most part, independent of the rate of growth abroad. There are no *a priori* grounds for assuming that policies appropriate in a world of rapid growth are less appropriate in a world of slow growth, as long as some access to world markets is maintained.

It is generally accepted that the orthodox view applies to the developed countries, even to the smaller among them, which rely on trade as much as, or more than, many developing countries. For developing countries, however, the orthodox claim of 'monoeconomics' – the view that economic analysis can be applied in the same way to all countries – is rejected. The view in the literature on development economics implies that 'underdeveloped countries as a group are set apart from the advanced industrial countries by a number of specific economic characteristics and that traditional economic analysis, which has concentrated on the developed countries, must therefore be recast in significant respects when dealing with developing countries' (Hirschman, 1981, p. 3). The key characteristics that set developing countries apart, according to development theory, are economic dualism and structural rigidity, which vitiate the price mechanism.

The relevance of the structuralist model of development, and in particular those aspects of the model relating to external economic relations, is not independent of time, as Findlay (1984) has pointed out: 'The hope of all concerned with the "development" of the Third World is that eventually its structural peculiarities will disappear as it approaches more closely to the levels of productivity and income of the presently more advanced countries' (Findlay, 1984, p. 222). In his masterful review of structuralist models of North-South relations, Findlay (1984) cautions that these models '. . . will one day, and perhaps even now, be of more historical than contemporary interest' (p. 222).

EMPIRICAL EVIDENCE ON TRADE AS AN ENGINE OF GROWTH

We now turn to an examination of the empirical relevance of the theory of trade as an engine of growth in the light of past changes in the structure of production and trade in developing countries. The focus of analysis will be the two key assumptions of the theory: that imports are essential for investment and growth in developing countries; and that the capacity of developing countries to earn foreign exchange is governed by the level, and rate of expansion, of income in export markets.

Economic growth

Discussion of the growth performance of developing countries in the period 1950-80 provides a useful perspective on the subsequent analysis of the changing structure of production and trade. Although the period was one of unprecedented growth in developing and developed countries alike, the post-war acceleration was even more pronounced in developing countries. As is shown in Figure 3.2, GDP in developing countries consistently grew faster than in developed countries, although growth in the latter is alleged to have been the driving force in the growth of the former. Particularly remarkable is the performance of developing countries after the mid-1960s, with growth of GDP averaging more than 6 per cent a year until early in 1970, and well over 5 per cent even after the oil price shocks. These rates of growth may be compared to those in the developed countries of an average 3.7 per cent a year in the period 1965-75. Thus, while the engine of the train

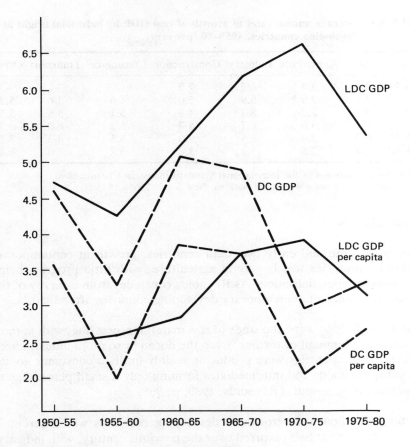

Source: United Nations, *Statistical Yearbook*, 1965 and 1981.

Figure 3.2 Average annual rates of growth of real GDP and real per capita GDP in developed and developing countries, 1950–80 (percentages)

was slowing down over the last decade and a half, the speed of its boxcars, the developing countries, appears to have been increasing!

In general, the developing countries have out-performed the developed countries even in terms of growth of income per head, although by a smaller margin. Nonetheless, this feat is remarkable, given the relatively high rate of population growth in developing countries in the post-war period – 2.3 per cent a year between 1950 and 1980 – as compared to the growth rate of less than 1 per cent a year in the nineteenth and early twentieth centuries, and also as compared to the population growth in developed countries in the post-war period of 1 per cent a year.[8]

TABLE 3.1　Average annual rates of growth of real GDP by industrial origin in developing countries, 1950–80 (per cent)

Period	Total	Agriculture	Industry[a]	Construction	Commerce	Transport	Other
1950–55	4.7	3.4	6.7	7.0	–	–	–
1955–60	4.6	2.9	6.9	5.0	4.6	5.6	5.2
1960–65	5.2	2.2	8.4	4.9	5.1	5.6	5.5
1965–70	6.2	3.0	8.7	6.7	6.2	6.0	6.3
1970–75	6.5	2.6	6.5	9.0	6.5	8.3	7.7
1975–80	5.4	2.5	5.1	8.2	5.2	7.6	6.3

[a] Comprising orders 2–4 of the International Standard Industrial Classification.
Sources: *Statistical Yearbook*, United Nations, New York, 1965 and 1981.

Industrialisation

In the nineteenth and early twentieth centuries, growth in contemporary developing countries was largely in agriculture, with little progress being made toward industrialisation. As Reynolds concludes from a survey of the growth experience of contemporary developing countries after 1850:

> Most (as of 1950) were at a stage of raw material processing, with at most a small development of textiles. Even the dozen or so more industrialized [developing] countries were producing mainly finished consumer goods, with capital goods and intermediates forming only a small percentage of manufacturing output. (Reynolds, 1980, p. 968).

After 1950, however, growth in developing countries was different in character from what had occurred over the previous century, with industry, construction, transport and other service sectors leading economic expansion. As is shown in Table 3.1, agriculture, on which the majority of the population of most developing countries depends, grew at rates far below those of industry and other major activities. The lagging rate of growth in agriculture was in part the consequence of the social and economic difficulty of introducing technical innovations in agriculture. As numerous studies have documented, however, a major obstacle to growth in agriculture was the policy adopted by most developing countries in the late 1950s of fostering industrialisation through import substitution (see Little, Scitovsky and Scott, 1970; Bhagwati, 1978; and Chapter 4 of this volume).

The damaging consequences of the strategy of import-substituting industrialisation are well documented, the retardation of agriculture being just one, albeit a major one. Nevertheless, the objective of transforming the structure of production was achieved to a significant degree. To what extent industrialisation proceeded because of, and to what extent in spite of, import-substitution policies is a matter of debate. Certainly, there was no

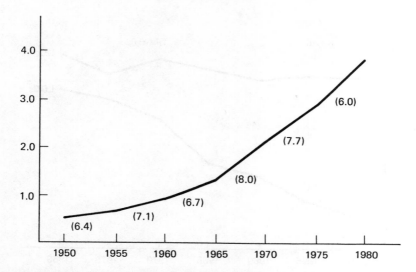

4.0

3.0 (6.0)

2.0 (7.7)

(8.0)

1.0 (6.7)

(7.1)

(6.4)

1950   1955   1960   1965   1970   1975   1980

Figure 3.3   Index of manufacturing production (average annual rate of growth)

diminution of growth in manufacturing after 1965, when many countries turned from policies of import-substitution towards a more outward-oriented approach. Indeed, as Figure 3.3 shows, manufacturing experienced its most rapid growth in developing countries between 1965 and 1975. It is important, however, not to overstate the extent of trade liberalisation in the mid- to late 1960s. For while most developing countries have attempted to ameliorate biases against exports, the complex of import-substitution measures remains very much in place in many of them, particularly in the larger countries. Many still believe in the structuralist view of the world that gave birth to the import-substitution strategy thirty years ago.

Nevertheless, the central feature of the structuralist model, the dichotomy between a primary-commodity-producing South and an industrialised North, has been significantly eroded over the past thirty years. As is shown in Figure 3.4, the share of manufacturing in the GDP of developing countries as a whole has steadily risen, to a level which fell short of that of developed countries by less than 3 per cent by 1980. Among developed countries there is, of course, considerable variation in the proportion of GDP accounted for by manufacturing, the share generally rising with income per head. Even among low-income countries, however, there are those with relatively large manufacturing sectors and, in general, these are the largest and most populous countries. Those countries in which the manufacturing share of GDP is less than 18 per cent, which was the level for India in 1980, are large in number but small in size and are mainly located in Africa (see World Bank, 1983, p. 152).

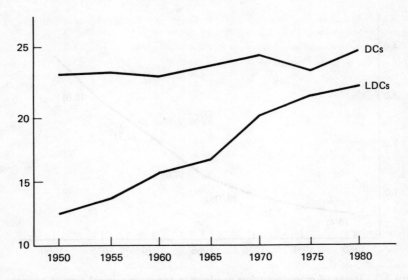

Figure 3.4 **Share of manufacturing in GDP in developed and developing countries, 1950–80 (percentages)**

Two 'gears' of the 'trade engine'

The view that growth in developing countries is more dependent on external conditions than is growth in developed countries rests on one, or both, of two propositions. The first is that investment in developing countries is more reliant on imported capital goods, and hence that their growth is more dependent on trade; the second is that exports of developing countries are tightly linked to growth and prosperity in developed countries to an extent that is not true for the developed countries themselves.

With regard to the first proposition, the level of imports in relation to GDP is no higher in developing countries than in developed countries when proper account is taken of the determinants of the ratio of imports to GDP apart from the level of development. Naturally, smaller countries import more in relation to GDP than larger countries, and countries with relatively high rates of investment also import relatively more. But income per head, a common proxy for the level of development, bears no statistically significant relationship to the level of import dependence.[9] Furthermore, as is shown in Table 3.2, the composition of imports in developed and developing countries is roughly similar. In both developed and developing countries, capital goods and intermediates, including fuels, constitute about 80 per cent of total imports. It is not apparent that trade is any more indispensable for investment in developing countries than it is in developed countries, although it may be the case that imports and domestically produced intermediate and

TABLE 3.2   Composition of imports by end-use, developed and developing countries, 1970 and 1980 (per cent)

	Developed countries	Developing countries
Consumer goods		
1970	25	22
1980	20	21
Capital goods		
1970	30	43
1980	23	30
Intermediate inputs		
1970	38	25
1980	29	29
Fuels		
1970	10	7
1980	27	18

Sources: *Yearbook of International Trade Statistics*, United Nations, New York, 1974 and 1983.

capital goods are closer substitutes in developed countries than in developing countries.

The thesis that the growth of developing countries is more vulnerable to external conditions must, therefore, rest primarily on the proposition that the capacity of developing countries to export is more dependent on external factors than that of developed countries. As was explained above, the proposition of the theory of the trade engine depends on the assumption that developing countries specialise in 'tropical' products for which close substitutes do not exist in their export markets. On this assumption, price competition, by which developing countries might increase their share in the markets of developed countries, is ruled out, and the economic relationship between developed and developing countries is reduced to a simple mechanical link. How relevant is the assumption and the implications which derive from it in the light of the structural changes in developing countries described above? This question is now considered.

Changing structure of exports

A look at the aggregate data on exports of developing countries would seem to dispel very quickly the notion that developing countries are heavily dependent on exports of agricultural products. As Table 3.3 shows, two dramatic changes have occurred in the structure of the exports of developing countries, reducing the share of primary products (that is, food, agricultural raw materials and minerals) to only slightly more than 20 per cent of total exports in 1982. One is the doubling of the share of fuels from 25 per cent of exports in 1955 to 62 per cent in 1980 and 57 per cent in 1982, a phenomenon largely attributable to increases in the price of oil since 1973.

The other change, far more profound in terms of the issues addressed in this paper, is the rising importance of exports of manufactures. The increase in the share of manufactures in exports of developing countries is not, as in the case of fuel, a phenomenon of higher prices, but is rather the consequence of three decades of sometimes painful and costly industrialisation. Moreover, although the most dramatic part of the expansion of manufactured exports has been accounted for up to now by a few small countries, the potential for all developing countries to share in the expansion of exports of manufactures distinguishes this trade from the oil boom, which can only be enjoyed by a limited number of countries because of the inequities of nature. Because the opportunity to export manufactures is more generally available and because major oil-exporting developing countries have not until very recently been constrained by their ability to export, whatever other problems they may face, the analysis below focuses on exports excluding fuel and countries other than those that earn the majority of their foreign exchange from oil. Hereafter, therefore, any reference to total exports should be understood to mean total exports excluding fuel.

A study of the figures for non-fuel exports of developing countries in the second section of Table 3.3 is even more revealing. Whereas in 1955 primary products, that is food, agricultural raw materials and minerals and ores, accounted for almost 90 per cent of all non-fuel exports of developing countries, with manufactures making up only just over 10 per cent, by 1970 the figures had changed to roughly 75 per cent and 25 per cent respectively. By 1982, however, manufactures accounted for more than half (52 per cent) of all non-fuel developing-country exports, and primary products for only 48 per cent. This can only be described as a dramatic shift in a period of less than thirty years, and there is no reason to doubt that the share of manufactures in developing-country exports will continue to increase in the years to come.

Were all or most developing countries to have similar structures of production and trade, therefore, the aggregate data alone might allow one to dismiss the models of the trade engine of growth as not only unrealistic but discredited by the facts. It has to be accepted, however, that developing countries share few economic characteristics other than income per head below some arbitrarily set level.[10] Not surprisingly, therefore, the aggregate data mask a wide diversity of export structures. Four countries in East Asia (that is, the Republic of Korea, Taiwan, Hong Kong and Singapore) alone accounted for more than 50 per cent of total exports of manufactures from developing countries in 1980, but they had only about 3 per cent of the total population of developing countries (excluding China). These four entities, together with Lebanon and Macao, are the only developing countries in which manufactures account for as much as 75 per cent of exports.

TABLE 3.3   Structure of developing-country exports, selected years, 1955–82 (per cent)[a]

	1955	1960	1970	1980	1982
Total exports	100.0	100.0	100.0	100.0	100.0
Food	36.5	33.6	26.5	11.4	12.5
Agricultural raw materials	20.5	18.3	10.0	3.6	3.0
Minerals, ores	9.9	10.6	13.6	5.1	4.8
Fuels	25.2	27.9	33.4	62.5	57.6
Manufactures[b]	7.7	9.2	16.3	17.4	22.1
Total non-fuel exports	100.0	100.0	100.0	100.0	100.0
Food	48.9	46.7	39.9	30.3	29.5
Agricultural raw materials	27.4	25.3	15.1	9.7	7.1
Minerals, ores	13.3	14.6	20.5	13.7	11.4
Manufactures[b]	10.4	12.8	24.5	46.2	52.0
Share of exports of developing economies to developed countries					
Total non-fuel exports	76.3	74.3	71.9	60.8	58.1
Food	79.0	77.7	74.0	59.2	53.0
Agricultural raw materials	74.3	67.8	64.4	59.0	56.0
Minerals, ores	94.5	92.0	89.2	73.2	68.1
Manufactures[b]	45.9	54.0	61.2	59.4	59.2

[a] The percentages do not always add to 100 because of rounding.
[b] Manufactures = SITC 5 to 8, less 68.
Sources: *Handbook of International Trade and Development Statistics*, UNCTAD Secretariat, Geneva, 1972, 1979, 1982, 1983 and 1985.

In the rest of the developing world, primary products, the traditional mainstay, are still the predominant export. As is shown in Figure 3.5, however, manufactures account for a growing share of exports even among countries relying heavily on exports of primary products. Among the fifty-four countries represented in Figure 3.5, the average share of manufactures in exports (excluding fuel) rose from 7 per cent in 1960 to 20 per cent in 1980. Moreover, it is particularly important to note that the increased share of manufactures reflected a decline in the share of the single largest primary commodity in total exports, so providing the greatest benefit from the diversification of exports arising from the expansion of manufactures.

Nevertheless, the picture presented in Figure 3.5 is also misleading because success in diversifying exports has varied widely even within this group of countries. Among the fifty-four countries, eleven managed to raise the share of manufactures from an average of 15 per cent in 1960 to almost 50 per cent in 1980.[11] This group of eleven 'balanced exporters', which includes most of South Asia, Egypt, Brazil, Mexico and some smaller Latin American countries is listed in Appendix 3A. The group accounts for about two-thirds of the population of the developing world, excluding the People's Republic of China, and consists of countries which were no longer highly

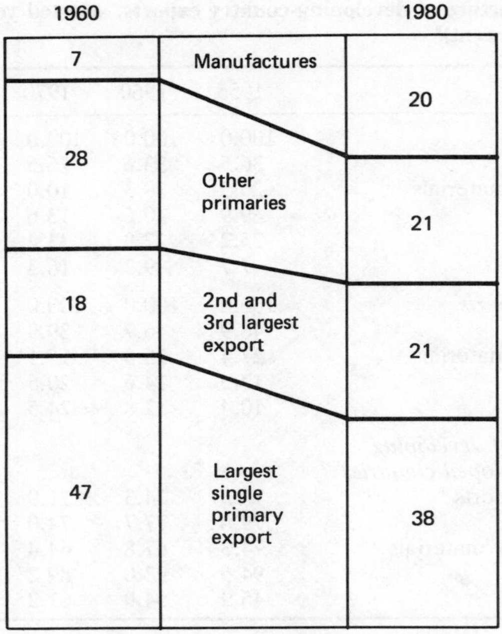

Trade as an Engine of Growth

Figure 3.5 Average export structure for total sample of LDCs (54 countries)

dependent on their traditional single largest primary commodity. As is shown in Figure 3.6, the average decline in the share of primary commodities in total exports was largely accounted for by the decline of the single largest commodity for this group of countries.

Developing countries in which exports of primary commodities continue to account for 80 per cent or more of total exports are large in number but relatively small in size, and together account for only about one-third of the population of developing countries, excluding the People's Republic of China. Even among these countries, however, there are important differences in diversification of exports, which deserve to be mentioned. Among countries still predominantly exporting primary products, only African countries appear to have been unable to reduce their dependence on their traditional, single largest primary export (as is shown in Figure 3.7).

In short, significant changes have occurred in the structure of exports of developing countries, particularly for countries outside Africa. Dependence on a single primary export, a key characteristic of the colonial economy, has declined greatly. Moreover, manufactures occupy an ever larger share of the exports of most developing countries and already possess a share in exports almost equal to that of primary products in countries which contain the majority of the population of the developing world.

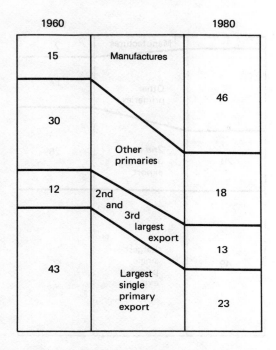

Figure 3.6   Average export structure for balanced exporters (11 countries)

Market shares of exports of developing countries

How has diversification of exports affected the link between the exports of developing countries and economic growth in developed countries? One thing it has not changed is dependence on the markets of developed countries. As is shown in Table 3.3, developing countries have come to depend on markets in developed countries for their exports of manufactures as much as for their exports of primary commodities. Nevertheless, although much has been made of a supposed bias against trade among developing countries, a thorough examination of the empirical evidence finds that developing countries' exports to one another of all non-fuel commodities, manufactures and non-fuel primary commodities all exceed what might be expected on the basis of their weight in the world economy (Harvylyshyn and Wolf, 1983). The share of the developed countries as markets for the exports of developing countries is, in other words, no more (and perhaps less) than proportionate to their share in world income. Moreover, since the aggregate income of developed countries is projected to exceed that of developing countries in the year 2000 by a factor greater than 2 to 1, even under the most optimistic scenario, developed countries will probably remain the major market for exports from developing countries for the foreseeable future (World Bank, 1980).

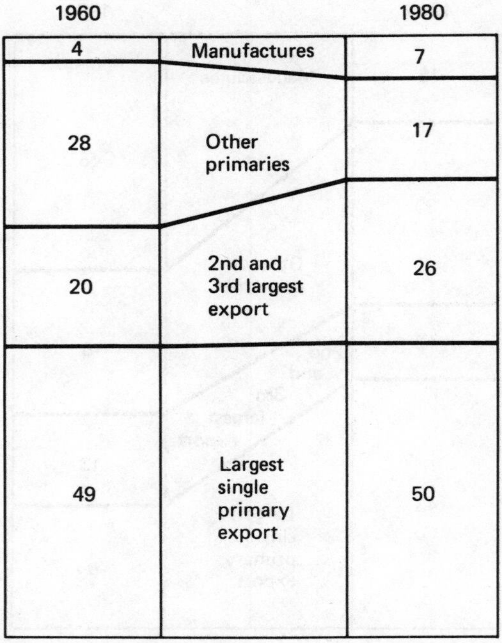

Trade as an Engine of Growth

	1960		1980
	4	Manufactures	7
	28	Other primaries	17
	20	2nd and 3rd largest export	26
	49	Largest single primary export	50

Figure 3.7 Average export structure for African primary exporters (20 countries)

Note: country groupings are given in Appendix 3a.
Source: M. Wolf, 'LDC Exports – key features of past performance; unpublished mimeo, February 1978; World Bank, *Commodity trade and price trends*, 1973, 1980; *Handbook of International Trade and Development Statistics*, 1979.

How, then, has the link been altered? The answer lies not in the destination of exports, but in the competitive position of the different exports of developing countries within the markets of developed countries. A crucial assumption of the theory of the trade engine is that of complete specialisation, which implies that there are limited possibilities for substituting the goods supplied by developing countries for those produced domestically in developed countries. Under this assumption, and as long as tastes and preferences remain fairly constant, exports from developing countries can only expand, more or less, in proportion to the markets themselves. Developing countries have little scope to expand exports simply by obtaining a larger share of the market through competition. In these circumstances, demand rather than supply determines an upper limit to exports. If the assumption of non-substitutability is relaxed, however, then the higher the elasticity of substitution among products of different origins and the lower

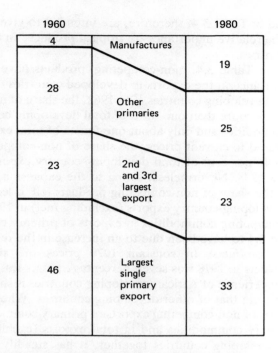

Figure 3.8 Average export structure for non-African primary exporters (23 countries)

the share of exports from developing countries in the market, the less important is the level, or rate of growth, of income in developed countries. Supply rather than demand would then be expected to be the main constraint on exports from developing countries.

Coffee, a product for which no close substitute is produced in developed countries, was traditionally and is still today the single largest export of developing countries, excluding fuel. But how important are coffee and other 'broadly non-competing' commodities in total exports (excluding fuel)? The classification of exports of primary commodities from developing countries into the categories 'directly competing' and 'broadly non-competing' is not easily done, since some important tropical products (natural rubber, for example) have close synthetic substitutes in developed countries. The procedure in Table 3.4 is to classify as 'broadly non-competing' those products for which the developing-country share of world exports exceeds 80 per cent. The criterion is obviously arbitrary and, in some important instances, misleading. For example, an exception has to be made for sugar, where developing countries dominate world exports, but account for less than half of the consumption of developed countries. The figures reported in Table 3.4, therefore, are intended to give only a rough indication of the relative importance of 'tropical products' in the exports of developing countries.

As is shown in Table 3.4, 'non-competing' products have long been of secondary importance in the exports to developed countries of the primary commodities of developing countries.[12] In 1962, the share of non-competing products was little more than one-third of total developing-country exports of primary commodities and only about one-fourth of total exports. excluding fuel. Measured in current prices, the share of non-competing products rose to almost 40 per cent of total developing-country exports of primary commodities in 1978. Nevertheless, owing to the expansion of exports of manufactures, the share of non-competing products fell to less than 20 per cent of total developing-country exports (excluding fuel) in 1978. The rising share of non-competing commodities in exports of primary commodities is shown in Table 3.4 to have been due to an increase in the relative price of non-competing products. In constant 1970 prices the share of non-competing products in 1978 was seven percentage points less than in 1962.

Again, the experience of African developing countries is shown, in Table 3.4, to diverge from that of other developing countries. Whereas the share at constant prices of non-competing exports of primary commodities in total exports of primary commodities and in total exports (excluding fuel) has fallen for all developing countries together, it has steadily increased for African developing countries. Indeed, beverages, the category accounting for the largest part of the decline in the share of non-competing exports for all developing countries, account for the largest part of the increase in the share of non-competing products in exports of primary commodities from African developing countries. This suggests that, while failing to share in the expansion of exports of manufactures, African developing countries have begun to replace the more successful developing countries as they abandon their traditional non-competing exports.

In the markets for manufactures of developed countries, developing countries play a minor role, in spite of growth in the volume of exports of manufactures to developed countries at more than 12 per cent a year over the last two decades. Table 3.5 shows the shares of exports from developing countries in the apparent consumption of manufactures in developed countries. The average share was only 3.4 per cent in 1979, up from a mere 1.7 per cent in 1970. Disaggregating to the five digit level in the International Standard Industrial Classification (ISIC), Hughes and Waelbroeck (1981) found only four categories (namely, leather, knitted apparel, furs and jewellery) out of a total of more than 150 in which the share of developing countries in the corresponding market of developed countries exceeded 25 per cent. In clothing and electrical machinery, the fastest growing categories, shares of the market in 1979 were 14.1 and 4.1 per cent respectively.

Some might argue that, although market shares of developing countries

TABLE 3.4 Shares of broadly non-competing and directly competing developing-country exports of non-fuel primary commodities to developed countries (per cent)

Commodity group	1962[a]		1970		1978[a]	
	Total	Africa	Total	Africa	Total	Africa
Broadly non-competing[b]	34.2 (39.8)	25.9 (25.9)	33.5	26.2	39.3 (32.3)	43.3 (30.6)
Food stuffs	22.0 (27.6)	14.6 (17.4)	21.1	18.4	27.5 (21.6)	32.8 (22.6)
of which beverages	17.0 (21.0)	12.4 (12.1)	15.1	15.3	21.4 (14.6)	30.1 (20.0)
Agricultural raw materials	9.3 (8.0)	5.6 (4.8)	8.5	3.4	7.8 (5.7)	3.1 (2.0)
Metals and minerals	2.9 (4.2)	5.7 (3.7)	3.9	4.4	4.0 (5.0)	7.4 (6.0)
Directly competing[c]	65.7 (60.2)	74.1 (74.1)	66.4	73.3	60.8 (67.7)	56.8 (69.4)
Food stuffs	32.5	39.3	29.4	22.2	33.3	21.8
Agricultural raw materials	14.6	10.8	9.5	8.6	9.1	9.4
Metals and minerals	18.6	24.0	27.5	42.5	18.4	25.6
Total primary commodities (excluding fuel)	100.0	100.0	100.0	100.0	100.0	100.0

Note: The percentages do not always add to 100 because of rounding.
[a] Figures in parentheses are shares in constant 1970 prices. In computing shares in constant prices, individual price indexes for each 'non-competing' product were used to derive values of exports in 1962 and 1978 at 1970 prices for each product. The aggregate non-fuel primary commodity export deflator was used to obtain total primary commodity exports, excluding fuel, in 1962 and 1978 at 1970 prices. The constant price shares for total 'directly competing' exports were derived residually. Since individual price indexes were not available for 'directly competing' products, constant price shares could not be derived.
[b] A list of commodities classified as broadly non-competing is given in Appendix 3B.
[c] The values of 'directly competing' exports were computed as the residual difference between the total and the sum of commodities defined as 'non-competing'.
Sources: IBRD computer tapes of GATT trade data system; *Commodity Trade and Price Trends*, World Bank, Washington, 1980; and *Monthly Bulletin of Statistics*, United Nations, New York, July 1980, Special Table I.

are low in manufactures, the threshold of tolerance of developed countries for penetration of their markets is equally low. Such arguments surfaced in the mid-1970s during a period of resurgent protectionism. However, a research project, sponsored by the World Bank, on the political economy of

TABLE 3.5 Shares of developing countries in apparent consumption of
manufactured goods in industrialised countries, by major product
groups, 1970, 1975 and 1979 (per cent)

Group (ISIC code)	1970	1975	1979
Food, beverages and tobacco (31)	3.4	3.5	3.9
Clothing, textiles and leather (32)	2.7	6.0	9.6
Wood products (33)	1.8	2.1	3.8
Paper and printing (34)	0.1	0.2	0.4
Chemicals (35)	2.0	3.0	3.4
Non-metallic minerals (36)	0.3	0.6	1.0
Basic metals (37)	3.2	0.9	3.5
Machinery (38)	0.3	0.9	2.0
Miscellaneous (39)	8.0	10.3	18.2
Total manufacturing (3)	1.7	2.4	3.4

Source: Hughes and Waelbroeck (1981), pp. 127–47.

protectionism in developed countries failed to find any significant correlation between the level or rate of change of market penetration and the incidence of protectionism (see Anderson and Baldwin, 1981). Moreover, the rising penetration of markets in developed countries by exports of manufactures from developing countries since 1974 suggests that 'The actual impact of the new protectionism of the 1970s . . . [was] not as large as was initially thought probable (Hughes and Waelbroeck, 1981, p. 143).

To summarise, the assumptions about elasticities of supply and demand, on which the theory of the trade engine is based, apply best to traditional exports of broadly non-competing, 'tropical' commodities. Such products, however, constitute a relatively small and declining share of exports for many developing countries, including the most populous ones. Although reliable estimates of elasticities of demand for export of manufactures to developed countries are unavailable, these elasticities are probably extremely high for most products in view of the small share of the market held at present by developing countries. The changing composition of exports from developing countries should, therefore, have relaxed the external constraint on export growth. Yet, according to Lewis (1980, p. 556), the link appears remarkably stable over time, namely 'quantitatively the same over a hundred years'.

Mechanical efficiency of the 'trade engine'

The mechanical efficiency of an engine depends on the tightness of fit of the gears that connect its moving parts. The efficiency of the trade engine is measured by the stability of the relationship between growth in developed countries and the export performance of developing countries. Estimates of the statistical relationship between the volume of exports of developing

TABLE 3.6 *Ex post* **elasticities of export volume of developing countries with respect to real income in developed countries**[a]

	1960–70	1970–8
Total non-fuel exports	0.86	1.74[b]
Manufactures	1.87	4.08[b]
Raw materials	0.95	0.07[b]
Food	0.49	0.65

[a] Based on estimation of the equation:

$$log\ X_t = a_0 + a_1\ log\ Y_t + a_2\ (D\ log\ Y_t) + a_3\ D$$

where X_t = volume of exports in year t ($t = 1960 \ldots 1978$)
Y_t = real income in OECD-North
D = 1 for observations 1970–8, zero otherwise.
[b] Statistically significantly different from the value for the period 1960–70.
Source: J. Riedel, 'Trade as an Engine of Growth in Developing Countries Revisited', *Economic Journal*, Vol. 94, March 1984, p. 68, Table 4.

countries and real income in developed countries in the 1960s and 1970s are presented in Table 3.6. The relationship has clearly been unstable. The 'income elasticity' of demand for exports from developing countries was found to have doubled between the 1960s and 1970s. This is largely attributable to the accelerated growth of exports of manufactures, which grew at twice the rate of income in developed countries in the 1960s, but almost four times as fast in the 1970s. The level of expenditure in developed countries, which grew at a diminished rate in the 1970s, clearly posed no effective constraint on the growth of exports of manufactures from developing countries; nor was protectionism in developed countries an overriding constraint on the expansion of exports of manufactures.

The relationship between the income of developed countries and exports of raw materials from developing countries was also unstable, but the shift was in the opposite direction to that of manufactures. Among other reasons for the inability in the 1970s of exports of raw materials (in particular raw cotton and iron ore) to keep up with even the reduced growth of economic activity in developed countries, was the decline of the cotton textile and steel industries in developed countries, itself in part the consequence of increased competition from exports of developing countries.

Exports of food show the most stable relationship to income in developed countries, but this observation, too, proves deceptive when individual commodities are analysed. Table 3.7 presents estimates of the *ex post* income elasticity of food exports from developing to developed countries. Not only are the elasticities unstable, but for only two of the six commodities is a positive relationship clearly indicated in the period 1970–8. In the case of coffee, the single largest export of developing countries (excluding fuel), no statistically significant relationship to income in developed countries was

TABLE 3.7 *Ex post* **elasticities for food exports of developing countries with respect to real income in developed countries**[a]

	1967–70	1970–78
Coffee	0.469	−0.179
Cocoa	0.073	−0.615
Tea	0.326	0.400
Sugar	0.220	0.952
Copra	−1.027	−0.952
Groundnuts	−0.121	−2.427

[a] Based on estimation of the equation:

$$log\ X_t = a_0 + a_1\ log\ Y_t + a_2\ (D\ log\ Y_t) + a_3\ D$$

where X_t = volume of exports in year t (t = 1960 . . . 1978)
 Y_t = real income in OECD-North
 D = 1 for observations 1970–8, zero otherwise.

The elasticities measure the percentage effect on exports of a per cent change in real income.
Source: J. Riedel, 'Trade as an Engine of Growth in Developing Countries Revisited', *Economic Journal*, Vol. 94, March 1984, p. 68, Table 4.

found. This is consistent with evidence from econometric studies of the world coffee market which invariably find extremely low price and income elasticities of demand for coffee (see deVries, 1982). For certain major markets, including the United States, the estimated income elasticity of demand is close to zero. As a consequence the slowdown of economic growth in developed countries will have little effect on the already dismal prospects for the growth of coffee exports.

Source of fluctuation in export revenues for food

An implication of the inelastic demand for coffee and other major exports of food is that the fluctuations in export revenue result primarily from supply shocks. Moreover, contrary to the tenets of the theory of the trade engine, one would expect that adjustments would predominantly take the form of changes in prices rather than quantities. These hypotheses are tested by analysing the variance and covariance of price and quantity movements for the major exports of food. The sign of the covariance of price and quantity is a commonly used indicator of the source of instability. The reason is that price and quantity would be expected to move together if demand shifts, so giving a positive covariance. If supply shifts, however, price and quantity would move in opposite directions and the covariance would be negative.

Measures of variance and covariance of prices and quantities for major food exports are presented in Table 3.8. The hypothesis that supply shocks are the primary source of variations in export revenue is supported in four of the six cases and is not ruled out in a fifth. In all cases variations in prices are

TABLE 3.8 Variance and covariance of price and quantity of selected food exports from developing countries, 1960[a]

Commodity	Variance of price	Variance of quantity	Covariance of price and quantity[b]	Correlation coefficient between variance of price and quantity[c]
Coffee	106.2	5.7	−39.3	−0.799*
Cocoa	108.1	6.6	−44.3	−0.829*
Tea	62.7	0.6	−0.5	−0.043
Sugar	384.5	7.5	35.8	0.332
Copra	80.2	35.3	−78.7	−0.740*
Groundnuts	43.9	34.8	−51.8	−0.633*

[a] Variance and covariance are measured as deviation from the log-linear trend for the period 1960–78. Values are multiplied by a factor of 1000 to make the table more readable.
[b] Covariance is multiplied by 2 to satisfy the identity: variance (revenue) = variance (price) + variance (quantity) + 2 covariance (price and quantity).
[c] Asterisks indicate that the correlation coefficient is significant at the 1 per cent level.
Source: *Commodity Trade and Price Trends*, World Bank, Washington, 1980.

found to be larger than variations in revenue. Only in the case of sugar is there evidence that shifts in demand are the predominant source of instability in export revenue. This finding is not surprising since only sugar, of the six commodities, faces significant trade barriers, behind which developed countries shelter a large and relatively volatile domestic industry.

The results reported in Table 3.8 for individual commodities are consistent with those based on a similar analysis of aggregate exports of individual developing countries. Analysing aggregate export price and quantity variations for twenty-five countries, one study concluded that 'for a majority of under-developed countries, supply fluctuations have been a more important cause of export earnings instability than demand fluctuations' (Murray, 1978, p. 68). Furthermore, as exports have become more diversified the level of instability has fallen and the relative importance of quantity (as opposed to price) as a source of instability has increased.

WHAT IS LEFT OF THE 'TRADE ENGINE'?

The widely held view that external conditions, principally growth and prosperity in developed countries, play a preponderant role in determining long-term growth in developing countries rests on assumptions that are increasingly inappropriate. In fact there is little left of the assumptions which generated the mechanistic conclusions of the theory of the 'trade engine of growth'. In the period since the Second World War developing countries have grown more rapidly than the developed countries, on which they are supposedly dependent. Furthermore, they have industrialised with extraordinary success, so ending the simple dichotomy between an industrialised North and a primary-commodity-producing South.

With regard to the model of the trade engine itself, two 'gears' are identified, one relating investment in developing countries to imports and the other relating exports from developing countries to levels of economic activity in developed countries. Much of the attention in the analysis is paid to the second gear, but it is made clear that developing countries are no different from small developed countries in their dependence on imported investment and intermediate goods. Small developing countries rely on trade no more than smaller developed countries.

The most important reason why the trade engine no longer works in the old way is the diversification of exports of developing countries, the main exception being the countries of Africa, which are still largely dependent on 'tropical' primary products. For both manufactures and many primary commodities, developing countries have either small or very small shares of world markets. They can expand their exports by increasing their market shares through price competition. Indeed, this is exactly what happened for manufactures when the growth of developed countries slowed down in the 1970s, the rise of protectionism notwithstanding. Thus market growth is not a binding constraint on exports from developing countries.

The one group of commodities that appeared to behave in the expected way is foodstuffs, but closer examination reveals that the behaviour of the aggregate is misleading. Of six major food exports, only two had consistently positive elasticities of export volume with respect to real income in developed countries, and, of these, only the elasticity of tea was stable. For the others there was no positive relationship at all. Given the negligible income elasticities of demand, it is not surprising that supply shocks rather than shocks to demand determine prices and that prices rather than quantities are the main mechanism of adjustment.

In short, the 'engine' for foodstuffs has no fuel, while there is no fixed gear for other products, especially manufactures. The economic relationship between developed and developing countries cannot be described meaningfully in simple mechanical terms. The 'stylised facts' that underlie the theory of the 'trade engine of growth' turn out on close examination to be little more than myths.

APPENDIX 3A

Fifty-two sample countries: primary commodities exporters

Eleven balanced exporters
Bangladesh
Barbados

*Twenty-one non-African
predominantly primary commodity
exporters*

Brazil
Egypt
Haiti
India
Jordan
Mexico
Pakistan
Tunisia
Uruguay

*Twenty African predominantly
primary commodity exporters*
Central Africa Republic
Chad
Cameroon
Ethiopia
Gambia
Ghana
Ivory Coast
Kenya
Liberia
Mali
Morocco
Mozambique
Niger
Senegal
Somalia
Sudan
Tanzania
Uganda
Zaire
Zambia

Afghanistan
Argentina
Bolivia
Burma
Chile
Columbia
Costa Rica
Dominican Republic
El Salvador
Guatemala
Guyana
Honduras
Jamaica
Malaysia
Nicaragua
Paraguay
Peru
Philippines
Sri Lanka
Thailand
Turkey

APPENDIX 3B

Broadly non-competing non-fuel primary commodities

Foodstuffs
Beverages
   Cocoa
   Coffee
   Tea
Bananas

Spices
Copra
Groundnuts
Palm Oil
Coconut Oil

Agricultural raw materials
Jute
Natural rubber
Sisal
Silk
Nonconiferous logs

Metals and minerals
Copper
Bauxite
Natural phosphates

4 Trade Strategies and Economic Development: Theory and Evidence

CHRIS MILNER

INTRODUCTION

The commercial policies that a developing country pursues may have a significant effect on the pattern and pace of economic growth and development, by influencing either directly or indirectly (via changes in relative prices) the allocation of resources between sectors (e.g. agricultural and manufacturing activities) and between industries (of differing factor requirements and for different markets either domestically or internationally). These policies intentionally and/or unintentionally influence the scope for and nature of the country's actual and potential 'performance'. The aim of this chapter will be to identify the nature and characteristics of alternative strategies that developing countries may pursue and have pursued in the last three decades. It will also seek to review the arguments (theoretical and other) that have been expounded in defence of particular strategies (import substitution, export promotion, 'mixed' strategies, etc.). Finally, it will seek to evaluate the extent to which empirical evidence demonstrates whether the intentions or objectives of particular strategies have been satisfied. Although these aims could be satisfied without recourse to any judgements about the relative merits of alternative strategies, normative judgement will be difficult to avoid.

The chapter is organised as follows. The next section describes the nature and characteristics of alternative strategies, and provides empirical evidence on the orientation of trade policies and a description of the changes of strategy that have taken place in the post-war period. We then go on to survey the arguments that can be derived from alternative trade theories and models regarding the relationship between trade policy and development that have been used to justify particular strategies. The penultimate section reviews the historical consistency and empirical validity of the arguments identified in the preceding section, by discussing the historical experiences

55

of alternative strategies and by offering a summary of the evidence on the relationship between trade policy and economic 'performance' (e.g. growth, employment) as it applies to developing countries. The final section offers a brief summary of the arguments and a judgement on the current state of our knowledge and understanding on this topic.

THE NATURE AND CHARACTERISTICS OF ALTERNATIVE TRADE STRATEGIES

Trade policies in *a narrow sense* can be classified into two major categories: those policies that directly (indirectly) influence the quantities (prices) of imports and exports, such as quotas and exchange controls, and those that directly (indirectly) influence prices (quantities) such as tariffs or subsidies. We may also distinguish between those measures that are transparent (e.g. tariffs imposed from a published tariff schedule) and those that are hidden. Hidden measures may have unintended effects on the prices and quantities of tradeable goods, but import-licensing procedures are often deliberately complex and slow in order to control imports and not merely to satisfy other stated objectives of the procedures. The less overt instruments of trade or commercial policy are in fact likely to multiply if we widen the sense in which we define trade policies. The instruments referred to above in the initial definition of trade policies are those which appear directly to affect the balance of payments (current account), i.e. at the 'border' or at the point of the international transaction. But just as instruments such as import tariffs influence domestic production and employment and can therefore be viewed as an element in a country's industrial policies, so measures which are apparently elements of industrial policy (e.g. production or employment subsidies and taxes) are also likely to influence the balance of payments, and the size and composition of the tradeable goods sector. In a wider sense, therefore, trade strategies can be viewed as being pursued by a whole gamut of overt and less overt trade and industrial interventions. Since strategic interventions by the government must be seen as an attempt to alter the size and composition of the tradeable goods sector, those alterations are possible only if relative prices within the tradeable goods sector and between tradeables and non-tradeables can be altered.

Measuring trade regime bias

In Chapter 5 the use of nominal and effective protection in giving incentives to particular industries or processes is discussed. The emphasis there is on the protection or disprotection of import-substitution activities via nominal tariffs on intermediate and final goods. But the same principles can be extended to the effective protection of exportables and to the calculation of effective rates of subsidy. But in the context of discussing wider issues of overall trade strategy, we need to abstract from the fact that the trade regime may offer varying levels of protection to different industries and aggregate across industries to identify the overall orientation of the trade regime.[1]

Consider the following index of trade regime bias (*B*):

$$
B = \frac{\sum_i w_i \, (P_{mi}/I_{mi})}{\sum_j w_j \, (P_{xj}/I_{xj})}
\tag{4.1}
$$

where *w* are weights, *P(I)* is domestic (international) prices, *i* is an index of import-competing products, and *j* an index of exportable products. Equation 4.1 gives the ratio of domestic relative prices to the international relative price of importables (*m*) relative to exportables (*x*). Under competitive free trade conditions domestic relative prices will not deviate from international relative prices and the index will tend to unity. As there are departures from free trade conditions and 'distortions' to domestic relative prices, so the index diverges from unity in accordance with the bias of the regime. Values of below unity for *B* are indicative of an export-oriented or promotion (EP) regime, and values above unity indicate an import-substitution (IS) regime.[2]

There are conceptual and measurement difficulties[3] which confront the empirical application of this bias indicator, but it is a guide which can be combined with other information on the level and structure of protection to classify countries' trade strategies on a cross-sectional and time series basis.[4] Some information on trade bias estimated using equation 4.1 is set out in Table 4.1. There is clear evidence of strong biases towards IS for a number of countries, even after some liberalisation (e.g. Turkey), but much less evidence of strong EP strategies. This may well be because countries are pursuing 'mixed' strategies rather than non-interventionist or free trade policies. A similar result is obtained by Balassa *et al.* (1982), who compare the ratio of effective subsidy (and protection) on sales in domestic markets to sales in export markets for a small sample of NICs.[5] Again, ratios above (or below) one indicate that incentives to sales in domestic markets are higher (or lower) than to sales in export markets. Table 4.2 sets out some results from this study, and a breakdown of the orientation of policy for a primary/manufacturing and traditional/non-traditional industry breakdown. In columns 4 and 5, although many of the observations are close to unity, the majority are greater than one, and there are examples of clear IS orientation (Argentina and Israel). There is also evidence of the 'mixed' strategy approach, Korea giving stronger relative incentives to exports in traditional primary activities, but the opposite in the case of non-traditional primary activities. We cannot, of course, tell from this schema whether the

TABLE 4.1   A cross-country comparison of trade regime bias

	At the start of the transition to export orientation[a]	After the transition[b] to greater export orientation[c]
Brazil	2.89	1.34
Chile	2.83	1.79
Philippines	1.67	1.16
South Korea	0.97	0.92
Turkey	3.05	1.80

[a] The years for which these estimates apply are as follows: Brazil (1957), Chile (1956), Philippines (1960–2), South Korea (1961), Turkey (1958–9).
[b] The transitional period, according to Krueger, is characterised by exchange rate 'correction' and the removal of detailed regulations.
[c] These are estimates for 1966 (Brazil and South Korea), 1967 (Chile) and 1972 (Philippines and Turkey).
Source: Krueger (1978), Table 6.2.

TABLE 4.2   Incentives[a] to sales in domestic and export markets by country and activity type

	Primary activities		Manufacturing and simple processing	All industries	
	Traditional (1)	Non-traditional (2)	(3)	Traditional (4)	Non-traditional (5)
Argentina	1.01	2.63	3.04	1.01	2.97
(1969)	(1.02)	(3.07)	(3.53)	(1.02)	(3.58)
Columbia	0.95	0.72	0.71	0.95	0.79
(1969)	(0.97)	(0.78)	(0.84)	(0.97)	(0.87)
Israel	1.10	1.47	1.63	1.10	1.38
(1968)	(1.00)	(1.29)	(1.63)	(1.11)	(1.39)
Korea	0.11	1.06	0.81	0.11	0.99
(1968)	(0.18)	(1.12)	(0.95)	(1.18)	(1.09)
Singapore	–	1.11	1.08	–	1.08
(1967)	–	(1.13)	(1.09)	–	(1.09)
Taiwan	0.75	0.91	1.01	0.75	0.91
(1969)	(1.11)	(1.05)	(1.34)	(1.11)	(1.13)

[a] The ratio of effective subsidy (protection) rates on sales in domestic markets (plus one) to that in export markets (plus one). Relative effective protection is shown in brackets.
Source: adapted from Balassa *et al.* (1982), Table 2.4.

products of particular activities are importable or exportable, and therefore whether the relative incentives given reflect a desire to protect in the home market or to promote in the export market. But since traditional primary activities tend to be exportables which can be given or need little protection, it is hardly surprising to find values close to unity for a majority of the countries. Similarly, we may safely assume that a substantial proportion of manufacturing activities in Argentina and Israel are unambiguously import-competing, whereas in the case of Korea export industries are more significant. But the trade policies employed are themselves likely to fashion what are import-competing or export industries – what would be importable and exportable in the absence of policy may be rather different – and we should employ these indices of bias to identify differences in the aims or orientation of policy, not to describe differences in circumstances or need which somehow dictate or justify different trade strategies.[6]

The form and origins of alternative strategies

We will stay for the moment with positive, rather than normative, issues and briefly describe the salient features of typical IS and EP policy packages or industrialisation strategies – production for the domestic market of previously imported goods in the former case and production of goods for external markets in the latter strategy. This is an over-simplistic categorisation, since most LDCs have employed elements of both strategies in their development/industrialisation efforts. The emphasis given to each strategy and the perceived orientation of policy has altered over time, however. In the 1950s and 1960s IS was the dominant strategy, in particular in the larger countries in Latin America (e.g. Brazil and Argentina) and Asia (e.g. the Philippines, India). A similar approach to industrialisation was subsequently adopted by smaller economies in Africa (e.g. Nigeria, Kenya) and Latin America and South-east Asia. The economic or theoretical rationale for this strategy will be considered in a later section. But in addition to this IS development literature, the origins or motivations for IS strategies might be explained by reference to other factors, e.g. prestige or the psychological appeal of self-sufficiency and the reduction of import dependency. Some writers (e.g. Hirschman, 1968; Ballance *et al.*, 1982) argue that early IS motivations were *externally reinforced*: depression and two world wars in the period 1914–45 restricted the flow of industrial goods from industrialised countries. But Schmitz (1984) feels that from the 1950s onwards IS was more a result of deliberate economic policies, often aimed at balance-of-payments control rather than industrialisation.

IS policies and processes

Whether import restriction was typically an emergency measure designed to deal with a balance-of-payments crisis, restricting primarily inessential imports, import restriction soon turned into a deliberate policy for encouraging new industries and for expanding established domestic industry. Tariffs, quotas and administrative controls were used extensively to restrict imports, with some countries relying primarily on import licensing[7] (e.g. India and

Mexico) and others on tariffs (e.g. Argentina). The degree of restriction was invariably much more severe than in advanced industrialised countries. By implication, currency overvaluation was also invariably more extreme and persisted for longer periods of time, thereby reinforcing the bias in the policy regime against exports. But in addition to the fear of inflationary spirals being induced by currency devaluations, this bias against exports was not so much the intention of policy as the price willingly paid to control economic activity. Undervalued imports of 'desired' goods (e.g. capital or intermediate goods) could be allowed into the country in line with (formal or informal) plans.[8] During this episode deliberate government intervention in economic affairs was much more pervasive in IS countries than in high-income industrialised countries. Much use was made of investment licensing, differential taxes, tax holidays, exemptions, and remissions to influence resource allocation between industries and sectors. Public sector investment also formed a large part of total investment in most countries.[9]

Although there are alternative ways of defining import substitution, it is the convention to say that it has occurred when the 'proportion of total supply of a particular commodity or group of commodities which is obtained through imports rather than through domestic production has declined in the country concerned' (Helleiner, 1972, p. 96). On the basis of Table 4.3, which provides information on changes in import shares by type of good for some IS countries, we may conclude that IS strategies did achieve some

TABLE 4.3 'Measured' import substitution[a] for selected countries, 1948–65

	Consumer goods (%)	Intermediate goods (%)	Capital goods (%)
Pakistan			
1951–2	77.5	73.2	76.3
1964–5	11.4	15.0	62.3
Philippines			
1948	30.9	90.3	79.7
1965	4.7	36.3	62.9
Brazil			
1949	9.0	25.9	63.7
1964	1.3	6.6	9.8
India			
1951	4.2	17.4	56.5
1961	1.4	18.4	42.4
Mexico			
1950	2.4	13.2	66.5
1960	1.3	10.4	54.9

[a] Imports as a percentage of total supplies in each year.
Source: Little, Scitovsky and Scott (1970), p. 60.

import substitution. Import shares fell for all countries and goods types covered in the period of the 1950s and early 1960s, except for the case of intermediate goods in India. Except for Brazil, dependence on imported capital remained high at the end of this period, but the 'observed' import substitution is substantial in some cases (Pakistan, the Philippines and Brazil). But import substitution was the means to an end, not the end itself. The success or desirability of this strategy depends on the consequences of IS for industrialisation, growth, employment, the balance of payments, etc. We will return to this issue in subsequent sections.

EP policies and patterns

Certainly there was a disenchantment with IS strategies, based presumably on a 'perceived failure' to achieve the objectives referred to above. From the mid-1960s onwards, this caused an increasing number of LDCs to adopt more outward-looking EP policies. Countries such as Korea, Taiwan, Singapore and Hong Kong led the way, and were joined later by a number of larger semi-industrialised LDCs. This group of countries, which adopted EP policies during the 1960s, subsequently became known as the 'newly industrialising countries' (NICs). Their exceptional growth rates (see Table 4.4) for manufactured exports and output have provided a 'model' which has been widely 'recommended'[10] by the World Bank, for example, to other lower-income LDCs.

The type of export orientation has varied between NICs. For countries with a substantial primary resource base, local processing has provided a means of substituting manufactured for primary exports. In countries with limited primary resources and domestic markets (e.g. Asian NICs), production of manufactures for exports was based on a relative abundance of

TABLE 4.4 Growth[a] of manufactured exports (by value) for a sample of semi-industrial countries

	1953–60	1960–66	1966–73
Argentina	–11.7	14.6	33.5
Brazil	9.9	27.5	38.5
Chile	3.2	15.6	0.0
Columbia	0.0	35.0	27.5
India	1.3	6.7	7.7
Israel	18.0	15.3	17.5
Korea	14.0	80.0	50.0
Mexico	5.6	12.7	20.0
Singapore	n.a.	24.5	42.0
Taiwan	29.5	36.5	47.0

[a] Average annual percentage growth rates.
Source: Balassa *et al.* (1982), p. 45.

cheaper labour. This type of production or component assembly activity has also been encouraged by multi- or transnational corporations (TNCs). 'Sourcing' has led to vertically integrated production processes, with (unskilled) labour-intensive stages (e.g. assembly) being located in lower-wage LDCs. In the larger NICs of South America, manufactured exports have also come in industries established or expanded in the earlier IS phase. Alternative schools of thought are likely to interpret this differently. Was IS a necessary precursor to exporting? Alternatively, did IS delay exporting? We will return to such issues later. For the moment we shall consider the form that more outward-looking EP policies took.

As the earlier discussion of Tables 4.1 and 4.2 suggested, it was not so much a question of dismantling protective structures in home markets as often selectively adding an incentive package for exports or lowering the disincentive structure, thereby reducing the bias in relative terms against exports rather than creating a bias in favour of exports. For some countries (e.g. the Asian NICs) an approximately equal incentive structure to export and import substitute was created. In Korea, for example, an almost free trade regime was created for exports, with general wastage allowances for duty-free and unrestricted imports of raw materials. But in order to reduce the remaining bias in favour of import substitution (given virtually unchanged import tariffs), it was necessary to give specific incentives to exports. The export incentives in place by 1967–8 included tariff exemptions on imports of machinery and equipment, allowances for accelerated depreciation, reduced prices for some overhead inputs, direct tax preferences, and subsidised credit. A similar package of policies was employed by most countries, even if the bias against exports was not removed. In Table 4.2 Argentina, for instance, is shown as having a marked bias in its incentive structure in favour of the home market, even for manufactures in 1969. But its incentive structure for non-traditional exports in this year included instruments such as a duty draw-back scheme (for tariffs paid on imported inputs), an export subsidy (12 per cent on the value of exports) and export credit at subsidised rates. The differential effect of these two EP packages on relative incentives may well be accounted for, however, by the fact that the average rate of effective protection for manufacturing industries (in domestic sales) was estimated at 54 per cent in Argentina (1969) and 1 per cent in Korea (1968).[11] Such information serves to emphasise the impossibility of protecting all activities in relative terms – protection of one activity inevitably disprotects in relative terms other activities in an economy.

Since pure strategies (IS or EP) are presumably concerned with altering relative incentives, mixed strategies (i.e. elements of both IS and EP) must be based either on a lack of appreciation of the effects on relative incentives and of the difficulties of promoting all activities simultaneously, or on a belief that the 'mix' can be applied selectively (so that some other exportables and importables are relatively disprotected), or on a recognition of the need to alter relative incentives without lowering previously applied protective measures. In making a choice between strategies we can appeal either to theoretical argument or to empirical evidence, including the experience of the recent episodes of IS and EP strategies discussed in this section. It is to the first of these, theoretical argument, that we now turn.

ECONOMIC THEORY AND THE CHOICE OF TRADE STRATEGY

A variety of theoretical perspectives can be brought to bear on the choice of trade strategy by a developing country. These may be categorised as follows: –

1. Given the existence of surplus productive capacity, production for export markets should be encouraged. The LDC can acquire imports and domestic activity virtually 'costlessly' and gain dynamic 'productivity' gains.
2. Free trade is a first-best policy for a small open economy and LDCs should pursue 'liberal' or non-interventionist trade and exchange rate policies.
3. First-best conditions rarely if ever prevail. Governments therefore should be encouraged to use optimal instruments of (remedial) intervention. Trade interventions, however, are not optimal instruments to deal with domestic distortions.
4. Not only do domestic structures in developing countries diverge from those assumed by liberal/neoclassical economists, but the trading relations of LDCs with industrialised countries bias the gains from trade against LDCs. In addition to the need for reform of international trading structures, LDCs should not be excessively dependent on external markets and should use trade instruments to encourage import substitution.

The first of these perspectives is derived from classical theory and lends itself to outward-looking and export promoting policies. The second and third views offer a neoclassical perspective which is outward-looking in the sense that specialisation should be according to international comparative advantage, but which calls for 'neutrality' in the treatment of importables and exportables. Finally, the fourth categorisation represents the structuralist and radical arguments in favour of inward-looking policies and structural reforms (in the case of structuralists) and reforms of the political and economic system (in the case of radicals).

This categorisation is not wholly satisfactory. There are similarities between approaches which cannot be brought out in a brief survey – for instance, Diaz-Alejandro (1975) identifies some similarities between neoclassical and structuralist thinking. The approach used here does, however, allow us to satisfy the present purpose, namely to rehearse the theoretical arguments for and against alternative trade strategies. Alternative and more comprehensive reviews or surveys of trade theories and development can be found in Findlay (1984), Little (1982) and Greenaway and Milner (1987), and of trade policies and development in Krueger (1984), Kirkpatrick (1987) and Greenaway (1986b).

The classical perspective

There has been a tendency to identify 'classical theory' with the (essentially static) comparative cost principles traditionally associated with Ricardo.[12] As we shall see shortly, the representation of the Ricardian model as a static one does not do justice to Ricardo's work. In its static representation, unfettered allocation of resources to reap the gains from specialisation and exchange (see Figure 4.1 and the accompanying discussion) is 'neutral' between production for foreign and domestic markets. But the 'vent for surplus' and 'productivity' doctrines of Adam Smith in *The Wealth of Nations* may be contrasted with the traditional comparative cost doctrine. The latter assumes full employment pre- and post-trade and high domestic substitutability. By contrast, 'vent for surplus' arguments assume the existence of surplus capacity and a lack of domestic substitutability. In mercantilist-sounding fashion there is a clear incentive to orientate activity towards external markets.[13] But there are also dynamic aspects to classical arguments. The 'productivity' doctrine aspect of the approach views international trade as a dynamic force which,

> by widening the extent of the market and the scope of the division of labour, raises the skill and dexterity of the workmen, encourages technical innovations, overcomes technical indivisibilities and generally enables the trading country to enjoy increasing returns and economic development. (Myint, 1971, p. 120)

Thus outward-looking policies are presented as a means of achieving 'export-led growth' and the cumulative gains of being receptive to new ideas, new wants, new techniques of production and methods of organisation from abroad.

These arguments are not derived, however, from a formal model of trade and development. Indeed, Ricardo is now best known for his static theory of comparative cost. But his main writings were concerned with examining how relative prices and income distribution changed with economic development. He provided, in fact, an implicit model of growth and trade, which has received attention recently.[14] The long-run predictions of Ricardo have not proved consistent with historical observation. Although dynamic Ricardian models can derive results that suggest asymmetrical gains from trade, nonetheless in standard classical fashion Ricardo was concerned not only with the gains from trade but also with those from growth – the dual forces of 'thrift' and 'productivity'.

Although classical theorists are usually presented as the nineteenth-century proponents of *laissez-faire* or free trade, the dynamic benefits of increased openness may argue for more active export promotion. It is presumably such 'engine of growth' arguments, and not neoclassical perspectives, that some commentators, implicitly if not explicitly, have had in mind in more recent times when they have advocated export-promotion strategies. The prevailing orthodoxy (as represented by the World Bank, for instance) is, however, invariably represented as deriving from a neoclassical perspective.

The neoclassical perspective

Dynamic factors of interest to this present debate have gained relatively little attention in neoclassical theory. There is a substantial literature on open-economy growth models of a neoclassical vintage. But these examine the effects of exogenous parameters (such as population growth and the savings rate) on growth and trade patterns. They do not establish the effects of trade on factor accumulation and productivity growth, and it is this which is of particular interest in any discussion of the role of trade and trade policy in economic growth and development. There are individual elements (borrowed from the optimistic 'classical' view) which have been emphasised by individual writers. Keesing (1967) argues that openness discourages complacency and improves the quality of entrepreneurship, while Krueger (1978) points to the benefits of scale associated with enlarged markets, the greatest competition and largest potential markets coming with free trade. But in similar and *ad hoc* fashion, and in the absence of an explicit model of the effects of trade on growth, one can hypothesise on *a priori* grounds in the opposite direction. In Schumpterian fashion, for example, one may argue that the incentive to innovate is inversely related to competitiveness. The question of trade-related dynamic efficiencies must ultimately be an empirical issue, and we return to it later. As far as neoclassical theory is concerned, we are left with the Heckscher–Ohlin (H–O) model, formalised within a marginalist/optimisation framework by Samuelson (e.g. Samuelson, 1948), which is concerned with the fundamentally (comparative) static criteria for efficient resource allocation and with the gains to be reaped from moving from autarkic to free trade equilibrium.

Given certain assumptions or 'first-best' conditions, the superiority of free trade in the small country case[15] can easily be demonstrated (see Figure 4.1). *FF* is the production possibility frontier for commodities *G* and *M*. Given full employment and domestic relative prices given by *dd*, then autarkic equilibrium is at *A*. Consumption and production are matched, and tangency of

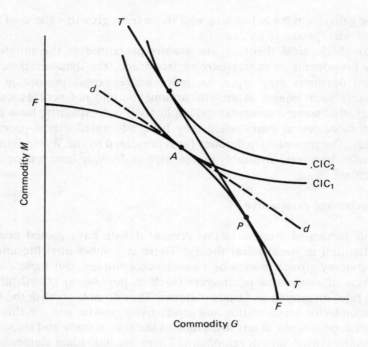

Figure 4.1 Static gains from trade

the production possibility frontier (*FF*) and a community indifference curve (*CIC₁*) guarantees that the marginal conditions for optimality are satisfied. With the opening of trade, the (exogenous) international price ratios or terms of trade are given by *TT*. Equilibrium is restored by the shift in production from *A* to *P* (incomplete specialisation in *G*) and by the shift in consumption from *A* to *C* – the marginal rate of transformation in production and the marginal rate of substitution in consumption are again equalised. The consumption possibilities of the country have been increased by the ability to transform at the international rather than domestic rate of exchange, and the communities' welfare is raised by the move to the higher indifference curve (*CIC₂*).

Note that, given 'first-best' conditions, any trade intervention – an import tax or export subsidy – will be welfare-lowering relative to the free trade situation. In its 'naive' form the neoclassical model of trade and specialisation offers a rationale for non-intervention, and for the avoidance of either import-substitution or export-promotion policies. The calls for export-promotion policies, associated with usually neoclassical economists, might be explained either by reference to omitted dynamic factors (mentioned above), or as a desire to compensate for existing (and presumed to persist) IS measures and thereby to move relative prices nearer to 'free trade' ones.

Strictly speaking, the call should be for non-inward-looking *attitudes*, not for EP *policies*, if it is the logic of the static, neoclassical model that we are seeking to apply.

Of course, 'first best' conditions often do not apply, especially in LDCs. There are factor and product market imperfections, including externalities and non-constant returns, which are likely to have to be taken as given in the short to medium term at least. This is seen by critics of neoclassical theory as a justification for alternative perspectives and models. But it is, in fact, possible to resurrect a (modified) free trade case, by reference to the principles of optimal intervention. Most arguments for protection – other than terms of trade arguments – can be accommodated within the neoclassical model in terms of some type of domestic market failure (which causes divergence from the optimal marginal conditions) without destroying the case for free trade. The central theme is that a distortion can be corrected without recourse to trade interventions; the intervention should be as close as possible to the source of the distortion. A production subsidy or tax should be used to deal with a production distortion, a consumption subsidy or tax with a consumption distortion, and so on. Thus direct, non-trade interventions in domestic product and factor markets may have indirect or incidental effects on trade flows, but the case for free trade is not destroyed.[16] The case for free trade has in effect been divorced from the case for intervention. (For a fuller discussion of the theory of domestic distortions, of the assumptions underpinning optimal intervention principles, and of the idea of a hierarchy of policies in the absence of first-best policies, see Corden, 1984.)

The infant-industry argument

One of the oldest and most popular arguments for protection is the infant-industry one. The argument is that some industries (individually or as a group) are initially uncompetitive (internationally), but in the longer term, and after temporary protection, they have a comparative advantage. It is, however, possible to analyse such arguments in terms of optimal intervention analysis, because the short term or temporary constraint on industry's development can be expressed as some form of domestic market failure. The use of a tariff to remedy such a distortion will involve a by-product consumption distortion, which can be avoided by the use of a non-trade intervention. Indeed, there will be a hierarchy of interventions depending on the nature of the distortion, trade interventions being low down in the rank order. Thus if there are learning-by-experience benefits which are internal to the firm and which the capital market imperfectly evaluates, then we should recommend capital market reforms as first best and perhaps subsidies to factor input or output as second best, and so on. The same hierarchy of non-trade interventions can be identified for dynamic external economies (e.g. benefits to the wider labour force from training subsequently mobile labour).

Thus a powerful literature has been developed in the post-war period, which offers a robustness to the apparently naive neoclassical model. Besides infant-industry considerations, it has also been applied to arguments for protection which rest on the presence of wage rigidity and unemployment (e.g. Brecher, 1974). Again the distortion is domestic, i.e. in the labour market, and trade interventions are non-optimal.[17] The best case that can be made for trade interventions in this framework is where there are existing, policy-induced trade distortions. In a (small) economy with tariffs *in situ*, the first-best policy is to remove the tariffs directly. If there are institutional rigidities which make the tariff irremovable (e.g. revenue-raising tariffs), an equivalent export subsidy (in a two-good case) will neutralise the tariff indirectly. We therefore have a rationale for recommending EP policies where import restrictions and taxes are viewed as given!

Structuralist and radical perspectives

We might interpret optimal intervention analysis as a defence of neoclassical theory and a reaction to the structuralist analysis which dominated much of the development literature in the 1950s. (For a discussion of the origins of structuralism, see Arndt, 1985.) Structuralists, in response to the clear naivety of the standard neoclassical model of trade, concluded that the model was largely inapplicable to LDCs and that the rigidities of markets in these countries provided a rationale for intervention, in terms of planning processes and administrative controls rather than of an incentive/fiscal form. Neoclassical economists would not, of course, disapprove of the need for structural reform to increase flexibility and lower constraints on resource reallocation and economic change, but they would offer alternative means to that end. There is a basic paradigm gap between those who believe in the potential efficiency of market processes/mechanisms, and those who eschew the neat theoretical elegance of neoclassical optimisation techniques, preferring instead less formal planning models and direct controls.

This alternative perspective on development, characterised by rigidities in domestic structures, capital accumulation constrained by limited domestic savings capability, and foreign exchange controls, was represented by 'two-gap models' (Chenery and Bruno, 1962; McKinnon, 1964). The approach was formalised theoretically by Findlay (1971), who applied Harrod–Domar type assumptions (fixed capital–output ratios) to an open economy in which growth is constrained by domestic savings. Thus the analysis, and the resulting policy prescription of import substitution, depends crucially upon the developing country's inability to translate increased savings into the foreign exchange necessary to sustain the required level of investment.

In addition to internal structural characteristics which were seen as deterrents to outward-looking policies, structuralists viewed the international trading structure as asymmetrical in its treatment of developed and developing countries. The best known exponents of this view that the gains from trade are biased against low-income LDCs are Prebisch (1950) and Singer (1950). Given technological improvements which raise the productivity of primary producers' (presumed to be LDCs) export industries for the benefit of consumers in industrial countries, and given a lower income elasticity of demand for primary than for manufactured goods, they argued that there would be a secular decline in the terms of trade against LDCs and a resulting transfer of income from poor to rich countries. This thesis lends itself to the policy prescription that the protection of LDCs' manufacturing industry will raise wages in all sectors and prevent the over-expansion of the primary export sector. There is not strong empirical support for the thesis, but the thesis can also be questioned on theoretical grounds, since the possibility of equilibrating forces arresting the secular decline is ignored. The most acceptable part of the argument may be the over-production of primary exports resulting from labour market imperfections which prevent productivity gains being translated into wage increases. But this is a production distortion which, as our earlier discussion of a hierarchy of instruments shows, does not provide a rationale for tariff intervention.

Much of the structuralist literature since the 1960s in fact avoids model 'competition', in view of the lack of robustness of the earlier theoretical work. It concentrates instead on questioning the generality or applicability of the neoclassical paradigm. Stewart (1977), for instance, addresses the issue of non-static technology and asymmetrical access to it. Helleiner (1979 and 1981) examines the implications of a range of imperfections in international markets, e.g. transfer pricing by multinationals in intra-firm trade and monopoly/monopsony situations. These and other structural imperfections in markets are 'seen'[18] as biasing the gains from trade against those with weaker bargaining power, i.e. the LDCs. The calls during the 1970s for a 'new international economic order' was an attempt to correct these imperfections through negotiations between developed and developing countries (see Kirkpatrick and Nixson, 1976).

The piecemeal critique of neoclassical economic analysis and piecemeal reform of international institutions associated with the structuralist perspective is viewed by more radical schools of thought (dependency, neo-Marxist, etc. theorists) as inadequate. These schools draw attention to what they see as more fundamental characteristics of social and economic processes in a global capitalist system which causes international trade to induce a polarisation between 'core' (developed) and 'peripheral' (underdeveloped) countries. (See Palma, 1978, for a more detailed survey.) Emmanuel (1972), for instance, elaborates the concept of 'unequal exchange': the periphery receives goods worth less than a day's labour in the 'core' in exchange for a day's worth of its own labour. In the context of Latin America in particular, these type of Marxist or neo-Marxist perspectives have spawned a literature on the contradictory needs of 'imperialism' and the development of backward, peripheral nations. (For a review of this type of literature see Bacha, 1978, and Little, 1982, and for a critique see Lall, 1975 and 1983.) The remedy proposed by these radical schools of thought is some form of 'delinking' of the 'South' from the 'North'.[19] This might be achieved by totally inward-looking IS policies or by some form of economic integration to encourage 'South–South' exchange.

On theory and trade strategy

There is a rich array of trade theories and models of trade that we might use to justify particular trade strategies in LDCs. There are, however, three broad approaches, which employ distinct methodologies and have distinct perspectives of the role of trade in economic development. The classical view of trade as the 'engine of growth' is likely to encourage EP (perhaps interventionist EP) policies; the neoclassical emphasis on allocative efficiency through 'correct' market pricing argues for free trade and 'neutrality' in relative incentives to import substitutes and exports; and the structuralist and radical view of structurally biased trade and asymmetrical development provides a rationale for inward-looking, including IS, policies. Neoclassical theory offers the most rigorous framework for analysis, and is the 'orthodoxy' offered by most economic textbooks and employed by the World Bank. But choice of trade strategy is likely to be fashioned by empirical evidence, as well as 'belief' and *a priori* reasoning. It is to the experience of alternative strategies and empirical evidence on the trade policy-development relationship that we now turn.

TRADE STRATEGY AND DEVELOPMENT: EXPERIENCE AND EVIDENCE

Experience of IS

By the early 1970s a large literature had been generated on the IS experience. The majority view was that IS had been a 'failure'. The most influential attack on IS came in the comparative study by Little, Scitovsky and Scott (1970).

The main aspects of the critique are as follows:

1. Average levels of effective protection for IS activities were in general very high. This induced currency overvaluation and a bias in the trade regime against exports. It also meant that protection was often achieved at very high domestic resource cost.

2. There tended to be an escalation of effective protection, with lower rates on intermediate and capital goods than on final consumption goods. This tended to induce the adoption of relatively capital-intensive, imported, techniques of production, and of imported, intermediate-input intensive products. Thus, while import substitution in consumer goods was often achieved, this was achieved at the expense of increased equipment and materials imports. Dependence on foreign supplies and susceptibility to foreign exchange problems was not removed, therefore.

3. Excessive capital-intensity and protection of product markets permitted the under-utilisation of capacity and restricted the growth of industrial employment. Low tariffs on capital imports, currency overvaluation and subsidised finance encouraged (discouraged) capital (labour) intensity. Alongside this, high protection of final products permitted good profitability even at low-capacity utilisation.

4. The high average levels of protection for manufacturing industry, which altered relative domestic incentives against agriculture and induced currency overvaluation, which in turn reduced domestic currency returns for agricultural exports, produced a clear bias against agricultural production.

5. The pattern of relative incentives induced income redistributions in favour of industrial sector profits, which aggravated income inequalities.

6. Resource misallocation was induced by trade interventions, which induced considerable variations in levels of effective protection between different sectors and industries, and by the inherent problems of pervasive government intervention. The excessive administrative requirements of the policies gave rise to excessive bureaucratisation, which in turn was a source of potential corruption, uncertainty and delays. The costs of this excessive administration were borne by the private sector and expressed themselves as reduced initiative and activity.

7. The inefficiencies induced by reduced foreign competition, by inappropriate technology, and by administrative procedures, restrict the ability to move into export markets as the constraint on growth imposed by limited domestic markets is experienced. Growth via import substitution is finite.

Points (1) to (7) constitute a neoclassical perspective on the experience of IS policies in developing countries. It would see the critique as offering a rationale for dismantling IS policies and 'liberalising' domestic markets and trade flows and for relying upon correct 'price' signals. Ironically many proponents of structuralist or radical approaches would agree with the *description* of industrial performance during the IS episode given by neoclassicists. They would, however, be more cautious in constructing a causal link between protection and economic performance (see Diaz-Alejandro, 1975). Indeed, they would argue that the sources of the failure of IS strategies can be traced to the nature of the structures and class formations which existed in

LDCs, but which need not have existed. IS strategies would have induced different effects if the distribution of income and pattern of demand had been different. Product specifications and production technologies were fashioned by high-income consumers. This encouraged the adoption of capital- and intermediate-input-intensive technologies and multinational activity. The latter forced out local producers, created monopolistic market structures and undesirable income redistributions in the form of remitted dividends. Although 'national welfare' may be lowered under this type of IS industrialisation, the radical view is that ruling classes in LDCs have a vested interest in accommodating foreign capital and in pursuing this particular type of industrialisation. Thus the non-neoclassical interpretation of the lessons of historical experience is that disenchantment with IS strategies was premature, and that reform of domestic structures (land ownership, income redistribution, etc.) is required, not reform of trade strategies (see Schmitz, 1984).

Clearly, historical experience is always capable of alternative interpretation. We have no means of re-writing history for an alternative set of given conditions. But it must be noted that neoclassical theory does not contradict arguments in favour of domestic reforms. It tends to say very little about the subject. However, reform of the trade strategy (i.e. the dismantling of IS policies) and reform of domestic structures do not have to be viewed as alternatives. The attempt at resurrecting a case for IS strategies, as set out above, is in danger of giving this mistaken impression.

Experience of EP

The performance of the NICs, and in particular South Korea, Taiwan, Hong Kong, Singapore and Brazil, has been impressive by any standards. They achieved annual growth rates of GDP (at constant prices) of 8–11 per cent and increases in manufactured exports of 20–40 per cent between 1965 and 1978, and manufacturing employment as a result increased annually by between 4 and 8 per cent over this same period. The orthodox and dominant explanation for this experience or juxtaposition of events is that the NICs adopted the 'right' policies – they reduced the 'bias' against exports by reducing import protection and providing incentives to exports, they adopted appropriate exchange rate policies, and they had factor prices which allowed specialisation according to genuine comparative advantage. Thus allocative efficiency (in neoclassical terms) is seen as having allowed these countries to use trade (in classical fashion) as an 'engine of growth'. Thus in an assessment of the Asian NICs' experience, Little concludes:

> The major lesson is that labour intensive export-oriented policies, which amounted to almost free trade conditions for exporters, were the prime

cause of an extremely rapid and labour intensive industrialisation. (Little, 1981)

Similarly, Tyler (1976) attributes Brazil's performance to liberalisation.

But again, not too surprisingly, the non-neoclassical schools do not accept the orthodox interpretation of the rise of the NICs. Their view is as follows. First, they would once again wish to be more cautious in constructing a causal link, this time between promotion and economic performance. Kirkpatrick (1987), for instance, questions whether export production is more labour-intensive when indirect as well as direct employment is taken into account. Bienefeld (1982) argues that the expansion of exports can be attributed to the relocation decisions of multinational enterprises. Given declining profitability and rising wages in industrialised countries, and the increasing feasibility of vertical fragmentation of production processes, the attractions of cheap labour and generous government incentives in a few specific locations induced industrial development as a response to 'external' market conditions rather than to local policy strategies. Second, they would argue that to attribute the NICs' success to getting prices 'correct' through liberalisation is to understate the extent to which government intervention has been used in several of the NICs to 'fashion' their comparative advantage. With the exception of Hong Kong, some planning and regulation has been a characteristic of the Asian NICs (Sen, 1983). Selective IS and EP measures have been employed in countries like Korea, and one may question whether this type of 'mix' of policies (which gives an absence of *measured* trade regime bias) is neutrality in the fashion of the neoclassical (two-good) model. Finally the non-neoclassical schools question whether the NIC model is capable of being widely replicated. The slow-down of growth in industrial countries, the increased protection in these countries, the more limited access to international finance since the debt-crisis[20] and the presence of already newly industrialised countries means that most other LDCs are unlikely to be able to break into international markets for non-traditional exports. To point, as this last argument does, to a fallacy of composition that all countries cannot increase their *share* of exports or that some countries cannot increase their share if the share of others remains constant, is of course mischievous. The exports of all countries in absolute terms can grow simultaneously. There is in any case a corresponding 'fallacy of decomposition' – an individual LDC should not rule out 'outward-looking' strategies on the grounds that if all other LDCs pursue the same strategy then their share of world markets will be smaller.

The above counter-arguments of the radical and structuralist schools to the neoclassical interpretation of the experience of EP serve to remind us of the dangers of using empirical evidence simplistically. But these counter-arguments must also be interpreted with care. To argue that the conditions of the neoclassical model were not fully satisfied in actual fact is not to establish that the policy recommendation is wrong. It may be that the success of the NICs may have been greater or the pattern of industrialisation somewhat different if the model had been properly applied! The reader can make a judgement in the light of the discussion thus far on the basis of either *a priori* reasoning from theory or of the interpretation of historical experience. The only remaining approach is to attempt to test empirically the impact of trade strategy on economic performance in developing countries.

Empirical 'tests' of the trade strategy–performance relationship

There have been various attempts to identify empirically whether the pursuit of a particular trade strategy has resulted in better growth performance. To support the hypothesis, for instance, that EP strategies result in higher growth strategies, three links would have to be empirically verifiable: –
1. The EP strategy must be distinguishable from a non-EP strategy.
2. A causal link between the EP strategy and export performance must be established.
3. A causal link between export performance and economic growth must be established.

Link (3) does have fairly good empirical support. Although it is not possible to specify a particular and generally accepted model of the growth process involved, different specifications of the relationship are identifiable. Michaely (1977), for example, identifies across countries a positive relationship between rates of growth of real GNP and of exports. Similarly, Balassa et al (1982) finds a high, positive rank correlation between GNP growth and export growth. (Further information on this relationship is discussed in Chapter 3 of this book.)

But export performance does not itself constitute an index of commitment to EP. We need to establish the link between policy orientation and export growth. The best that can be done in this direction is to identify separate phases of policy and to compare growth performance in different periods. The casual empiricism earlier in this section is certainly supportive of this interpretation of the NICs' 'success' and is widely interpreted in this fashion. Greenaway (1986b) also finds support for this view. Krueger (1978) gives more formal support by comparing deviations of countries' growth rates (for pooled time series and cross-sectional data) from their trends (estimated as a function of the growth of export earnings) for different time periods or policy episodes. The liberal economist interprets this evidence as clear support for the view that export performance is a function in large part of pursuing non-IS policies (e.g. Krueger, 1980). However, an alternative interpretation is that IS was an important and necessary feature of the early stage of industrialisation in the NICs (Chenery, 1980), which provided a foundation (the learning required) for the export stage. Teitel and Thoumi (1986) argue that the Argentinian and Brazilian experiences give support to the view that countries tend to acquire a comparative advantage in the goods they import! In terms of this view we would be required to formulate a more complex hypothesis: industrialising countries will grow more quickly in the long run if they pursue IS policies for the optimal duration before switching to EP or non-IS policies.

The ambiguities that arise from relying upon empirical evidence in this context are compounded by the difficulties of distinguishing EP from non-EP policies. The studies cited earlier suggest that countries that reduce the 'bias' against exports have registered improved export and growth performance. But does reduced 'bias' against exports constitute:

1. a 'mixed' strategy of selective interventions of some EP and some IS policies;
2. a 'neutral' incentive structure which approximates to free trade/optimal conditions;
3. genuine export promotion?

If we accept the earlier information on a positive trade policy–economic performance relationship, we would recommend selective, interventionist policies in case (1) (the 'revised' structuralist perspective), liberal, non-interventionist policies in case (2) (the neoclassical perspective), and in-terventionist export-promoting policies in case (3) (a quasi-classical perspective).

The weight of the available empirical evidence is not in favour of the structuralist/radical perspective, and the orthodox interpretation of the evidence is that provided by the neoclassical perspective. More satisfactory empirical testing awaits more systematic and formal modelling of the trade of growth relationship.

CONCLUSION

The issue of trade strategy and growth and development in LDCs has been the subject of exhaustive empirical and analytical investigation in recent decades. For many observers this work has not served to resolve the choices offered by the clear differences in perspective of the main schools of theory, at least not for those who eschew the theoretical elegance and simplicity of neoclassical theory. For these people the process of industrialisation and development is a complex one, fashioned by a multitude of economic and non-economic factors. Reynolds (1983), for instance, argues that the politi-cal organisation and administrative competence of government is a domi-nant influence on economic development. They therefore counter the neo-classical case, which has a powerful theoretical tool-box of optimisation analysis, and the evidence of the NIC experience to support it, on two grounds. First, they would argue that representing IS and EP strategies as mutually exclusive choices is misleading. The issue is rather one of selecting the optimal sequence of strategies. Second, they would argue that the inefficiencies that are frequently identified in import-substitute activities (which are just as possible in promoted export activity) are due to poorly implemented policies rather than resource misallocation. But herein lies the strength of the liberal case. Given the complexities of economic structures and processes in an industrialising economy and given the inherent administrative inefficiencies in LDCs, it is unlikely that selective state intervention will approximately achieve either an optimal resource allocation (at any one moment or over time) or induce the efficient use of resources once allocated. Given appropriate concern for the competitiveness and efficiency of markets, allocative and X-efficiency is more likely to be achieved by reliance on the price mechanism than by pervasive state intervention. There may well be important insights into the growth process that are not offered by static neoclassical theory, and that may justify a reappraisal and formalisation of classical analysis. But this argues for 'open' economies and allocative efficiency, not for an emphasis on 'inward-looking' policies and administered allocation. If 'active' export promotion could achieve gains in excess of free trade 'neutrality', then the optimal sequence of policy may be free trade policies (in order to identify genuine comparative advantage) followed by interventionist EP policies. However, comparative advantage changes through time, and governments are unlikely to be better pickers of new export 'winners' than they have been of 'infant industries' to substitute for imports. Absence of trade regime bias can help to insulate LDCs from policy-induced distortions. Governments should be encouraged to remedy known sources of 'market failure', rather than to predict future events! It is not only the choice of trade strategy, but also the appropriate role for government policy, which is at the heart of this development issue.

5 Evaluating the Structure of Protection in Less Developed Countries

DAVID GREENAWAY

INTRODUCTION

Trade policy involves the use of tariff and non-tariff interventions which seek to discriminate in favour of domestic firms and against foreign-based firms. As we saw in Chapter 4, at the strategy level the orientation of policy can be described as export-promoting or import-substituting, depending upon whether the net impact of policies is to engender an orientation to the 'world' or domestic market.

It is rarely, if ever, the case that policy measures are systematically thought out and implemented as part of some coherent trade strategy. In general, trade policy tends to be fashioned by responses to short-term expedients (such as tariff surcharges designed to alleviate budgetary pressures), or as a response to the pressures of particular interest groups. Even when a particular posture is adopted, interest group activity can result in the strategy being implemented in a wholly indiscriminate fashion.[1] For instance, most commentators would endorse the judgement that India has actively pursued a strategy of import substitution over the entire post-war period. It has been argued by many, however, that although this objective is clear and unambiguous, its implementation has been indiscriminate in the sense that in principle *any* activity can obtain import protection (see, for example, Balasubramanyam, 1984). Since the essence of protection is to provide one activity with an advantage *relative* to other activities, indiscriminate intervention is inherently problematic.

The theory of protection suggests that, in a situation where distortions are absent, tariff and non-tariff barriers will have a number of readily identifiable resource allocation effects. Moreover, theory also allows us to isolate the effects of intervention in many 'second best' situations where distortions exist, and to rank alternative instruments for correcting a particular distortion.[2] In this chapter we shall assume that the reader is familiar with

77

these issues. Consequently an awareness of the arguments for intervention, and the economic effects of that intervention, will be taken as read. This allows us to focus in this chapter on attempts to evaluate empirically the impact of intervention in less developed countries (LDCs). In particular we shall focus on two techniques that have been used by practitioners in policy evaluation, namely effective protection analysis and incidence analysis. The former is the most widely used technique and has been extensively deployed over the past twenty-five years. The latter is of more recent vintage, but has nevertheless been applied to a number of countries over the last decade. It shoud be emphasised that these are not the only techniques that have been used in policy evaluation in LDCs; domestic resource cost analysis and bias estimation have also been implemented in many cases.[3]

Space constraints, however, dictate some selectivity. The principal advantages of focusing on effective protection analysis and incidence analysis are, first, that an extensive array of empirical analysis is available for comment; second, they are both tractable from an analytical standpoint; and third, they are to some degree complementary techniques.

The remainder of this chapter is organised as follows. In the next section we focus on effective protection analysis. There we will look at the concept of effective protection, comment on some measurement problems, and finally evaluate some results for LDCs. The following section focuses on incidence analysis, again under the headings of theory, measurement and empirical results. The final section provides a summary and overall evaluation.

EFFECTIVE PROTECTION ANALYSIS

Theory

The refinement of the theory of effective protection has been one of the most significant developments in international trade theory of the last twenty-five years. The concept recognises that in order to comment sensibly on the potential resource allocation effects of intervention, one has to focus on the entire protective structure, and not just on any protection which is afforded to the final stage of the production process. Thus in the case where tariffs are the only form of intervention, whereas an output tariff acts like a subsidy to the producer of a given commodity, an input tariff acts as a tax on value-added. The net protection to value-added in an activity therefore depends on the relative magnitude of output and input tariffs.

The effective protection provided to a particular activity j, can be stated as follows:

$$e_j = \frac{V_j^* - V_j}{V_j} = \frac{V_j^*}{V_j} - 1 \tag{5.1}$$

where

e_j = effective protection to activity j

V_j^* = value added in j at tariff-distorted prices

V_j = value added in j at world prices.

Another way of writing this, assuming a single imported input and a fixed relationship between input and output, is:

$$e_j = \left[\frac{P_j - z_{ij}P_j}{\dfrac{P_j}{1 + t_j} - \dfrac{z_{ij}P_j}{1 + t_i}} \right] - 1 \tag{5.2}$$

where

P_j = price of the final product at tariff distorted prices;

z_{ij} = share of imported inputs in the final value of j;

t_j = nominal tariff on the final product;

t_i = nominal tariff on the imported input.

Clearly the numerator in equation (5.2) refers to value-added at tariff-distorted prices, and the denominator refers to value-added at world prices. Expressing effective protection in this way, however, has several merits. First of all, it emphasises the dependence of e_j on both t_j and t_i. Secondly, it makes the exact relationship between e_j and t_j, t_i and z_{ij} perfectly clear. Other things being equal, a higher t_j is consistent with a higher e_j, while a lower t_i is consistent with a higher e_j. In other words, effective protection varies directly with the height of output tariffs, but inversely with the height of input tariffs. For given values of t_j and t_i; e_j and z_{ij} vary directly. A higher z_{ij} means a lower value-added in absolute terms, and therefore a greater proportionate effect of the given nominal tariffs. (As we shall see below, this effect is important in explaining some of the spectacularly high estimates of effective protection found in some countries). The third merit of expressing e_j as in equation (5.2) is that it provides a clue as to how effective protection can be measured in empirical studies. Given information on final value, the value of intermediate inputs and nominal tariffs, one can obtain an estimate of value-added at tariff-distorted prices and then deflate this figure by the relevant nominal tariffs to obtain an estimate of value-added at world prices.

The fourth merit of expressing e_j as in equation (5.2) is that the possibilities of *negative effective protection* and *negative value-added* can be identified. Negative effective protection is the easier of the two concepts to comprehend. Clearly, e_j will be negative if the numerator in equation (5.2) exceeds the denominator. Thus, if the tariff structure results in tariff-distorted value-added exceeding value-added at world prices, effective protection will be negative. This state of affairs could arise if a zero tariff applied to final output while positive tariffs applied to imported inputs, a situation which is commonly found in industries which produce principally for the export market. The concept is useful because it helps to highlight the potential impact of import protection for export activities.

Negative value-added is a more subtle concept. This describes a situation where the denominator in equation (5.2) is negative. In other words, once value-added at tariff-distorted prices is deflated by the relevant tariffs, it becomes negative at world prices. This occurs if the deflated value of inputs exceeds the deflated value of the output. In principle, the degree of effective protection provided by the tariff structure is infinitely high. The importance of the concept lies in identifying activities which in principle could be eliminated and yet result in an increase in GNP. As we shall see later in this section, instances of negative value-added have been discovered in several economies.

Measurement

Equations (5.1) and (5.2) express effective protection in its simplest form. As already noted, we can use (5.2) as a basis for estimation. As one might anticipate, however, there are a number of technical and practical problems associated with the implementation of the measure. Such measurement problems are not a central concern of this chapter. Nevertheless, it is important to comment briefly on the principal problems in view of the discussion of empirical results which follows. The principal difficulties relate to the following:

Multiple inputs. For expository purposes equation (5.2) is cast in terms of a single importable input. In practice, of course, a given production process will involve the transformation of many inputs into a given output. So long as one can obtain information on the shares of individual inputs in final value, and any tariffs which pertain to these inputs, this problem is easily overcome. The dearth of input-output information in many LDCs can, however, mean that obtaining data is not in itself straightforward.[5]

Non-traded inputs. Equation (5.2) assumes that all inputs are importable. In practice some inputs are non-traded. If protection serves to influence the price of non-traded inputs, then estimates of effective protection which do not take account of this will be biased. Post protection prices of non-tradeables could increase either because protected importables are inputs into the production of non-tradeables, and/or because substitutional relationships within the economy may result in upward pressure on the prices of non-tradeables. Analysts have responded to this difficulty in a variety of ways. One could lump non-tradeables with primary factors and in effect ignore the problem. Alternatively, one can estimate the price-raising effect of protection by estimating the traded inputs required to produce non-tradeables, and their associated price effects.

Fixed input coefficients. Related to the previous point is the fact that in equation (5.2) z_{ij} is assumed to be fixed. The presence of tariffs on imported inputs, however, may stimulate input substitution. Primary factors could be substituted for imported inputs and/or non-tradeable inputs could be substituted for imported inputs. The former creates no real difficulty, since effective protection estimates are essentially an attempt to gauge the degree of protection to primary factors. The latter, though, is more of a problem.

Tariff averaging. In equation (5.2) t_j and t_i refer to unique rates of tariff which pertain to specific products. In practice, this is not always so. Conceptually, there are two quite separate problems. First, a given product may be subject to different tariff rates depending upon its origin (due, for instance, to preferential trading arrangements); or the status of the domestic purchaser (for example, duty drawback schemes often allow some firms to claim back import duty). Second, inputs to and outputs from a particular process may come under a variety of tariff headings and may therefore be subject to a variety of rates. What tends to happen is that a trade-weighted average tariff is used in the calculations, although several commentators have pointed to biases which result from so doing (see, for instance, Tumlir and Till 1971; Kitchin 1976).

These and other problems such as tariff redundancy and non-tariff barriers often have to be faced in estimating rates of effective protection. No further comment will be made in discussing the results reported below, since the relative importance of each problem is not fixed across all studies. Armed with the knowledge that measurement is imperfect, we can now proceed to consider why we are interested in estimates of effective protection, and examine some of the results which are currently available.

Interpretation of effective protection estimates

Assuming that a tractable data set is available and a set of effective protection estimates can be obtained, we are essentially interested in three aspects of the results – the *average* level of effective protection across all industries, the *ranking* of effective rates across industries, and the *variance* of rates across industries.

The industry average is of interest because it provides an indication of the average extent to which the tariff structure permits domestic producers to raise value-added above the levels that would prevail in the absence of protection. This can be used for comparison with the average nominal tariff to provide an indication of the extent to which nominal tariffs may understate effective protection. Moreover, it may be a useful summary statistic for cross-country comparisons as a benchmark for comparing 'high' and 'low' protection regimes. However, averages, even weighted averages, can be misleading. Therefore one would supplement information on averages with information on the variance of effective rates. This latter information is important for at least two reasons. First, protection is essentially a relative concept: one uses instruments to protect (or disprotect) some activities relative to others. Variance therefore provides information on the extent to which the most highly protected industries benefit from the protective structure relative to the least protected. Second, if protection succeeds in inducing resources to move from one activity to another, the variance of rates provides an indication of the potential for resource misallocation in the tariff structure. Other things being equal, this potential will be greater the wider the variance of rates.

Since a primary objective of protection is to stimulate resource movement into the protected activity, information on the ranking of effective rates is useful. Other things being equal, one would anticipate that resources would be pulled from activities with relatively low rates of effective protection towards those with relatively high rates. Details of the ranking of rates across industries facilitates inferences regarding resource pulls between industries.[6]

Empirical evidence

Table 5.1 reports details of some studies of effective protection in LDCs and NICs. The studies encompass economies for various years between 1958 and 1980–1. For some economies (such as Brazil and Pakistan) several studies have been completed, which facilitates some inter-temporal comparisons. In most cases, however, the studies pertain to a single year. Thus most of our remarks will be of an inter-country nature.

Before commenting on the detail of Table 5.1, it is important to make a number of *caveats*. As we saw in the previous section, the measurement of effective protection is not uncontroversial. Complications exist relating to, *inter alia*, the treatment of non-tradeable inputs and the treatment of exportable output. Conventions on the resolution of such complications vary from study to study. Where this is so it is difficult to make direct comparisons. Having said this, many of the studies reported in Table 5.1 were prepared as part of larger projects. As a result, some standardisation with regard to methodology has taken place across some of the studies. For instance, the first thirteen studies in Table 5.1 were prepared as part of a National Bureau of Economic Research (NBER) research programme and

TABLE 5.1 Evidence on effective protection in LDCs and NICs

Country	Year	Number of Industries	Average EPR	Range of EPRs	Negative Effective Protection	Negative Value Added	Source
1. Brazil	1958	n.a.	108*	17→502	n.a.	n.a.	Krueger et al. (1981)
2. Brazil	1963	n.a.	184*	60→687	n.a.	n.a.	
3. Brazil	1967	n.a.	63*	4→252	n.a.	n.a.	
4. Pakistan	1963–4	n.a.	356*	-6→595	n.a.	n.a.	
5. Pakistan	1970–1	n.a.	200*	36→595	n.a.	n.a.	
6. Korea	1968	n.a.	-1	-15→82	n.a.	n.a.	
7. Uruguay	1965	n.a.	384*	17→1014	n.a.	n.a.	
8. Colombia	1969	n.a.	19*	-8→140	n.a.	n.a.	
9. Chile	1967	n.a.	175*	-23→1140	n.a.	n.a.	
10. Indonesia	1971	n.a.	119*	-19→5400	n.a.	n.a.	
11. Thailand	1973	n.a.	27*	-48→236	n.a.	n.a.	
12. Tunisia	1972	n.a.	250*	1→737	n.a.	n.a.	
13. Ivory Coast	1973	n.a.	41*	-25→278	n.a.	n.a.	
14. Korea	1968	150	10	-67→164	(76)	n.a.	Balassa et al. (1982)
15. Israel	1968	94	76	-943→750	(9)	n.a.	
16. Singapore	1967	69	6	-1→86	(29)	n.a.	
17. Taiwan	1969	61	46	-18,728→89	(26)	(6)	
18. Argentina	1969	82	94	-596→1308	(15)	0	
19. Colombia	1969	-2	46	-51→215	(10)	0	
20. Brazil	1980–1	22	46	-16→97	(6)	n.a.	Tyler (1985)
21. Pakistan	1980–1	90	60	-799→1543	(22)	(13)	Naqvi et al. (1983)
22. India	1968–9	69	n.a.	27→3354	n.a.	(4)	Bhagwati and Srinivasan (1975)

Notes:

* sample includes only manufacturing industries.

n.a. = not available.

figures in parenthesis indicate number of activities falling into this category.

used a common methodology. This is also the case for studies 14–21, which were prepared as part of a World Bank Study. Other things being equal, some comparisons between these studies can be made. However, there are further complications which frustrate direct comparisons. One difficulty is that the level of aggregation is not constant across studies. Thus the UNCTAD (1986) study relates to twelve sectors in Jamaica, while the Balassa et al (1982) study relates to 150 industries in Korea. Other things being equal, more highly aggregated studies are likely to be downward biased. Finally, in addition to methodological differences and differences in the level of aggregation, most of the studies pertain to different years, and there is no guarantee that in all cases we have representative years.

All of these complications make generalisation from the information in Table 5.1 difficult. Notwithstanding this, however, some comments are possible. In summarising each of the studies we have provided information on the average rate of effective protection, the range of effective rates, details of whether or not evidence of negative effective protection was found, and details of whether or not evidence of negative value-added was found. (For an analysis of a larger number of effective protection studies, alongside information on non-tariff barriers and exchange rate misalignment, see Greenaway, 1986b).

Inter-country comparisons. If we take first of all studies 1–13, since these use a common methodology, we observe a minimum *average* effective rate of −1 per cent, Korea in 1968, and a maximum average of 384 per cent, Uruguay in 1965. For the former economy the suggestion is that the protective structure is, on average, almost neutral with regard to effective rates. In Uruguay, however, it would seem that the structure of protection resulted in very high average levels of effective protection in the mid 1960s – on average, value-added in Uruguayan manufacturing industry would appear to have been some three and a half times world value-added. Of the thirteen studies, the average ERP exceeded 100 per cent in eight cases (Brazil in 1958 and 1963, Chile in 1967, Indonesia in 1971, Pakistan in 1963–4 and 1970–1, Tunisia in 1972), suggesting highly protective incentive structures. In four cases the average rates were moderately low, suggesting more neutral incentive structures (−1 per cent in Korea in 1968, 19 per cent in Columbia in 1969, 27 per cent in Thailand in 1973, and 41 per cent in the Ivory Coast in 1973).

Although studies 14–21 apply to roughly the same time period as studies 1–14, the reported average ERPs are somewhat lower. The maximum for this group of studies is recorded as 94 per cent (Argentina in 1969). The minimum here seems to be −300 per cent, for Taiwan in 1969. This, however, is a misleading estimate and is biased by the inclusion of activities which produce negative value-added, and whose ERP rates are estimated as negative. If one excludes the largest of these rates (−18,728) the average changes to a more realistic 46 per cent, which is the figure reported in the table. (The same remarks apply, *mutatis mutandis*, to Korea). The most highly protected economies in this group appear to be Argentina, Israel and Korea, with average ERPs of, respectively, 94, 75 and 61 per cent; the least protected appear to be Columbia, Singapore and Taiwan with averages of −2, 22 and 46 per cent respectively.

As we noted in our earlier discussion, the range of ERPs is of interest because it provides some guide as to the potential resource allocation effects of the protective structure. Referring first to studies 1–13, it would appear to be the case that the range of estimates is wider in the more highly protected economies. Thus in Indonesia the range is −19 per cent to 5400 per cent, for Chile it is −23 per cent to 1140 per cent and for Uruguay it is 17 per cent to 1014 per cent. Those economies with relatively low average ERPs also appear to have somewhat narrower ranges. In the Ivory Coast it is reported as −25 per cent to 278 per cent, in Colombia −8 per cent to 140 per cent and in Korea −15 per cent to 82 per cent. The potential for protection-induced resource misallocation would seem to be greater in the high-protection economies than in the low-protection economies. This inference can also be supported by studies 22 and 21 on India and Pakistan, two highly protected economies, where the ranges are −27 per cent to 3354 per cent and 799 per cent to 1543 per cent respectively. The results from studies 14–21 are more ambiguous, however. The ranges for this group of studies are consistently wider than those for the NBER studies (1–13). This may be due to the fact that the data set for these studies is more disaggregated. Notwithstanding this, there is further support for more highly protected economies having ranges which are wider than those recorded for the less highly protected cases – compare, for instance, Argentina and Israel with Colombia and Taiwan. The association, however, is not as clear as with the NBER studies.

Table 5.1 also provides information on negative effective protection and negative value-added for cases where these are reported. The former is not at all unusual. In Korea no less than seventy industries seem to have negative rates, almost half of the entire sample. There were over twenty instances in Taiwan, Singapore and Pakistan. It would seem, then, that cases where the protective structure works to the disadvantage of activities, i.e. disprotects them, is not at all unusual. Moreover, as we noted earlier, it will often be the case that these activities are (actual or potential) export activities which do not benefit from protection of their output but are subject to tariffs on their inputs. (The way in which import protection may impact upon the export sector will be explored more explicitly in the next section, when we discuss incidence analysis.)

It will be recalled that negative value-added describes a situation where domestic value-added at world prices is negative. In other words, the value of the inputs exceeds the value of the industry's output, and the activity would not exist in the absence of protection. Such activities actually make a negative contribution to GNP. Some of the studies have discovered evidence of the phenomenon. In India in 1968–9, four instances were recorded, while in Pakistan in 1980–1, thirteen cases were identified. What is particularly interesting in this context is the fact that the phenomenon is not confined to the most highly protected economies. In both Taiwan in 1969 and Singapore in 1967 six cases of negative value-added were identified. It is often assumed that the phenomenon only arises in the most highly protected regimes. Clearly, this would appear not to be the case.

Inter-temporal comparisons. It is not possible to say very much by way of inter-temporal comparisons. As can be seen from Table 5.1, there are only two economies for which studies pertaining to several points in time exist, namely Brazil and Pakistan. Moreover, even in these cases, the same data set has not been consistently used, nor the same methodology. Any remarks must perforce be tentative, therefore. Bearing this in mind, a few comments can be made on each. The evidence on Brazil seems to suggest that the economy has become less protected between 1958 and 1980–1. The average ERP rose from 106 per cent to 184 per cent between 1958 and 1963, but has fallen since then to 46 per cent. Furthermore, the range, which increased between 1958 and 1963, has subsequently fallen, and in 1980–1 was −16 per cent to 97 per cent. This evidence of an economy which has liberalised to some degree during the last twenty-five years or so is corroborated by other evidence (see, for example, Teitel and Thoumi, 1986). The evidence on Pakistan is more difficult to interpret. There are two average rates for the earliest years, 1963–4, which are significantly different – 95 per cent and 356 per cent. Comparing the 1980–1 figure with either does suggest a fall in the average ERP to 60 per cent. However, the range for 1980–1 is wider than that reported in both of the 1963–4 studies. Clearly there must be some ambiguity in deciding whether or not the economy is more or less highly protected than in the earlier period.

Taking all of these results together, it is clear that the structure of protection varies from one country to another, and in a given country from one period to another. Some economies are highly protected, others less so. In most economies there appears to be evidence of negative effective protection, suggesting that some activities are actually disprotected by commercial policy. This is an issue we take up further in the next section. The question of whether or not more highly protected economies are less successful in some sense (e.g. in terms of growth performance) than less protected economies was discussed in Chapters 3 and 4.

INCIDENCE ANALYSIS

Theory

As we have seen, effective protection analysis is a partial equilibrium approach to evaluating trade policy which is generally applied at the 'industry' or activity level. Focusing on the industry provides detailed information on the impact of protectionism at a relatively disaggregated level of economic activity. It may, however, be of interest to track the effects of trade policy at a more aggregated level. For instance, one might wish to focus on broad sectors of economic activity such as the export and import sectors in order to comment on the way in which protection of one sector may impact upon the other.

Incidence analysis is a technique which attempts to do just this. By focusing on three broad sectors, namely the importable, exportable and non-tradeable sectors, it attempts to establish how interventions intended to protect the first of these sectors may be shifted to the other two. The technique attempts to accomplish this by evaluating the impact of protection on relative prices rather than value-added. By so doing it constitutes an attempt to formalise the notion that in order to protect one sector, one inevitably disprotects some other sector.

The essential features of the incidence model can be outlined by reference to Figure 5.1. The model assumes a small open economy where output can be produced in one of three sectors, an importable, an exportable and a non-tradeable sector. Markets are assumed to be competitive, so that prices respond quickly to changes in demand and supply. With three sectors, two domestic relative price ratios can be identified, P_m/P_h and P_x/P_h. The former refers to the price of importables relative to non-tradeables, the latter to the price of exportables relative to non-tradeables. P_m/P_x is the international terms of trade. For simplicity, all of these price ratios are initially set at unity. The schedule labelled HH traces out combinations of the two domestic relative prices, which are consistent with equilibrium in the market for non-tradeables. Its negative slope reflects the fact that a fall in P_m relative to P_h must be offset by a rise in P_x relative to P_h for equilibrium to be maintained. This follows because the fall in P_m relative to P_h would serve to create an excess demand for tradeables and an excess supply of non-tradeables. The rise in P_x relative to P_h removes this disequilibrium. Points above and to the left of HH are consistent with a situation of excess demand for non-tradeables (excess supply of tradeables), while points below and to the left reflect excess supply of non-tradeables (excess demand for non-tradeables). The general equilibrium nature of the model ensures that for points along HH, trade is balanced. The final feature of the model to note is that the negative slope of HH reflects the implicit assumption that non-tradeables are substitutes for, rather than complements to, tradeables.[7]

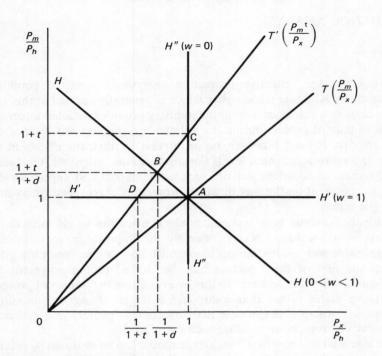

Figure 5.1   The incidence of protection

Commencing from an initial equilibrium at A, suppose an import tariff is introduced. Given the small open economy assumption, P_m/P_x will rise from unity to $1 + t$, where t is the *ad valorem* rate of tariff. This much is clear from the analysis of a tariff in the basic Heckscher–Ohlin model of international trade. Since, however, we have a non-tradeables sector, it is important to enquire as to how the tariff affects the price of non-tradeables. To see this we can focus on the impact effect of the tariff which would take us to point C. At C, not only has P_m/P_x risen to $1 + t$, but so too has P_m/P_h. However, point C is clearly above and to the right of HH. There is an excess demand for non-tradeables and excess supply of tradeables, i.e. a trade surplus. For these excess demands/supplies to clear, P_h has to increase relative to both P_m and P_x. If we label the change in P_h as d, it should be obvious that equilibrium is re-established at point B, at the intersection of HH and OT'. P_m/P_h is now $1 + t/1 + d$, while P_x/P_h has fallen to $1/1 + d$.

The exact magnitude of the change in the price of non-tradeables which is required to restore equilibrium depends upon the slope of HH. Clearly, the steeper the slope of HH, the greater the induced price increase of P_h. In the limit, if HH were vertical, P_m/P_h would increase to $1 + t$. At the other extreme a horizontal HH would ensure that the relative price ratio P_m/P_h is wholly unaffected by the tariff. Thus the slope of *HH* is determined by substitutional relationships in the economy. If non-tradeables and import-ables are close substitutes, their relative price ratio will not be much affected by the tariff, and the slope of *HH* will be relatively shallow. By contrast, if importables and non-tradeables are poor substitutes for each other, a tariff will drive a wedge between their prices, and *HH* will be relatively steep.

The importance of focusing on what happens to P_h is simply this: since we are dealing with a small open economy we must treat P_x as parametric. An import tariff raises P_m relative to P_x *and* may also cause P_h to increase relative to P_x. In other words, the import tariff causes P_x to fall relative to *both* P_m and P_h. As a result the incidence of the import tax is shifted at least in part to the export sector. The extent to which this shifting occurs can be summarised as:

$$\Delta \left[\frac{P_h}{P_x} \right] = w \, \Delta \left[\frac{P_m}{P_x} \right] \tag{5.3}$$

where $0 \leq w \leq 1$.

In equation (5.3) w is the so-called *shift parameter*.[8] Clearly, if w is equal to one, any increase in P_m relative to P_x is fully reflected in an increase of P_h relative to P_x. The import tariff is in effect fully shifted as an export tax. Given price data on P_m, P_h and P_x, it is possible to estimate this shift parameter and make inferences regarding the extent to which import protection may be shifted as implicit export taxes. Moreover, the same data can be used to estimate 'true' protection to a given sector, where true tariffs describe the extent to which P_x increases relative to P_h, while true export subsidies refer to the extent to which P_x increases relative to P_h, i.e.:

$$t^* = \Delta \left[\frac{P_m}{P_h} \right] = \frac{t - d}{1 + d} \tag{5.4}$$

and

$$s^* = \Delta \left[\frac{P_x}{P_h} \right] = \frac{s - d}{1 + d} \tag{5.5}$$

These, then, are the basic ideas of incidence analysis. We have dwelt at greater length on examining the framework because the technique is not nearly as well known as effective protection analysis and cannot therefore be easily referenced in the textbooks. We will comment further on its uses shortly. For the moment, some remarks on measurement are appropriate.

Measurement

Even a casual inspection of equations (5.2) and (5.3) should provide an indication of the fact that data requirements for incidence analysis are far less exacting than those pertaining to effective protection analysis. This is so for two reasons. First, as we have already noted, effective protection analysis is executed at the industry level, while incidence analysis is implemented at the sectoral level. With the latter one is only dealing with three sectors; with the former one deals with many more than three industries. Second, effective protection analysis requires detailed information on nominal tariffs, output values and input values. Incidence analysis only requires information on output prices.

Having said this, one still faces difficulties in estimating the model. In particular, the following tend to be problematic.

Sector identification. In theory it is straightforward to distinguish between different sectors of economic activity. In practice it is very much more difficult. It is not always obvious what should comprise the components of a price index for importables or exportables. In principle the price indices P_h, P_m and P_x should exhaust all productive activities in the economy. In practice one has to work a sub-set of information. Price data will often not be available for all possible importables, non-tradeables and exportables. Thus, for example, in a study of Mauritius, Greenaway and Milner (1986) construct a price series for importables from data on furniture, furnishings, household appliances, alcoholic drinks and cotton yarns; their non-tradeables index comprises household operations, shoe repairs, medical care, entertainment and education; and two separate series for exportables are used, one for 'traditional' exportables (comprising sugar and tea) and one for 'non-traditional' exportables (comprising finished clothing). The choice of these sub-sets was fashioned by data availability.

Weighting of components. Having decided on the components of a particular index, it is necessary to decide on whether the aggregate sectoral index to be used should be a simple average of the components, or a weighted average. In the event of the latter, one then has the problem of selecting an appropriate weighting system. Should weights be selected by reference to the importance of each component in the overall consumer price index, or its share in output, or its share in value-added, or its share in trade? In practice, either an unweighted average is used, or, where weighted averages are used, some experimentation with weights takes place as a test of robustness.

Lag structures. It seems reasonable to suppose that changes in P_h which are induced by changes in P_m will materialise after some adjustment period. In a smoothly operating economy the transmission lags could be relatively short. In an economy where distortions exist and frustrate market clearing, the transmission lags could be relatively long. Theory provides no reliable guide as to the length or structure of lags, and this issue tends to be resolved by reference to the data.

Observational equivalence. Most empirical analysis in economics is subject to the problem of observational equivalence. This simply refers to the fact that even where a set of results which appears to be supportive of the theory being tested is found, this does not in itself constitute decisive proof for that theory, since the same set of results could be consistent with some other explanation. Incidence analysis is not free of this problem. Thus, although a given estimate of the shift parameter may suggest that a certain proportion of the incidence of protection is shifted to the export sector, the result could also be consistent with some other explanation of changes in relative prices. As will be argued further below, however, despite this the estimates may contain useful information from the standpoint of evaluating trade policy.

Interpretation of incidence estimates

Taking the complications mentioned above as given and assuming that suitable price data are available, it is possible to estimate w in equation (5.3) to gain some idea of the incidence of protection. In addition, once one has information on ΔP_h, it is possible to estimate true protection to the import-able and exportable sectors. There are several uses to which this information can be put. First, by focusing on relative price changes, one is explicitly highlighting relative incentives to invest in different sectors. Second, the estimate of the shift parameter provides an indication of the extent to which the export sector finds itself bearing the burden of import protection. Arguably, the technique highlights this shifting of protection more directly than other approaches. Thus, the possible inconsistencies of policy are explicitly highlighted. Third, by generating estimates of true tariffs and true subsidies it is possible to demonstrate that very complicated protective structures sometimes confer relatively little by way of net, or true, protec-tion. For instance, where the shift parameter is relatively high and the price of non-tradeables increases in proportion to the price of importables, the latter sector gains little benefit, relative to the former sector, from any protectionist interventions. Finally, the methodology helps to demonstrate that often the actual and intended effects of policy intervention may be rather different. Thus, although the information content of incidence analysis may not be as full as with effective protection analysis, it is nevertheless potentially a valuable technique in policy evaluation.

Empirical evidence

On pp. 82–6 above we reviewed an extensive array of empirical evidence relating to effective protection analysis. As we have already noted, incidence analysis is of more recent vintage than effective protection analysis. As a result, the volume of empirical studies relating to applications of the technique in LDCs is relatively small. To date six studies on Latin American countries have been completed, and two on African economies. Sjaastad (1980a) and (1980b) applied the technique to Argentina and Uruguay; Diaz (1980) to El Salvador; Fendt (1981) to Brazil; Garcia (1981) to Colombia; Sjaastad and Clements (1981) to Chile; Greenaway and Milner (1986a) to Mauritius; and Greenaway (1986a) to the Ivory Coast. All of these studies, with the exception of the last two, provide estimates of the shift parameter. In addition, Greenaway and Milner (1986a) offer some hypothetical calculations for true tariffs and subsidies using the estimated shift parameter, actual data on nominal tariffs and assumed values for nominal subsidies. Greenaway (1986a) provides estimates for the shift parameter and estimates of true tariffs and subsidies using estimates of nominal tariffs and subsidies.

Table 5.2 provides summary information on these estimated shift parameters. As can be seen from the table, the studies cover a range of data periods and data sets, with some relying on quarterly data, some on monthly data and some on annual data. Most of the studies use price indices of 'traditional' exportables, basically exports of primary commodities. Greenaway and Milner (1986a) and Greenaway (1986a) do attempt to estimate shift parameters for models using information on non-traditional as well as traditional exportables. Some of the studies use single-product price indices, while others employ multi-product indices.

TABLE 5.2 Estimates of the incidence of protection

Country	Period	Data set	Shift parameter	Exportables
Uruguay	Jan. 1966–Oct. 1977	Monthly	0.53	Traditional
Chile	July 1959–Dec. 1980	Monthly	0.55	Traditional
Argentina	1935–1979	Annual	0.57	Traditional
El Salvador	1962 (Q1)–1977 (Q4)	Quarterly and monthly	0.70	Traditional
Brazil	1950–1978	Annual	0.70	
Colombia	Jan. 1970–Dec. 1978	Monthly	0.95	Traditional
Mauritius	July 1976–Dec. 1982	Quarterly	0.85	Traditional
Mauritius	July 1976–Dec. 1982	Monthly	0.59	Non-traditional
Ivory Coast	1960–1984	Annual	0.69	Traditional
Ivory Coast	Jan. 1970–Dec. 1984	Monthly	0.56	Non-traditional

Source: compiled from Sjaastad and Clements (1981), Clements and Sjaastad (1985), Greenaway and Milner (1986a) and Greenaway (1986a).

It will be recalled that the shift parameter can vary between zero and one. The implication of w being at the upper end of the scale is that the incidence of protection is borne largely by the export sector. At the lower end of the scale incidence is shared between the exportable and non-tradeable sectors, in the sense that P_m rises relative to P_x and P_h by the same proportion. As we can see from Table 5.2, all of the estimates reported so far have exceeded 0.50, with the lowest being 0.53 for Uruguay. This suggests that for those countries examined, the exportable sector bears the largest share of the incidence of protection.[9] In one case, Columbia (for traditional exportables), the shift parameter comes close to unity, suggesting that protection is shifted in its entirety to become an implicit export tax. The variation in the shift parameter is determined entirely by substitutional relationships in the economy. In this respect it is significant that for those two cases where estimates are made for both traditional and non-traditional exportables (Mauritius and the Ivory Coast), the estimates for non-traditional exportables are considerably less than for traditional exportables. This suggests that there is a greater degree of substitutability between importables and non-tradeables in a setting where the primary exportable is assumed to be 'traditional'. Alternatively stated, there is greater substitutability between exportables and non-tradeables when the former are non-traditional. This accords with *a priori* expectations, since there are likely to be more sector-specific factors in the traditional sector than in the production of non-traditional exportables.

These results are of some interest. Although they pertain to a range of economies with differing production structures and at different stages of economic development, they are unanimous in suggesting that there may be a significant degree of 'disprotection' for the export sector associated with protecting the import substitute sector. This helps explain why import protection is often associated with the contraction of traditional activities like agricultural production. It may often help to explain why there is frequently disappointment on the part of policy-makers at the apparent inability of export incentives to promote significant expansion of the export sector. Such incentives as are often offered to producers in export-processing zones may do little more than partially offset the disincentives created by the existence of import controls.[10] This point can be supported more directly by reference to estimates of true tariffs and true subsidies. Unfortunately, very little information is available here, although Greenaway (1986a) does report some results for the Ivory Coast. Here a nominal tariff of 20 per cent and a nominal subsidy to traditional exportables of 14 per cent, i.e. an export tax, are in fact consistent with a true tariff of 0.7 per cent and a true subsidy of −31.5 per cent. If one takes non-traditional exportables, the nominal tariff on importables is again 20 per cent, but the nominal subsidy to exportables is 2 per cent. However, the true tariff and subsidy rates are 11 per cent and −7.1 per cent respectively. The actual and intended effects of policy would therefore appear to diverge quite markedly, particularly when we take the traditional exportables case.

One final remark should be made regarding incidence analysis. We noted above the problem of observational equivalence. It could be claimed that these estimates of shift parameters are consistent with other explanations, and might even be explained by different trends applying to different series. Even if that were so, estimates of the shift parameter can still be used in discussions of the structure of protection. This value of the shift parameter is determined by substitutional relationships in the economy. In turn these substitutional relationships determine the transmission of price movements from one sector to another. In a way, therefore, the source of the price shocks pertaining to the data set used for estimation is irrelevant. As long as import protection impacts upon the domestic price of importables in a predictable way, we can still use estimates of the shift parameter to make inferences regarding the ultimate incidence of protection.

CONCLUDING COMMENTS

In this chapter we have examined two distinct approaches to the evaluation of commercial policy, namely effective protection analysis and incidence analysis. In addition, we have discussed applications of both techniques. Effective protection analysis is an approach which has been developed over the last twenty years or so, while incidence analysis is of more recent vintage. We have argued that the two approaches are complements rather than substitutes. Effective protection analysis is generally applied at the industry or activity level and provides us with a means of tracking the impact of commercial policy at a fairly disaggregated level of analysis. As such it is potentially very useful in commenting on the potential resource allocation effects of protection. By contrast, incidence analysis is intended to focus on the relative price effects of protection at the sectoral level and, in so doing, to comment on the potential for commercial policy to alter relative incentives to invest in different sectors of the economy. Both techniques have been deployed in the context of LDCs and have helped provide some insights into the operation of commercial policy in a number of countries. Some general comments can be made on the results of these analyses. For instance, it would seem that the structure of protection varies considerably from one economy to another. It would also seem that more highly protected economies have a wider spread of effective protective rates than less well-protected economies. In addition, it seems clear that although some activities are unambiguously protected by commercial policy, it is equally clear that others are actually disprotected. Finally, the empirical evidence suggests that the actual and intended effects of commercial policy may not always be the same.

6 Export Instability and Growth Performance

A. I. MACBEAN and D. T. NGUYEN*

INTRODUCTION

Whether economic growth in developing countries is significantly damaged by short-term fluctuations in their exports remains an important and unresolved question. It is important, because the belief that such instability does hinder growth underpins the continued demands of the Group of 77 for widespread intervention in commodity markets through international commodity agreements and for export diversification, backed by a reformed and more generous International Compensatory Facility in the International Monetary Fund (IMF) or the creation of a new Complementary Financing Facility.

Developing countries' goals are, of course, much broader than simple growth, and they vary among countries in their importance. Nevertheless, growth seems paramount in most developing countries. The attainment of many of the other goals is either dependent on growth or is required in order to sustain growth. For example, the creation of job opportunities for a growing labour force requires growth in national product, and the avoidance of serious balance-of-payments deficits is likely to be a necessary condition for sustained growth. In this survey growth in per capita income is taken to be the overriding objective of governments, and the effect of export instability upon subsidiary goals will only be considered in so far as these may influence growth.

Export instability also needs definition. Much of the confusion in the literature and the inconsistencies in statistical evidence stem from the lack of precision about the particular type of instability being studied, and the selection of statistical measures which can approximate the theoretical concepts. There is agreement in the literature that we are concerned with averages of movements above and below the trend in prices or earnings. There consensus ends. Various trends are possible and various methods of computing the indices of instability are available.[1] Even if, as often appears, they correlate with each other quite well, they are usually conceptually

95

different. They measure different aspects of export instability. We shall return to this issue after considering theories which seek to explain how export instability can affect growth and what data are available for testing these theories. Between them, the hypotheses we seek to test and the data available for econometric testing will determine the indices of instability which can approximate the ideal.

There is no lack of theories concerning relationships between fluctuations in either prices or earnings of exports, and economic growth in less developed countries (LDCs). Most imply that export instability will, via one route or another, reduce growth below what it would have been with a more stable set of export prices or revenues.[2] But a few economists have taken the opposite view and suggested mechanisms which could result in growth being stimulated by unstable prices or earnings.[3]

To complement these hypotheses there is no lack of empirical literature.[4] Some of it is well related to explicit hypotheses, some rather less so. Despite a relatively large number of statistical studies, it has proved extremely difficult to produce convincing refutations of either view of the likely overall effect on growth of export instability in developing countries in general.

In attempting to test the various hypotheses, several different approaches have been attempted:

1. Cross-sectional (cross-country) regression analyses which attempt to sum up the experience of large samples of countries over a number of years.
2. Case studies of individual countries using time series analyses to study relationships between export earnings and domestic variables which seem likely to determine growth.
3. Formal statistical modelling of countries, either with a general model (with few structural differences) to explain growth (Rangarajan and Sundarajan, 1976) or with a different model specifically designed for each individual country (Adams and Behrman, 1982). Such models seek to uncover the main functional relationships in the determination of national product. These are then used for statistical experiments which compare either their actual behaviour with what is inferred would have occurred if their export earnings had been stabilised, or what would have happened with predetermined economic changes in exports up and down, with the effects of stable exports.

One further preliminary point is necessary. Should the discussion focus on the instability of export earnings in total (perhaps in terms of real purchasing power) or should it be confined to, say, non-oil primary commodity exports? In the 1950s this distinction may not have been so important. It could be assumed that the export earnings of practically all LDCs were dominated by primary commodities. This is no longer so. For many countries manufactures now form the dominant, or at least a significant, proportion of exports. There is also the growth in value of oil plus the much larger number of countries for which it is the major export. These facts have drastically altered the situation for the 1970s and 1980s. Quite apart from Hong Kong,

TABLE 6.1   Manufactures as a percentage of merchandise exports

	1960 (%)	1980 (%)	Population (millions), mid-1981
India	45	59	690
Pakistan	27	50	85
Brazil	3	40	121
Argentina	4	23	28
Mexico	12	39	71

Source: World Bank, World Development Report, 1983, Tables 10 and 1.

Singapore, South Korea and Taiwan, which are clearly industrial exporters, approximately a further twenty LDCs are significant exporters of manufactures, among them several very populous nations (see Table 6.1).

Most of the policy proposals and most of the debate on export instability and growth in international forums seems to focus on commodity exporters. International commodity agreements, the European Community's STABEX scheme, The Common Fund and the Complementary Financing Facility proposal all concern instability in commodity exports. Most of the discussion about the vulnerability of LDCs' economies to instability focuses on their dependency upon commodities. This could suggest that both the theoretical and the empirical analyses should concentrate on the relationship between instability in commodity export prices and/or earnings, and domestic growth.

However, for reasons discussed below, there is no justification for singling out fluctuations in the export earnings of commodities as having special adverse effects on economic growth. It is the large sudden swings in total export earnings, rather than earnings from one source commodities, that may raise investment risk and disrupt imports of capital goods. It is not surprising, therefore, that much of the academic discussion and empirical work has concentrated on the macroeconomic impact of variations in total export earnings on growth, or on factors believed to determine growth.

International interest in commodity exporters partly reflects the belief that export prices and earnings are more unstable for commodities than for manufactures or other categories, and partly the fact that many very poor LDCs are heavily dependent on the export of a very few commodities. Given such interest, there is a case for investigating whether for those LDCs exporting mainly commodities, economic growth did in fact suffer as a result of excessive export earnings fluctuations. Even in this case, total export earnings rather than commodity export earnings is the more meaningful or relevant variable. However, there is also a good case for investigating the hypothesis that excessive fluctuations in the total export earnings would retard the economic growth of LDCs generally, irrespective of whether or not commodities contribute a substantial share to total export earnings.

HYPOTHESES

There are at least three different possible hypotheses, each of which implies a different population of countries from which any sample would be drawn and so suggests a certain criterion (or set of criteria) for selecting the sample of countries for investigation.

Hypothesis 1: Fluctuations in total merchandise earnings damage economic growth in developing countries generally – it would be appropriate to include in the samples of countries studied even those which were mainly dependent on exports of manufactures, or oil and gas, so long as they met some generally accepted criteria for being regarded as LDCs.[5]

Hypothesis 2: Export instability only damages the economic growth of those countries which are mainly exporters of primary products – this would require the exclusion of LDCs not specialising in commodity exports.

Hypothesis 3: Instability in commodity exports is damaging to economic growth only for those LDCs where, *prima facie*, income from commodity exports forms either a large part of the total foreign exchange available to the country and/or a large part of its national product – this would restrict still further the maximum number of countries that could be included in the study.

The possible reasons for Hypothesis 2 are (a) commodity exports tend to be more unstable than non-commodity exports, (b) fluctuations in earnings could be more troublesome for commodity sectors than for non-commodity sectors, (c) commodity sectors could have greater forward and backward linkages than other sectors and (d) LDCs mainly dependent on commodity exports tend to be poorer, more dependent on trade, less able to earn adequate foreign exchange or borrow to pay for import needs, and have other characteristics which render them more vulnerable to export fluctuations.

Let us consider each of these reasons in turn. Reason (a) is not necessarily true in practice, and even if true does still raise the question of why countries with less unstable export earnings should be excluded. To find out whether greater instability is associated with slower growth across countries, both stable and unstable countries are required.

Reason (b) need not generally be true. The adverse effects of earnings instability need not be greater for commodity sectors than for non-commodity sectors and could vary considerably across countries and commodities. In sectors exporting commodities such as tea, sugar, rubber or minerals, where a large proportion of output comes from large plantations or mines owned by the state or foreigners, *output and employment may not fluctuate much* because variable costs tend to be small relative to total costs. Output in plantations will be reduced in response to a fall in prices/earnings only if prices fall below harvesting costs (a very rare occurrence). Similarly, in mining, varying short-run output by continually laying off and recruiting labour or closing down and re-opening mines would seldom be economic. *Employment and wages are unlikely to vary much* in response to fluctuations in mineral prices. For sectors exporting commodities such as cocoa, coffee, groundnuts and jute, a large part of output is produced by small farmers whose *money* incomes would normally vary in line with export fluctuations. But would their sufferings be reflected in any slowing down in economic growth?

It is obvious that reason (c) can hardly hold in practice. The costs of farm inputs such as fertilisers, pesticides and fuel for irrigation pumps are usually not large relative to the value-added in agriculture. Most mineral processing has substantial energy costs, but energy consists mainly either of imported fuel or hydro-electricity. The production of either has few linkages with the rest of the economy.

Reason (d) is debatable. Many LDCs which are major exporters of commodities are not poor, e.g. Argentina, Brazil, Colombia, Uruguay and Malaysia. Whether instability is more serious for countries exporting mainly commodities than for others remains open to question.

Thus none of the above reasons for confining the study to LDCs which export mainly commodities seem convincing. As discussed below, export instability may hinder economic growth partly via increased uncertainty and risk and partly via short-term foreign exchange constraints on imports. For both headings, fluctuations in total export earnings rather than those in export earnings from commodities alone seem to be more relevant, and there is no clear justification for excluding LDCs which are less dependent on commodity exports.

It might be considered sensible, according to Hypothesis 3, to exclude countries which have ratios of commodity exports to GDP below a certain minimum on the ground that variations in commodity exports would be likely to have insignificant effects on national income, let alone economic growth. However, countries with small ratios of exports to GDP tend to have large income multipliers associated with any change in export earnings, because their import leakages also tend to be small relative to their national incomes. Undoubtedly, it makes good sense to exclude those countries whose economic growth appears, *prima facie*, to be unlikely to be hampered by export earnings instability. These countries are likely to be those which can either afford to hold large amounts of international reserves relative to their annual total imports, or have easy access to international borrowing. They need not necessarily be those whose exports are small relative to their national incomes.

The hypotheses to be set up for testing depend on the particular questions we want to answer. The models formulated and the data examined depend on the hypotheses. Are we concerned with, say, the relative importance of export instability to the growth of LDCs in general, as compared with other problems, such as those associated with slow growth rate in their export revenues or their ill-conceived domestic economic policies? Or is our concern to discover whether, for those countries where commodity export instability is *prima facie* likely to be significant, does it in fact retard their growth? As these last countries are the only ones which might be helped by international policies to stabilise commodity prices or receipts from commodity exports, there would seem to be a case for confining the analyses to this last group. However, as noted above, to find out whether countries whose exports are relatively unstable also tend to have a low rate of economic growth, it is necessary to include both those with stable as well as those with unstable exports in order to compare their rates of growth.

THEORETICAL CONSIDERATIONS

Economic growth can usefully be conceived (in terms of Harrod–Domar terminology) as the product of investment to national income ratio and marginal efficiency of investment (or the inverse of the marginal capital output ratio). Export instability may reduce economic growth because it adversely affects both the level and efficiency of investment. Investment may be *larger* and *more efficient* with stable export earnings for the following reasons:

1. With unstable incomes, it is more difficult to estimate the expected returns on yields; export fluctuations encourage business speculation and miscalculation and generate risks and uncertainty for entrepreneurs.
2. Fluctuations in government expenditure on the infrastructure and the stop-go policies resulting from export instability raise the risks associated with investment and cause inefficiences in delayed construction work, etc.
3. Fluctuations in imports of capital goods and raw materials result in fluctuations in investment which would reduce the efficiency of investment.
4. In so far as wages and prices are inflexible downwards (but not upwards), export instability increases inflationary pressures, with inflation encouraging spending, discouraging saving and possibly distorting the allocation of resources further away from optimum.
5. The country may under-produce the unstable commodities in which it otherwise enjoys comparative advantages and may thereby forgo some of its potential trade gains. Of course, high risks associated with investment for reasons (a)–(c) above could deter inward investment and make foreign borrowing more expensive.

However, it has also been contended that export booms generate optimism, leading to increased investment which is not matched by disinvestment in years of export slumps. According to Reynolds (1963, p. 108), investors in the export industry (copper mines) regard upswings as beginnings of trends rather than as temporary phenomena, and behave accordingly; downswings, on the other hand, are apparently considered short-run phenomena, since no major disinvestment occurred even during the severe depression of the 1930s. But if an industry is to expand, then we should expect it to increase its investment during booms at a rate unmatched by disinvestment during slumps when faced with unstable income, rather than to maintain investment continuously at a high level, irrespective of the movements of its income. Thus increased investment in upswings which is unmatched by disinvestment in downswings may simply reflect two facts: the industry is growing and its income is unstable. Instability produces this stop-go pattern of investment, but the reason for growing capital formation may be long-term profitability rather than instability. Hence, investment in the boom unmatched by disinvestment in the recession cannot be regarded as convincing evidence that unstable earnings lead to a higher average level of investment.[6]

The view that export instability favours investment was also held by Sir Sidney Caine (1958, p. 188) who maintained: 'There is in fact plenty of evidence on the other side in, for example, the high level of investment which has prevailed in such countries as Malaya and Indonesia during periods of very sharp fluctuations in the prices of their principal products.' Investment is expected to be related positively to the expected mean of returns and negatively to risks (as indicated by the variance of returns). A high level of investment in Malaysia and Indonesia during periods of high risks (owing to unstable prices) may simply reflect high expected returns rather than risk-addicted investors. Investment in these periods may have been high *despite* rather than *because of* high price instability.

Higher risks and uncertainty would induce firms and individuals to hold larger precautionary balances; to raise these, savings have to be higher. This view is stressed by Knudsen and Parnes (1975), who contend, on the basis of Friedman's permanent income hypothesis, that a large variance in transitory income (caused by export instability) will stimulate savings and so investment, since savings are the primary source of capital formation in LDCs. However, while it is true that savings are necessary for investment, it does not automatically follow that a decline in consumption will induce capital formation, for the fall in consumption could contract the market and so discourage private investment. Even if this did not occur, most of these savings would, as we suggested above, be held in the form of liquid assets and could fail to be turned into long-term investment. Generally, saving from a transitory increase in income in one period would be matched by dissaving to support consumption in the next. Furthermore, income instability leading to a high level of demand for precautionary balances would increase savings only temporarily while this balance was being built up, but would not raise long-term saving.

EMPIRICAL RESEARCH

Whether export instability generates observable adverse consequences on the domestic economy or not depends a great deal on the policy reactions of governments. The adverse consequences can largely be avoided if the country holds adequate reserves (or is willing and able to borrow abroad) and pursues domestic stabilising policies to insulate exporters and the rest of the economy from its effects. The cost of export instability, which in this case is simply the cost of borrowing or holding reserves, seems likely to be lower than unmitigated adverse consequences of export instability spreading throughout the economy. In the latter case, adverse effects of export instability can probably be observed in the forms of fluctuations in income, investment and employment, and possibly higher inflation. The marginal costs of holding reserves are the opportunity costs involved in forgoing investments which would have been undertaken, less the returns on the overseas assets in which reserves are held.

Where investment and its efficiency are allowed to be affected adversely by export instability, it is still by no means easy to measure the detrimental effect of instability on economic growth in practice either by cross-country comparison or time series analysis.

Methodology

Cross-country analysis. Even if we exclude from the sample all countries which choose to isolate the effects of export instability on their economies by holding large reserves, etc., the multiplier effects of export fluctuations can be very different for different economic structures, and a cross-country regression (or rank correlation) analysis may not reveal any relationship. A given shock may produce different income and investment instability in different countries. The effect of a given degree of investment instability on its efficiency may also differ among commodity sectors. Furthermore, the efficiency of investment, the investment/income ratio and hence the rate of economic growth may be determined by many factors which are more powerful than export instability. Technological changes and international capital flows have recently transformed the pattern of tastes, factor endowments and comparative advantages of individual countries, and these are likely to be more powerful determinants of economic growth than export instability. Other powerful influences include the savings habits of the people, the tax and trade policies pursued by the government, and the level and pattern of domestic investment. Suppose a country suddenly finds itself possessing substantial comparative advantage in the production of a number of commodities with stable export markets, then its economic growth would be high and its exports would be stable. By comparing only growth and instability across countries, we would wrongly attribute its high growth to its export stability. Conversely, had these commodities had unstable markets, then its high growth would be associated with high export instability and we would conclude, equally wrongly, that export instability, if anything, favours growth. Thus cross-country comparison can easily fail to reveal the true relationship between economic growth and export instability.

Time-series analysis. Could time series analysis of each country do better? Suppose we examine the case of a small country, e.g. Zambia, which derives most of its export earnings from a single commodity, e.g. copper. By virtue of its small size, the country contributes only a small fraction of world exports of this commodity, so that for all practical purposes, it is a price-taker in the world market. The most satisfactory approach to studying the effects of export instability on the country appears to involve the construction of an econometric model, consisting of the sector exporting this commodity with links to a macro-model of the whole economy. Since short-run output can be treated as very inelastic with respect to price, i.e. output moves more or less along a trend, fluctuations in export earnings would largely reflect fluctuations in export prices (which are exogenously given). By comparing the results for GDP levels and growth rates in two simultaneous runs – one with stable export prices and one with unstable export prices around the same smooth trend – one could, in principle, measure the effects of export instability on the economic growth of this country.[7]

The question is, how do we model the effects of export instability on investment and its efficiency? *A priori*, we would expect random fluctuations in export prices/earnings to produce results different from those of a smooth trend because of risk aversion on the part of producers and consumers, disruption to investment programs, the presence of non-linearities (arising from summing the constraints), lags in the functional forms and rigidities in the money wage, or asymmetric responses of certain variables to export fluctuations. It is possible for investment to respond symmetrically to an export shortfall and yet at the same time to be lower, say, because of frequent disruptions to capital goods imports. Hence, the effect of export instability on investment may not be reflected in asymmetric responses of investment (or other variables) to export swings. In the absence of such asymmetric responses, simulation runs would probably fail to detect any effects of export instability on investment or economic growth.

In any case, export instability may have a significant long-term impact on investment and its efficiency, but a negligible short-term (year-to-year) impact. The presence of lagged responses of investment level and efficiency and income growth to export instability make it very difficult to observe or measure the impact of export instability on growth when other variables affecting growth and investment are also changing and have lagged effects on them.

REVIEW OF EVIDENCE

Cross-country approach

The hypothesis investigated is whether export instability hinders economic growth. The cross-country regressions produced by MacBean (1966), using a sample of twenty-five countries, indicated a non-significant positive relationship (rather than the expected significant negative relationship) between an index of export instability and the growth rates of domestic capital formation. Simple regressions showed that neither the ratio of investment to income nor the rate of growth of investment was negatively related to export instability. In fact, multiple regression with the growth rate of import capacity as an additional explanatory variable showed a positive relationship between the growth rate of investment (the dependent variable) and export instability.

Maizels (1968), by excluding five countries from MacBean's sample of twenty-one LDCs and relating the growth rate of GDP to export instability and the growth rate of fixed investment (rather than that of import capacity), produced an equation which would appear to provide 'a reasonably good explanation of inter country differences in rates of economic growth' and which 'also strongly suggests that highly unstable exports are likely to be a significant constraint on the rate of economic growth of many developing countries'. Unfortunately Maizels did not provide any rationale for replacing the growth rate of import capacity by that of investment, and in so far as export instability affects income growth via its impact on investment, the inclusion of both export instability and the growth rate of investment as two explanatory variables in determining income growth appears to be somewhat confusing. Furthermore, the grounds for excluding the five countries from MacBean's sample were not given. In general, the exclusion of observations which weaken one's chosen hypothesis without strong justification is not an acceptable scientific procedure. For these reasons, the results from Maizel's regression should best be disregarded.

Using a slightly larger sample of countries, a different index of instability and two decades of data (1950–66), Kenen and Voivodas (1972) found that their results in general do not contradict those of MacBean. They found *no consistent association between export instability and economic growth*. What they found was that instability hindered investment in the 1960s, even though it appeared, contrary to expectation, to stimulate investment in the 1950s. One can object to their chosen index of instability. It is a measure of 'forecast errors' rather than of fluctuations around a trend, since deviation is measured around a 'forecast' which contains, in addition to a time trend, a component associated with the previous year's export earnings. The use of this forecast in the place of a smooth time trend in the definition of the instability index suggests that only *unpredictable* changes are included in the definition of instability. But although predictable changes may be easier to deal with than unpredictable changes, both types affect the economy depending on policy reactions and therefore should be included in the definition of instability. The index should measure *unstable* earnings rather than merely *unpredictable* earnings.

Another problem is their inclusion of a coefficient of autocorrelation in all their regressions, which seems difficult to justify. The forecast used in the instability index is obtained by regressing current export earnings against the previous year's export earnings and time. The resulting regression coefficient of the previous year's export earnings, R, is called the 'autoregressive coefficient'. To avoid the estimation bias which arises because of the dependence between lagged export earnings and the residual term, Kenen and Voivodas (1972) in fact obtained the estimates for the growth rate and the autoregressive coefficient by regressing the first difference of exports (i.e. current exports minus the previous year's exports) against the first difference of exports lagged by one year. They refer to the coefficient of this lagged first difference as R' and use R' in all of their multiple regressions, which also include the instability index for exports and a measure of inflation. R' is used as a measure of the *duration of export disturbances*. But no economic rationale for including R' is given (nor is it self-evident).

By contrast, Glezakos (1973) found a significant negative effect of export instability on the real per capita growth rate of the LDCs included in his sample over the 1953–66 period. However, some doubts can be raised about the validity of his results. First, seven of the forty countries placed in the LDC sample were countries not normally considered to be LDCs: Cyprus, Greece, Iceland, Portugal, Spain, Turkey and Yugoslavia. Second, while per capita growth rates were in real terms, there is no indication that the instability indices relate to exports in real terms. The mixing of monetary and real variables could cause serious bias in Glezakos's results. Instability indices calculated in current prices may differ from those calculated in constant prices. Third, although for most purposes per capita income is a better indicator of welfare than national income, there are reasons for doubting its suitability as the dependent variable in this case. The plausible relationship is that growth of income should be influenced by the growth of the workforce, which in turn is related to the growth of population, and other variables such as export growth and instability. To regress the growth rate of per capita income on export instability implicitly assumes that the partial elasticity of income with respect to population is unity, which is unlikely. It should also be noted that ten countries whose imports were found not to depend on their exports were excluded from Glezakos's sample, and this has helped to strengthen the negative relationship between instability and growth. The reason given was that most of the effects of export instability on economic development stem from its impact on imports. Hence, countries whose imports were not sensitive to their exports were excluded. The relative insensitivity of imports to exports in a country suggests that it may have been insulating its economy from export instability by policy measures. This would mean that in such a country the effects of export instability on risks, uncertainty and growth may have been largely prevented. That would seem good grounds for exclusion, but one should remember that the results can no longer be extended to LDCs in general.

Knudsen and Parnes (1975), using a sample of twenty-eight developing countries, in a multiple regression equation with income growth as a dependent variable and both export instability and domestic instability as independent variables, found that the coefficients of these indices were positive and statistically non-significant. They also found that the coefficient of a weighted average of these two indices (with export instability weighted by export share in GNP and domestic instability, one minus export share) was positive and statistically significant. They maintained that a positive effect of instability on growth is not surprising because transitory income is largely saved, not consumed, and therefore adds to investment. But the *a priori* reasoning is not convincing. If savings are higher out of positive transitory income than out of permanent income, then dissavings should also be higher out of negative transitory income, and effects on saving should even out. Instability may also increase the need for a larger precautionary cash balance and hence savings, but, as argued earlier, this is a stock change and need not lead to a higher flow of savings or investment over time.

Voivodas (1974) postulated that the investment to income ratio, I/Y, is positively related to the ratio of capital goods imports to income, MK/Y_1, and negatively to its variance in a linear equation, and that MK/Y is a linear function of export earnings, X, and net capital inflows, F. Since income growth Y_g is proportional to I/Y, Voivodas obtained a linear equation relating Y_g to X/Y, F/Y, variances of X/Y and F/Y and the covariance of X/Y and F/Y:

$$Y_g = a_1 (X/Y) + a_2 (F/Y) - a_3 \, Var \, (X/Y) - a_4 \, Var \, (F/Y)$$
$$- a_5 \, Cov \, (X/Y, F/Y) \tag{6.1}$$

Lim (1976) claimed that $Cov \, (X/Y, F/Y)$ has no distinct economic meaning *vis-à-vis* the instability issue. We disagree. Since a positive (negative) Cov $(X/Y, F/Y)$ measures the extent to which movements in X and F are reinforcing (offsetting), given $Var \, (X/Y)$ and $Var \, (F/Y)$, a smaller value of $Cov \, (X/Y, F/Y)$ would imply a more stable capacity for importing capital goods than a large value. Hence we would expect Y_g to be negatively related to $Cov \, (X/Y, F/Y)$. Lim's reformulation to get rid of this variable in the estimating equation makes less sense.

Replacing variables X/Y and F/Y by dX/Y and dF/Y, Voivodas produced the following alternative estimating equation:

$$Y_g = b_1 (dX/Y) + b_1 (dF/Y) - b_2 \, Var \, (X/Y) - b_3 \, Var \, (F/Y)$$
$$- b_4 \, Cov \, (X/Y, F/Y) \qquad \qquad (6.2)$$

The regressions $X = a + b(t) + u_t$ and $F = a_1 + b_1(t) + u_t$ were run to obtain dX and dF respectively, and these were divided by Y to obtain dX/F and dF/Y. Voivodas proceeded (p. 411) to estimate equations (6.1) and (6.2), using the data from thirty-one LDCs and six primary producing developed countries, over the period 1956–68. He found that the coefficients of the variance terms in (6.1) have the expected negative sign but are non-significant, and the coefficients of the covariance terms and the ratio of exports to GNP have positive signs instead of the expected negative ones. He found that the coefficients associating the growth rate and the variance of the ratio of capital inflows to income and the covariance terms are not significant. By dropping the variables relating to foreign capital inflows he found that R^2 increases, suggesting that the inclusion of foreign capital inflow as an independent variable does not improve the explanatory power of the regression and that the coefficients of the growth in the ratio of exports to income and the variance of this ratio have the expected negative signs and are statistically significant.

Using data from a sample of twenty-nine LDCs and six primary producing developed countries, Lim (1976, p. 320) re-estimated equations (6.1) and (6.2) both with and without $Cov \, (X/Y, F/Y)$ and found the results are very poor for equation (6.1), with $R^2 = -0.04$ with $Cov \, (X/Y, F/Y)$ and $R^2 = -0.02$ without $Cov \, (X/Y, F/Y)$. For equation (6.2) the results are much better: R^2 is 0.32, significant at 1 per cent level with $Cov \, (X/Y, F/Y)$, and 0.23, significant at 5 per cent level without $Cov \, (X/Y, F/Y)$. In equation (6.2), the coefficient of $Cov \, (X/Y, F/Y)$ has the expected negative sign and is significant at 5 per cent; those of the variances of X/Y and F/Y have the right signs but are not significant. When $Cov \, (X/Y, F/Y)$ is dropped, the coefficients of both variances retain the *correct* signs and that of $Var \, (X/Y)$ becomes significant at 5 per cent. Thus, it appears that countries whose capital inflows tend to be compensatory for export earnings fluctuations, i.e. negative $Cov \, (X/Y, F/Y)$, have a higher growth rate of income. However, when the sample period was extended by five years, i.e. the period became 1956–73, the R^2 for all equations became statistically non-significant, suggesting that over the longer period the impact of export instability on the economic growth of LDCs became weaker.

Recently, Lancieri (1978, p. 147), using a large sample of 101 countries over the period 1961–72 to test the relationship between export instability and GDP growth rates (both in real terms), obtained a negative rank correlation of –0.33, which is significant at the 1 per cent level. Lancieri (1979, p. 304) also tested the relationship between the real GDP growth rate and the instability of real total agricultural exports using a sample of seventy countries for the period 1961–72 and obtained an even higher rank correlation of –0.59 per cent, which is significant at 1 per cent. Lancieri's results reinforce Glezakos's earlier finding of a negative impact of instability on growth. However, since his results are based on a simple correlation between growth and instability, instability (the independent variable) may have spuriously captured the effects of other influences on growth which are omitted from the equation. Moreover, although the relationship between GDP growth and export instability is statistically significant, variation in instability explains only 11 per cent of the variation in growth (implied by a correlation of –0.33), a rather small proportion. This suggests a rather weak relationship between growth and instability.

Lam (1980a) produced statistical results which show a significant, positive rank correlation between export instability and export growth for a sample of fifteen Western Pacific countries and nine developed countries for two time periods, 1961–72 and 1961–74. This positive correlation between export instability and export growth was later shown by Glezakos (1983) and Tan (1983) to be the result of a systematic bias caused by the manner in which the instability index was calculated.

The instability index used by Lam is the 'normalised standard error of estimate' of the 'linear regression of exports against time'. Examination of the data for merchandise export values of the countries in the sample reveals that they are in fact non-linear with respect to time. The standard error of estimate derived from fitting a linear trend to data with a non-linear trend will result in countries with a higher export growth rate having larger standard errors of estimate. Hence, the instability index as calculated by Lam contains a positive bias, in that countries with higher rates of growth of exports will have spuriously higher instability indexes. In order to test whether suitable correction for bias in the instability index affects the results reported by Lam, Tan fitted non-linear trends to the export values of all the countries in his sample, using the same data sources and covering the same time periods, and found that there is no statistically significant correlation between export instability and export growth or income growth. Glezakos (1983) also re-estimated the instability indexes for the fourteen Western Pacific countries over the 1961–72 and 1961–74 periods, using both linear and exponential trends. He found that, over the 1961–72 period, export instability is negatively correlated to income growth (but not significant) when either an index with exponential trend or an index with the trend being linear or non-linear, depending on the 'best-fit' criterion, is used. Over 1961–74, the correlation of export instability with these same indices becomes positive, but statistically non-significant. Thus Lam's study and the comments by Tan and Glezakos illustrate how the choice of a linear or non-linear trend in the calculation of an instability index can seriously affect the results.

More recently, Moran (1983), on the basis of a cross-section analysis for a sample of thirty countries, found that export instability (as measured by several formulae to give emphasis to different aspects of instability) does not have a significant effect on domestic savings or income growth over the 1954–75 period as a whole. However, the effect of export instability on domestic savings and income growth was found to be negative and statistically significant over the 1954–65 period, but not significant over the later 1966–75 period, suggesting that the results are highly sensitive to the period of analysis.

Savvides (1984) used the same method as Glezakos to estimate the three variables, income growth (Y_r), export growth (X_r) and export instability index (I_x) for the same sample of countries but for the later period 1967–77. He found that in a regression equation relating Y_r to X_r and I_x, the coefficient of I_x is positive and non-significant, and that of X_r is positive and significant. This is in marked contrast to the earlier results of Glezakos. However, in a reply, Glezakos (1984) drew attention to the inordinately high real per capita GDP growth rates reported in the statistical appendix of Savvides's paper. On closer examination of Savvides's data, a number of countries (Chile, El Salvador, Ethopia, Ghana, etc.) known to have had stagnating economies during the time period under consideration, are shown to have real per capita growth rates ranging from 4.5 per cent to 11.5 per cent per annum. Also, according to Savvides's data, over 60 per cent of the LDCs attained annual real per capita growth rates of over 10 per cent. This bias could be due to Savvides's attempt to convert each country's GDP from domestic currency into dollars, using foreign exchange rates which could be inappropriate, rather than using the UN Basic Series of National Accounts in constant (1975) US dollars. Using the latter data series and a different instability index (which is based on the trend, linear or non-linear, which best fits each country's time series of exports), Glezakos obtained an equation determining the growth rate of per capita income which shows a significant negative coefficient for export instability and a significant positive coefficient for export growth rate for the 1967–77 period, i.e. results which basically confirm those of his previous study for the earlier period, 1953–66.

Limitations of the cross-country approach

Most of the studies reviewed above investigate the effect of export instability (as well as inflation and export growth) on economic growth using a cross-country approach. Adams and Behrman (1982, p. 44) consider these studies as 'reduced-form representation of the impact of changes of commodity exports (or total exports) on various summary statistics relating to the macro-economic goals of the developing countries.' But, alas, Adams and Behrman did not explain what they meant by 'reduced-form representation'.

We would call such an equation a derived equation rather than a reduced-form equation, as it contains more than one endogenous variable.

It is misleading to call it a reduced-form equation since, in doing so, one destroys the usefulness of the reduced-form concept by making it mean two quite different things. It is better to reserve the concept of reduced-form equation for an equation which involves only one endogenous variable, i.e. according to its strict econometric meaning.

The parameters of the *derived* equation relating income growth to export instability and other variables are combinations of the parameters of the original equations. Adams and Behrman suggest (p. 50), as a criticism of the cross-country approach, that the parameters of the *derived* equation may be unstable even if the *original* parameters are stable. The converse is also possible that, owing to offsetting movements in *original* parameters, the *derived* parameters may turn out to be more stable than the *original* ones. Instability in parameters may be just as much a problem for either original or *derived* equations.

In most of the cross-country studies, very few variables apart from export instability are included in the equation determining economic growth. The omission of important variables determining economic growth would reduce the explanatory power of the overall equation (R^2) but need not necessarily cause a bias in the estimate of the effect of export instability, unless the omitted variables are correlated with export instability.

If the omitted variables are correlated with export instability, their omission will bias the estimation of the effect of export instability, but without knowing the signs and magnitudes of these correlations, one cannot say anything about the direction of the bias. Although this criticism may be valid against particular cross-country studies, it is not valid against the cross-country approach as such. The bias caused by the incorrect omission of variables is as much a problem for time-series analysis or country modelling as it is for cross-country analysis. Thus Adams and Behrman were perhaps disingenuous in regarding this as a problem peculiar to the cross-country approach.

The aim of most studies is to determine whether export instability hinders growth. For this purpose, the simpler *derived* form of the estimated equation would do. Although for other purposes mentioned by Adams and Behrman, knowledge of the *original* parameters may be required, it is not necessary for the specific issue of effects on growth. Their criticism that the derived form 'suppresses the overall constraints on the economy due to factor availabilities, national identities, government and central bank budgets, and so forth' is similar to their above criticism. Of course, the *derived* form only answers the very limited question it is set; it can hardly be criticised for not providing other answers, however useful they might be. The coefficient of the export instability in a cross-country equation determining economic growth may well reflect all the constraints and identities mentioned above.

Both export instability and low growth may be caused by a set of exogenous variables, so that any observed relationship between them need not indicate a causal relationship. This is true, but is quite another matter. In practice, we always have an identification problem, i.e. the problem of distinguishing a structural relationship we are interested in estimating and that of a *mongrel* equation representing a combination of other equations in the model. The identification problem again applies equally to both time-series and cross-section approaches.

The final criticism made by Adams and Behrman (p. 52) is valid. They correctly point out that 'even if the underlying structural relations have the same form across countries, the *reduced forms* may differ because of different structural parameters or different predetermined variables'. More-over, owing to different policy reactions by the governments in different countries, the underlying structural relations may well have very different forms. The coefficient of export instability in the *derived form* equation relating it to income growth would therefore be likely to vary a good deal across countries, so that even if it were significant and negative for every country, the estimate of it on the basis of an across-country regression would probably have a large variance. The probability is, therefore, that this estimate would not be significant. This is an *important* weakness of the cross-country approach which has already been discussed. Despite this weakness, the approach may still have to be used to assess the kinds of impact export instability has on growth which time series analysis, by its nature, would fail to estimate, e.g. the effect of export instability on investment and growth via its effect on risk and uncertainty.

Time series–country modelling approach

This approach relies on the estimation and simulation of econometric models of national economies, commodity sectors and, sometimes, com-modity markets to assess the impact of export instability on the various goals of the countries. It appears successful in estimating the short-run effects of changes in commodity prices, quantities or earnings on the main macro variables, but largely fails to measure the long-term impact of instability on the *trends* of these variables.

When the econometric model is used to estimate what would happen when export prices are first stable over a number of years, and then unstable, domestic income, investment, the price level and other macro variables may show considerable differences in fluctuations between the two cases, but the trends in these variables may show little or no difference. This could simply be reflecting non-linearities, constraints, lags or the weakness of any ratchet effects.

Rangarajan and Sundarajan (1976) estimated highly aggregated macro-econometric models for eleven LDCs. They obtained long-run export multi-pliers above 2 for nine out of eleven countries and found growth rates improved with greater export stability in about half of the cases. Their results suggest that while export growth assists economic growth, export instability is just as likely to help as to hinder economic growth.

Rangarajan and Sundarajan's approach is superior to the cross-country approach in the sense that they at least allow for some structural differences among countries. However, their model can be criticised for being grossly oversimplified, since it is an extreme Keynesian demand-determined one, lacking supply constraints normally considered relevant for LDCs. Furthermore, usual policy reactions are ignored and overall fiscal and monetary constraints are left out of their models. Given these weaknesses, it is not exactly clear what their results really show. Their approach may reveal even less about the relationship between economic growth and instability than does the cross-country approach, which is based on much larger samples of countries and where the estimate of the cross-country coefficient of export instability and its distribution reflects in part the different policy reactions among countries.

The recent country studies by Adams *et al.* (1979) (coffee and Brazil), Priovolos (1981) (coffee and the Ivory Coast) and Obidegwu and Nziramasanga (1981) (copper and Zambia) have overcome some of these weaknesses by investigating the impacts of export instability within the wider context of econometric models in which the relevant primary sectors and their linkages with the rest of the economy are explicitly specified. Adams *et al.* (p. 168) demonstrate, on the basis of simulations, that 'fluctuations in the coffee market have magnified impacts on the macro variables of the Brazilian economy'. The predominant effects are through the demand linkages, with some supply impacts via capital formation, because 'the Brazilian macro model does not contain capacity constraints on industrial and tertiary sector output, reflecting the significant industrial underutilization which exists in Brazil'. However, Adams *et al.* make no attempt to measure the impact of instability on economic growth. Priovolos and Obidegwu and Nziramasanga found that fluctuations in commodity prices (coffee for Ivory Coast and copper for Zambia) had little impact on the growth of their respective economies. According to Obidegwu and Nziramasanga (p. 108), while fluctuations affected the value of output of mining from the export sector negatively, 'the rest of the economy is insulated by net international reserves, the foreign share of net export revenues, and balance on current account. They seem to absorb most of the up-and-down movements, leaving the real variables on their long-term trend rate'.

Adams and Behrman (1982) summarise the major results of the country and commodity studies by Priovolos and Obidegwu and Nziramasanga, as well as those by Adams and Priovolos (1981) (coffee and Brazil), Siri (1980) (coffee and Central America), Lasaga (1981) (copper and Chile) and the commodity models by Pobukades (1980, copper) and Ford (1978, coffee). On the basis of simulation exercises designed for comparing the combined effects of an upward and downward movement of 10 per cent in the prices of coffee and copper and sustained price changes, they produce many useful results. Depending on policy reactions, the direct and indirect impacts of an upward (or downward) change in the international price of a commodity, or a sustained change in direction, can be very large for most countries, but *the impacts of a combined upward and downward change of a given size on the macro variables are small, suggesting that ratchet effects are negligible as transmitters of the effects of export instability on investment and growth.* A sustained increase in a commodity price powerfully assists investment, growth and capacity utilisation, but has adverse effects on inflation and income distribution.

Limitations of time-series approach

It appears that these studies fail to detect any adverse effects of instability on investment in the form of asymmetrical responses of investment (or other macro variables) to instability. If this is because asymmetrical responses are weak or absent in practice, any time series analysis would fail to detect adverse effects on investment. But long-term investment could still be lowered by high export instability through causing a higher risk discount and lowering incentives to invest by disrupting imports of capital goods over a long period of time. Such adverse effects of instability can only be picked up in a cross-country analysis and not in a time-series analysis, involving relationships between annual observations on different variables. Thus the results reported by Adams and Behrman really produce *no* evidence on the effects of instability on growth rather than evidence that the effects are weak or absent.[8]

CONCLUDING REMARKS ON CONSEQUENCES OF INSTABILITY FOR ECONOMIC GROWTH

Empirical evidence in the form of time-series analysis and country modelling, together with *a priori* reasoning, clearly suggests that any upward or downward change in commodity export prices or earnings would have important effects not only on the export sectors but also, if the export sector is large, on the rest of the economy, unless offset by policy actions. Such offsetting policies backed by adequate reserves of foreign exchange and/or easy access to international borrowing could substantially mitigate the impact on the rest of the economy of changes in export prices or earnings.

A priori reasoning suggests that where the adverse effects of export instability on growth take the form of ratchet effects (e.g. asymmetrical responses of investment to an upward *vis-à-vis* downward change in exports), time-series analysis could capture them, but where these effects take the form of reducing the trends of variables affecting growth (e.g. the investment/income ratio and investment efficiency), then time-series analysis and country modelling would fail to detect them. Only cross-country analysis can hope to capture any such adverse effects of instability on growth using suitably chosen samples of countries which are homogeneous in terms of economic structures and policy reactions.

Since in general there are other more powerful influences on economic growth than export instability, responses of relevant variables such as investment and imports may be very different for different countries, and policy reactions in different countries may also vary considerably – it is unlikely that the effects of instability on economic growth would consistently be revealed in different cross-country studies, using different samples of countries, and over different periods of time.

Indeed, this review of empirical literature on the relationship between export instability and economic growth, using a cross-country approach, suggests some support for the view that instability is an obstacle to growth, but the results are shown to be sensitive to the samples of countries, the periods under investigation, and the manner in which export instability and the trends in exports are measured. Table 6.2 gives a summary of cross-country results. The differences in the results produced by different studies do not appear surprising – they simply confirm the difficulty of capturing, in practice, adverse effects (which could be slight) of export instability on economic growth, even though *a priori* grounds suggest some adverse effects are likely.

Over twenty years ago one of the author's of this review wrote that, 'The case for viewing export instability as a severe deterrent to economic growth in most underdeveloped countries is not proven' (MacBean, 1966, p. 127). We see no reason to change that conclusion, but would remind the reader that the Scottish verdict of 'not proven' does not mean 'not guilty'. The difficulty of proving a causal relationship does not mean that it does not exist. There is evidence in other fields of economics that higher returns are required for investments with higher risks, and that repeated disruptions to investment programmes reduce their attractiveness to investors. Even in the absence of direct evidence confirming the detrimental effect of export instability on economic growth, *a priori* reasoning and indirect evidence still strongly suggest that those countries whose economies seem likely to be sensitive to export fluctuations should be encouraged and assisted to insulate their economies from the effects of export instability. The costs of instability to them and to the international community at large may considerably outweigh the cost of such devices as a generous international compensatory financing scheme.

TABLE 6.2 Effects of export instability on economic growth: a summary of cross-country results

Authors	Dependent variable	Sign	Significance	Correlation	Number of countries (LDCs)	Period	Comments
MacBean (1966)	$\dot{I}$	+	°	S	21	1950–8	Sample size too small.
	$\dot{I}$	+	°	M	"	"	Period too short.
	I/Y	+	°	S	"	"	Index trend: 5-year moving average.
	$\dot{Y}$	–	°	S	"	"	
	$\dot{Y}$	–	°	M	"	"	
Maizels (1968)	$\dot{Y}$	–	*	M	16	"	As above, plus: arbitrary exclusion of data; dubious rationale for inclusion of I.
Kenen & Voivodas (1972)	$\dot{Y}$	–	°	M	22	1950–9	Instability around a forecast. Unclear rationale for inclusion of autoregressive coefficient.
Glezakos (1973)	$\dot{Y}pc$	–	*	M	40	1953–66	$\dot{Y}pc$ as dependent variable is unsuitable. Incl. some non-LDCs in sample. Mixing money & real variables.
Voivodas (1974)	$\dot{Y}$	–	°	M	31	1956–68	Instability of export–income ratio. Results suggest offsetting capital flows help.
Lim (1976)	$\dot{Y}$	–	°	M	29	1956–68 1956–73	As above, except without covariance of export & capital flows as a regressor.
Lancieri (1978)	$\dot{Y}$	–	*	Rk	101	1961–72	Correlation is significant but small. Instability may capture effects of omitted variables.
Lam (1980)	$\dot{X}$	+	*	S	24	1961–72	Index with linear trend is spuriously correlated with growth if trend turns out to be non-linear.
Tan (1983)	$\dot{X}$	+	°	S	"	1961–74	Re-estimate of above but using instability around exponential trend.
	$\dot{Y}$	+	°	S	"	"	

continued on p. 116

Table 6.2 continued

Authors	Dependent variable	Sign	Significance	Correlation	Number of countries (LDCs)	Period	Comments
Glezakos (1983)	$\dot{Y}$	–	°	S	"	1961–72	Instability around best-fit
	Y	+	°	S	"	1961–74	trend.
Moran (1983)	$\dot{Y}$	–	*	S	30	1954–65	Different formulae used
	$\dot{Y}$	–	°	S	"	1966–75	to stress different aspects of instability.
Savvides (1984)	$\dot{Y}pc$	+	°	M	39	1967–77	$\dot{Y}pc$s are too high: use of inappropriate exchange rates to convert GDP in domestic currencies into \$.
Glezakos (1984)	$\dot{Y}pc$	–	*	M	38	1967–77	Re-estimate, using UN Basic Series of Constant \$ GDP.

Notes: $\dot{Y}$, $\dot{Y}pc$, $\dot{I}$ and $\dot{X}$ are growth rates of income, per capita income investment and export respectively, and Y and I are the levels of income and investment respectively; * and ° denote significant and not significant, at 5 per cent respectively; S, M and Rk denote simple, multiple and rank correlations respectively.

7 The Debate Over Trends in the Terms of Trade

DAVID SAPSFORD*

INTRODUCTION

This chapter is concerned with the debate over the long-run behaviour of the net barter terms of trade between primary products and manufactures. Defined as the ratio of the price of primary commodities to the price of manufactured goods, the net barter terms of trade between ·primaries and manufactures (referred to hereafter as NBTT) may alternatively be interpreted as a measure of the *real* price of primary commodities (e.g. Ray, 1977). The next two sections of this chapter survey the existing literature, while the penultimate section presents a simple trend analysis of the behaviour of the NBTT over the period since 1900, which is designed, among other things, to resolve the controversy which surrounds the direction of its long-run trend. In the final section, the chapter's main findings are summarised.

PREVIOUS STUDIES

Classical economics predicted that as a consequence of diminishing returns occurring in the production of primary products from a fixed stock of land (including mineral resources) as population increased and capital was accumulated, the price of primary products would inevitably rise over the long run in relation to the price of manufactured goods, thus giving rise to an upward drift in the NBTT.[1] In consequence, classical thinking up to and including John Stuart Mill took it for granted that there was a tendency for the prices of primary commodities to increase in relation to those of manufactures, especially since the pressures of surplus population and the process of urbanisation would hold wages and production costs down in manufacturing (Singer, 1986). This argument, which is essentially Ricardian in character (although it can also be found in the writings of both Malthus

117

and Jevons), has recently been extended in the context of a two-sector model of the world economy by Kaldor (1983).

However, in the early 1950s the classical prediction of a secular improvement in the NBTT was challenged by both Prebisch (1950) and Singer (1950). Both argued forcefully that in direct contravention of the classical prediction, the NBTT had actually been, and could be expected to continue to be, subject to a *declining* long-run trend. Being contrary to traditional thinking, this finding was criticised on a number of grounds. In particular, the problems raised by transport costs and improvements in the quality of manufactured goods were seized upon by critics (e.g. Viner, 1953; Haberler, 1961; Ellsworth, 1956; Morgan, 1957) in an attempt to contest the empirical basis of the Prebisch–Singer declining-trend hypothesis. However, it should be noted that subsequent analysis (Spraos, 1980; 1983) has demonstrated that correction for both shipping costs and changing quality does not destroy the empirical basis of the hypothesis.

A number of explanations have been put forward in the literature to account for the observed downward movement, and these have recently been conveniently summarised by Singer (1986) under the following four headings.

(a) Differing elasticities of demand for primary commodities and manufactured goods

Those primary commodities which are used as inputs tend to have a lower price elasticity of demand than manufactures because a given percentage change in the price of a primary input will result in a lesser percentage change in the price of the finished product, with the consequence that no great influence in quantity demanded can be expected. Similarly, food commodities have a low price elasticity of demand due to the fact that food is a basic need. Consequently, a large proportion of the income released by a fall in the price of food is likely to go to other consumption goods rather than to an increase in food consumption. The price inelasticity of demand for commodities implies that in the case of a fall in price there will be no compensation in balance-of-payments terms as a result of increased export volume. The inelastic nature of the demand for primary commodities is of direct relevance to the declining NBTT hypothesis because it implies that the effects of increases in the conditions of commodity supply have tended to be felt more in price *decreases* than in quantity increases. In addition, the low demand elasticity, particularly when combined with the low elasticity of supply as emphasised by classical analysis, also implies that there will be marked instability in primary commodity prices and hence the terms of trade.

(b) Differing rates of expansion in the demand for primary commodities and manufactured goods

Singer (1986) argues that the demand for primaries is bound to expand less rapidly than the demand for manufactured products. This, it is argued, is due in part to the lower *income* elasticity of demand for primary products, especially agricultural commodities (Engel's Law) and in part to the techno-logical superiority enjoyed by the industrial countries which export manu-factures. Two aspects of this technological superiority which are relevant to the declining NBTT hypothesis are, first, economies in the use of primary commodities as inputs in the production process, and second, the develop-ment of synthetic substitutes for primary commodities (Sapsford, 1985a; 1986). Although attention was drawn to this latter feature of economic development by Singer (1950), it has accelerated markedly since that date. Moreover, as emphasised by Singer (1986), the resulting tendency towards balance-of-trade deficit for developing countries which arises from such divergent demand trends will tend to enforce currency depreciations which will result in further deterioration in the NBTT.

(c) Technological superiority

The technological advantage enjoyed by the industrialised/manufactures exporting countries means that their exports embody a more sophisticated technology, the control of which is concentrated in these countries, and particularly in large multinational firms located in these countries. In conse-quence, it is argued that the prices of manufactured exports embody a Schumpeterian rent element for innovation, plus an element of monopolistic profit arising because of the size and power of multinationals.

(d) Differences in market structure

The structure of both goods markets and labour markets differs markedly between the industrialised (or 'centre') countries and the developing (or 'peripheral') countries. This type of explanation for the Prebisch–Singer (P–S) hypothesis of a declining long-run trend rests on the idea that differences in market structure (with primary commodities being produced under competi-tive conditions, while manufacturing in industrial countries is characterised by a high degree of monopoly by organised labour and monopol-istic firms) mean that the fruits of technical progress in the form of in-creases in labour productivity are differently divided. Thus, it is argued that while improvements in labour productivity in the production of primary commodities were, given the unorganised nature of the labour force and the existence of a rural surplus population, reflected in lower product prices, improvements in labour productivity in manufacturing were appropriated by organised labour and capital as higher factor incomes rather than lower prices for the consumer.

Policy implications

As pointed out by Singer (1986), all four of the explanations for a deteriorating trend in the terms of trade of developing countries relate as much, or more, to the characteristics of different types of countries – differences in technology, labour market organisation, and so forth – as to the characteristics of different commodities. This observation suggests a shift in emphasis, particularly from the development policy viewpoint, away from the terms of trade between primary commodities *versus* manufactures and more towards the exports of developing countries – whether primary commodities or (simple) manufactures – *versus* the exports of industrial countries (predominantly sophisticated manufactures and capital goods as well as skill-intensive services). One interesting implication is that the policy advice of *export-substituting industrialisation* to divert exports away from primary commodities (whose prices were deteriorating in relation to those of manufactures) given by some early followers of the P–S thesis to countries like India failed to solve the problem because the causes of the deteriorating terms of trade were to be found in the characteristics of the countries themselves and not in the products they produced. In short, it has been argued that the types of manufactures exported by developing countries in relation to the different types exported by the industrial countries share some of the disadvantages originally highlighted by Prebisch and Singer for primary commodities in relation to manufactured goods. Singer (1986) develops this argument further, and presents some statistical evidence to suggest that the deterioration in the terms of trade experienced by developing countries since the mid-1950s can be attributed to three, perhaps equally important, causes: first, the deterioration in the price of primary commodities in relation to manufactures (as emphasised in the early P–S literature); second, a more rapid deterioration in the prices of the primary commodities produced by developing countries than in the prices of the primary commodities produced by developed countries; and finally, a fall in the price of the manufactures exported by developing countries relative to the manufactures exported by industrial countries.

The current debate

Although a number of subsequent developments and criticisms of these explanations have appeared in the literature (e.g. Higgins, 1968; Meier, 1968; Spraos, 1983), current debate seems to have largely converged on two main themes. The first of these concerns the adequacy, or otherwise, of the historical series available as measures of the NBTT, while the second concerns the statistical evidence surrounding the sign and statistical significance of the NBTT's long-run trend. The first of these themes has been well covered in the work of Spraos (1980, 1983) and Sarkar (1985), and it is to the second theme that we now turn.

THE STATISTICAL EVIDENCE

Despite the fact that when launching the declining-trend hypothesis both Prebisch (1950) and Singer (1950) obtained their evidence of secular deterioration from straightforward data inspection, the subsequent re-appraisal of the pre-Second World War evidence by Spraos (1980) seems to bear out their conclusion. On the basis of a painstaking analysis of the various available NBTT series, Spraos (with the aid of regression analysis) demonstrated that the balance of the evidence for the approximately seventy-year period ending with the outbreak of the Second World War offered support for the declining long-run trend hypothesis of Prebisch and Singer.

Two points of particular importance to arise from Spraos's (1980) study are as follows; first, the particular data series selected by Prebisch (1950) himself[2] did appear to overstate, possibly to a considerable extent, the rate of deterioration, and second, once the sample period is extended to include the post-Second World War experience, the evidence becomes rather less supportive of the P–S declining-trend hypothesis. In respect of the latter point, Spraos concluded that 'while the deteriorating tendency cannot be decisively refuted, it is open to doubt . . . when the record of the 1970s is taken into account' (1980, p. 126). It should be noted, however, that Spraos's finding of trendlessness referred to the period ending in 1970, and in this section we explore the question of whether the post-1970 evidence provides further support for, or raises additional doubts about, the declining long-run trend hypothesis.

Following Spraos (1980), the estimates of the long-run trend rate of growth in the NBTT reported in this section were obtained by regression analysis of the following simple semi-logarithmic trend model, which follows straightforwardly from the assumption of continuous trend growth in NBTT at a constant proportional rate of 100r per cent per annum.

$$In\ NBTT_t = a + rt + u_t \qquad (t = 1, \ldots, n) \qquad (7.1)$$

where In denotes natural logarithms, t denotes time, $a = In\ NBTT_o$ (where $NBTT_o$ denotes the base period value of NBTT) and u_t denotes a disturbance term). On the basis of the usual assumptions regarding the statistical

TABLE 7.1 Estimated long-run trend growth rates in NBTT

Period	Series[a]	Estimated trend growth rate (% per annum)	R^2
1876–1938	Prebisch (1950)	−0.95 (18.2)	0.91
1876–1938	League of Nations	−0.64 (9.6)	0.74
1871–1938	Lewis (1952)	−0.46 (9.7)	0.62
1900–1938	United Nations	−0.73 (3.9)	0.33
1900–1970	United Nations	0.13 (1.4)	0.04
1900–1970	United Nations/ World Bank hybrid	−0.14 (1.5)	0.04

Notes
[a] The various actual series analysed by Spraos are presented in his Tables 1 and 2. For detailed
   discussions of the construction and coverage of the alternative series, see Spraos (1980,
   pp. 107–19).
All estimates were obtained by ordinary least squares regression, but no Durbin–Watson
statistics were reported by Spraos.
Figures in parenthesis are absolute t values, but see the caution expressed in the text regarding
serial-correlation problems.
Source: derived from Spraos (1980, Table 2).

properties of the disturbance term u_t, an estimate of the long-run proportional trend growth rate (say r) may be obtained by fitting model (7.1) to the
data using standard regression procedures.

Existing evidence

Table 7.1 provides a summary of the trend growth rates (expressed in per
cent per annum) estimated by Spraos for his various study periods. As can
be seen, his pre-war analysis considered the behaviour of four principal
alternative NBTT indices, while his evidence for the period ending at 1970
focused on two particular series. These were (a) the United Nations series
which was extended from its initial coverage of 1900–38 to include observations covering the period 1950–70, and (b) a World Bank index covering the
post-1950 period. Spraos (1980, p. 121) considered the World Bank index
superior to the UN Index on a number of grounds, namely its more
comprehensive coverage, its closer adherence to the primary products/
manufactures dichotomy, and the fact that it weighted primary products
according to their shares in developing country exports rather than world
trade as a whole. In view of this alleged superiority, Spraos resorted to

splicing this on to the earlier UN data for the post-1956 period in order to provide what he referred to as a 'hybrid' series covering the period 1900 through to 1970.

Although Spraos regarded his regression equations as little more than rough descriptions of the NBTT's long-run behaviour (see Spraos, 1985, p. 789), it is important to approach his estimates (as summarised in Table 7.1), all of which were obtained by straightforward ordinary least squares regression, with a degree of caution. Since Durbin–Watson statistics[3] were not reported by Spraos, it is not possible to appraise his estimates properly. However, replication of his estimated equations (see Sapsford, 1984) showed the presence of positive first-order autocorrelation, suggesting that superior estimates on econometric grounds could have been obtained by using one of the techniques for handling serially correlated residuals, such as the Cochrane–Orcutt (1949) iterative estimation procedure.[4] In particular, the presence of positive autocorrelation implies that the *t* ratios reported by Spraos (as set out in Table 7.1) should be approached with caution, since it is well-known that the presence of *positive* serial correlation in the disturbance term can be expected to lead to an underestimate of the sampling variance of the ordinary least squares estimators, giving rise to overoptimistic *t* values which therefore overstate the significance of the estimated coefficients.

The pre-war results reported in Table 7.1 imply estimated trend rates of deterioration of between 0.46 (Lewis's series) and 0.95 (Prebisch's series) per cent per annum. According to Spraos's *t* ratios, each of the estimated pre-war trend growth rates reported in Table 7.1 achieves significance at the 1 per cent level. However, it can be clearly seen from Table 7.1 that once the post-war experience (up to 1970) is introduced into the picture, both the UN and hybrid series fail to reveal any evidence of a significant trend.

More recent evidence

In this sub-section we investigate whether Spraos's finding of trendlessness holds up when the study period is extended to include post-1970 observations. Table 7.2 reports the results that were obtained by fitting trend model (7.1) to data covering the period 1900 through to 1980 and 1975 for the UN and hybrid series respectively. In both cases, the series were updated using the most recently available editions of the sources used by Spraos. However, while it was possible to update the UN series to 1980, it was not possible to update the precise hybrid series examined by Spraos past 1975. This was because the World Bank index used by Spraos in the construction of his hybrid series, which was compiled on a petroleum-inclusive basis, was discontinued in 1975. After this date the World Bank's Commodity Studies and Projections Division only compiled the relevant NBTT series on an energy-exclusive basis.

TABLE 7.2 Further estimates of long-run trend growth rate in NBTT

Equation number	Period	Series	Estimated trend growth rate (% per annum)	R^2	D–W	Estimation method
2.1	1900–80	United Nations	0.355** (3.9512)	0.2038**	0.458	OLS
2.2	1900–75	UN/World Bank hybrid	0.0476 (0.4062)	0.00294	0.495	OLS
2.3	1900–80	United Nations	0.6095* (2.0153)	0.6681*	1.966	C–O iterative
2.4	1900–75	UN/World Bank hybrid	0.534 (1.1615)	0.5492	1.813	C–O iterative
2.5	1900–82	UNCTAD	−0.2437** (3.2781)	0.1457**	0.720	OLS
2.6	1900–82	UNCTAD	−0.295* (1.7868)	0.4874	3.193	C–O iterative
2.7	1900–80	United Nations (fuel-exclusive)	0.0686 (0.9381)	0.01422	0.541	OLS
2.8	1900–80	United Nations (fuel-exclusive)	0.0755 (0.3995)	0.5339	1.99	C–O iterative
2.9	1900–82	UN/World Bank (petroleum-exclusive) hybrid	−0.0954 (1.2643)	0.02474	0.636	OLS
2.10	1900–82	UN/World Bank (petroleum-exclusive) hybrid	−0.137 (0.7558)	0.47	1.907	C–O iterative

Notes
Figures in parenthesis are absolute *t* values.
A single asterisk denotes a coefficient which is significantly different from zero at the 5 per cent level; a double asterisk denotes significance at the 1 per cent level.

Equations (2.1) and (2.2) in Table 7.2 report the ordinary least squares (OLS) results which can be seen to imply *appreciating*, rather than deteriorating, trends in both NBTT indices. However, in view of the unsatisfactorily low values of the Durbin–Watson statistics, both of these equations were re-estimated by the Cochrane–Orcutt (C–O) iterative procedure, yielding the results set out in equations (2.3) and (2.4). As can be seen, both (2.3) and (2.4) likewise give positive estimated trends when the post-1970 experience is brought into the picture. In the case of the hybrid series, the estimated trend is not significantly different from zero at conventional levels, but the positive trend in the UN series achieves significance at the 5 per cent level.

One obvious influence brought into play by inclusion of the 1970s into the estimation period is that of the 'oil crisis' of 1974 and thereafter, and it is to this issue that we turn in the next section. However, an interesting picture emerges from a third index (compiled by the United Nations Commission on Trade and Development, UNCTAD) which was presented but discussed only briefly by Spraos. This particular NBTT index, which is constructed on a petroleum-exclusive basis, was updated from recent data published by UNCTAD and the World Bank to include the period ending in 1982. The ordinary least squares and Cochrane–Orcutt results which were obtained by fitting trend model (7.1) to this series are reported in equations (2.5) and (2.6). In each case the estimated trend growth rate of the NBTT is both negative and significant and therefore in agreement with the P–S thesis. The numerical value of the estimated trend is quite similar in both equations, implying a trend rate of deterioration in the NBTT over the period 1900–82 to the order of between 0.24 and 0.29 per cent per annum.

Comparison of the UNCTAD results with those obtained from both the UN and UN/World Bank hybrid series indicates quite clearly the potential sensitivity of the evidence regarding both the direction and significance of the long-run trend in the NBTT to the inclusion, or otherwise, of petroleum price fluctuations during the 1970s. This question is investigated in more depth in the following sub-section.

Oil versus non-oil commodity prices

The 'special' nature of petroleum price movements since 1973 is well known. To give an indication of the orders of magnitude involved, it is relevant to comment on some recent estimates (Chu and Morrison, 1984, Table 2). They put the trend growth rate of the price of manufactures at 9.8 per cent per annum for the period 1972–82, with the corresponding trend rate of growth in non-oil primary commodity prices being estimated as 6.5 per cent per annum. This gives rise to an estimated trend rate of *decline* in the ratio of non-oil primary commodity prices to manufactures prices (i.e. the NBTT between non-oil primary commodities and manufactures) of 2.7 per cent per annum. Over this same period, oil prices rose dramatically in relation to the price of manufactured goods, with their trend rate of growth over this period being estimated as 28.3 per cent per annum. When seen alongside the above-mentioned trend growth rate of manufactures' prices over this period (of 9.8 per cent per annum), this indicates a very pronounced increase in the NBTT of oil *vis-à-vis* manufactures. Clearly, then, the empirical evidence regarding the P–S declining-trend hypothesis may prove to be highly sensitive to the exclusion or inclusion of oil and petroleum.

Equations (2.7) through to (2.10) report the results that were obtained when trend model (7.1) was fitted to the oil-exclusive counterparts of the UN and UN/World Bank hybrid series analysed by Spraos. Although the adjustment for oil prices involved in the construction of these series is an extremely crude one – removing only what might be termed the direct effects of petroleum price movements in the sense of merely excluding petroleum from the group of primary commodities whose prices enter into the construction of the numerator of the NBTT series[5] – the sensitivity of the estimated trend to the influence of recent oil price fluctuations is clearly illustrated. Equations (2.9) and (2.10) illustrate that exclusion of recent petroleum price movements results in the emergence of a negative, but insignificant, trend in the hybrid series for the period 1900 to 1982. Equations (2.7) and (2.8) show that although the exclusion of recent fuel price movements from the UN series does not reverse the previous positive trend in the UN index, it does render it not significantly different from zero.

Thus the petroleum-adjusted evidence for both the UN and hybrid series support, for the longer period ending 1980 and 1982 respectively, Spraos's earlier finding of trendlessness. In contrast, however, our results show that the behaviour of the UNCTAD series over the period ending 1982 offers support for the P–S thesis.

Structural instability

Closer inspection of Spraos's results reveals a somewhat puzzling finding. As seen from Table 7.1, Spraos's 1900 to 1970 UN and hybrid evidence (like the corresponding evidence for the longer period ending in the early 1980s reported in Table 7.2 above) reveals no significant trend. However, if one examines the separate pre- and post-war sub-period results presented by Spraos for both of these series, it is immediately seen that the sub-period regressions both yield negative and significant trends consistent with the P–S thesis.

Table 7.3 summarises Spraos's own estimated equations for the separate pre- and post-war sub-periods and indicates quite clearly that while his whole period regressions (as summarised in Table 7.1 above) reveal no significant trend, each of his sub-period regressions reveal negative and significant trends.[6] Note, in particular, that a negative and significant trend emerges from the post-war World Bank series in both its petroleum-inclusive and -exclusive forms.

The question immediately arises as to why Spraos's whole-period regressions tell a different story from that told by each of their constituent parts. One possible answer to this question, which is investigated in some depth in Sapsford (1985b), lies in the econometrics of the estimation procedure adopted by Spraos.

The argument presented in Sapsford (1985b) recognises that the method of trend estimation employed by Spraos, involving the fitting of the simple trend model (7.1) to various NBTT series, rests on the assumption that the underlying parameters of the NBTT's growth path remain unchanged over the period of estimation. In econometric terminology, this assumption is generally referred to as *structural stability*. Over recent years, an extensive

TABLE 7.3 Sub-period estimates

Period	Series	Estimated trend growth rate (% per annum)	R^2
1900–38	United Nations	−0.73 (3.9)	0.33
1950–70	United Nations	−1.52 (19.3)	0.95
1950–70	World Bank (petroleum-inclusive)	−2.3 (11.6)	0.88
1950–70	World Bank (petroleum-inclusive)	−1.1 (4.4)	0.44

Notes: as for Table 7.1 above.

econometric literature has developed to cover situations where this assumption is violated (for a useful survey see Goldfeld and Quandt, 1973). This literature suggests that results obtained from estimation across a study period within which structural instabilities occur (or switches from one regime of parameter values to another) should be treated with appropriate statistical caution since it is easily shown that under such circumstances, the whole period parameter estimates will, in general, provide *biased* estimates of the true parameter values during each of the separate sub-periods.[7]

The simplest case is that of a single discontinuity in the underlying parameters of the NBTT's growth path, and the investigations reported in Sapsford (1985b) suggest that the above-mentioned discrepancies between Spraos's whole- and sub-period results are a consequence of the existence of a structural instability in the parameters of equation (7.1) as between the pre- and post-Second World War sub-periods. For example, it was found that the usual Chow (1960) test for structural instability rejected decisively the hypothesis of constancy in the underlying parameters of the NBTT's growth path (equation 7.1) as between the pre- and post-Second World War sub-periods.

The following sub-section presents some evidence which emerges once the appropriate econometric action is undertaken to overcome this problem of structural instability as between the pre- and post-war sub-periods.

Some new evidence

Dummy variables provide a particularly straightforward means of treating the problems raised in the present context by structural instability. Accordingly, the whole-period regressions for each of the UN, hybrid and

UNCTAD series were re-estimated with the addition to specification (7.1) or slope and intercept dummy variables (denoted by D_s and D_i respectively), constructed so as to capture parameter instability. Experiments with a number of alternative temporal specifications of these dummies are reported in Sapsford (1985a), and the equations set out in Table 7.4 summarise some of the results which appear to fit the observed statistical facts most satisfactorily. Table 7.4 reports the results which emerged when the various series were extended as far as existing sources allowed, and excludes recent petroleum price movements as a special case (Spraos, 1980, p. 126).

Equations (4.1) and (4.2) summarise the results thus obtained, for both the hybrid and the UNCTAD series. Both equations show the existence of a significant upward shift in the growth path's intercept during the post-war period accompanied by no significant change in the trend rate of deterioration. These results indicate that in both cases, structural instability takes the form of an upward intercept movement accompanied by no change in slope. These equations would therefore seem to provide some quite strong evidence in support of the P–S declining-trend hypothesis, in that they both show that once the structural instability problem has been recognised and dealt with, we find that the significant pre-war downward trend actually continued throughout the post-war period up to 1982 without any significant change from its pre-Second World War value. The estimates reported in equations (4.1) and (4.2) imply long-run trend growth rates in the NBTT of -1.2926 and -1.2659 per cent per annum (both of which are significantly different from zero) for the hybrid and UNCTAD series respectively. In a detailed investigation of an alternative (petroleum-exclusive) NBTT series constructed by the International Monetary Fund (see Sapsford, 1985a) the author found that this alternative NBTT index also exhibited the same pattern of structural instability (i.e. an upward post-war intercept shift accompanied by no significant slope change) and yielded an estimated (and statistically significant) long-run trend rate of deterioration over the same period 1900–82 of -1.2315 per cent per annum (see Table 7.4, equation 4.3).

Equation (4.4) reports the evidence that emerged from the UN data. Although this evidence tells a slightly different story from that which emerges from the other series, it is, nevertheless, still supportive towards the P–S thesis. As can be seen from (4.4), structural instability in the UN case appears, in contrast, to take the form of a significant upward movement in the trend rate of deterioration during the post-war period, accompanied by no significant intercept alteration. However, the magnitude of this upward movement in the trend is insufficient to reverse the previous negative trend. This is clearly illustrated by the relevant *t* test which rejects, at the 1 per cent level, the restriction that the coefficient of D_s and the trend growth rate in (4.4) sum to zero. Accordingly, the UN evidence also offers support for the P–S secular deterioration hypothesis in that both the pre-war trend and the *net* post-war trend which emerge from (4.4) are negative and

TABLE 7.4 Some new evidence on NBTT

Equation number	Series	Period	Intercept	Estimated long-run trend growth rate ($\hat{r}$)	Estimated coefficient of D_i	Estimated coefficient of D_s	R^2	D–W
4.1	UN/World Bank (petroleum-exclusive) hybrid	1900–82	4.71031** (50.2411)	−0.012926** (3.70096)	0.725228* (2.61018)	−0.001554 (0.277058)	0.4129**	1.827
4.2	UNCTAD	1900–82	4.69858** (51.3153)	−0.012659** (3.66715)	0.82297** (2.97490)	−0.005533 (0.763058)	0.4129**	1.831
4.3	UN/IMF (petroleum-exclusive) hybrid	1900–82	4.69628** (52.6734)	−0.012315** (3.67721)	0.584676* (2.18353)	0.0011253 (0.2095)	0.6631**	1.818
4.4	UN (fuel-exclusive)	1900–80	7.16249** (14.076)	−0.05931** (6.65374)	−0.485022 (0.86627)	0.0330269** (2.7769)	0.6478**	1.622

Notes:
All estimates were obtained by the C–O iterative technique.
Figures in parenthesis are t values; a single asterisk denotes significance at the 5 per cent level, and a double asterisk denotes significance at the 1 per cent level.
Dummy variables D_i and D_s are defined as follows: $D_i = 1$ for 1950 and thereafter;
$D_i = 0$ otherwise;
$D_s = D_i \cdot t \; (t = 1, \ldots, n)$.

Source: Sapsford (1985a, 1985b).

significantly different from zero. Equation (4.4) implies trend rates of deterioration to the order of approximately 5.9 and 2.6 per cent per annum for the pre- and post-war periods respectively (Sapsford, 1985c).

The picture that emerges from our analysis of all but the UN series is clearly illustrated in Figure 7.1. Taking the IMF series as representative, Figure 7.1 provides a plot of the actual NBTT series, together with the estimated trend growth paths for the pre- and post-war periods implied by equation (4.3).

CONCLUDING REMARKS

This chapter has considered the debate surrounding the long-run behaviour of the net barter terms of trade between primary commodities and manufactured goods. We began by surveying the existing literature and set out in some detail the various explanations that have been put forward to account for the declining long-run trend thesis originally advanced by both Prebisch and Singer. The remainder of the chapter has been concerned with the statistical evidence surrounding the long-run trend behaviour of the NBTT. The statistical evidence reported detected the existence of a structural instability in the parameters of the NBTT's underlying growth path and suggested that once appropriate action is undertaken to overcome this problem, the evidence for the period from 1900 to the early 1980s appears to be very much more supportive towards the Prebisch–Singer secular deterioration hypothesis than that which emerged from earlier research.

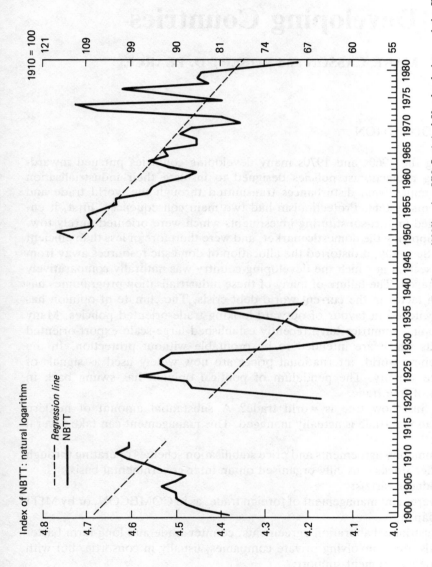

Source: this NBTT was obtained by updating the UN series given by Spraos (1980) using UN *Statistical Yearbook* data and the IMF Research Department index of prices of non-oil primary commodities deflated by UN index of price of manufactures.

Figure 7.1 Long-run trend in NBTT

8 Intra-Firm Trade and the Developing Countries

MARK CASSON and ROBERT D. PEARCE

INTRODUCTION

During the 1960s and 1970s many developing countries pursued inward-looking protectionist policies designed to insulate their industrialisation programmes from disturbances transmitted through the world trade and payments system. Protectionism had two main consequences. First, it encouraged import-substituting investments which were oriented purely towards supplying the domestic market, and were therefore of less than efficient scale. Secondly, it distorted the allocation of domestic resources away from those sectors in which the developing country was naturally comparatively advantaged. The failure of many of these industrialisation programmes has been a factor in the current world debt crisis. The climate of opinion has now switched in favour of outward-looking trade-oriented policies. Many developing countries have recently established large-scale export-oriented projects which are intended to be profitable without protection. In the developing world, international prices are now widely used as signals of relative scarcity. The pendulum of political opinion has swung back in favour of free trade.

But just how free is world trade? A substantial amount of modern international trade is actually managed. This management can take several forms:

1. commodity agreements and price stabilisation schemes operating through buffer stocks – usually organised on an inter-governmental basis;
2. producer cartels;
3. government management of foreign trade, as in COMECON, or by MITI in Japan;
4. industrial collaboration agreements, counter-trade and long-term barter deals, often involving private companies, usually in consortia, but with some government support;
5. control over trade by multinational enterprises; and
6. influence over trade through networks of interlocking joint ventures and informal understandings between large firms.

This list is by no means exhaustive. The focus of this chapter is on the last two aspects of trade management, and most especially on the phenomenon of intra-firm trade by multinationals. Intra-firm trade is exemplified by shipments of components and semi-processed materials between a parent company and a foreign subsidiary, or between different subsidiaries of the same firm.

There is a suspicion that intra-firm trade is not susceptible to the same competitive pressures as trade between independent parties – so-called 'arm's length trade'. It has been alleged that intra-firm trade strengthens the monopoly power of large multinational firms (Murray, 1981). Developing countries are often forced to rely on multinationals for exporting, for example, because of these firms' control over the consumer markets in industrialised countries. Multinationals can also avoid taxation and tariff payments due to developing countries by manipulating the prices at which intra-firm sales are invoiced (so-called 'transfer pricing'). It is often suggested, too, that these problems are becoming more acute, because intra-firm trade is increasing, and that world trade will soon be dominated by a relatively small number of large multinational firms.

This chapter presents some recent evidence on the growth of intra-firm trade and examines the determinants of it. It is suggested that while intra-firm trade has been growing in absolute terms, it is not growing as a proportion of world trade as a whole. The incidence of intra-firm trade, it is argued, is largely industry-specific. The propensity of an industry to engage in intra-firm trade varies with the life-cycle of its product (Vernon, 1966, 1979), and is the result of two opposing effects. When a product is newly developed, the extent of international trade in components and semi-processed material tends to be small, but the incentive for this trade to be conducted within the firm is high. When the product matures, becomes standardised, and enters into mass production, components and other intermediate products enter more extensively into trade, but the tendency for trade to be intra-firm is lower. On balance, it seems that the share of intra-firm trade in total trade within the industry falls as its products mature.

The fastest growing industries at any one time tend to be those with the most novel and complex products, and these are the industries where intra-firm trade is highest. But as these industries mature, the expansion of demand slackens, the age of their products rises, and other industries take over the leadership in market growth. Thus although, at any one time, the fastest growing industries have the highest levels of intra-firm trade, intra-firm trade overall may be relatively static because of an offsetting decline in the role of intra-firm trade in slower growing industries. The pattern of intra-firm trade therefore alters as the world economy undergoes structural change. Such changes have already occurred, and are still occurring. The 1960s growth of intra-firm trade in the European motor industry, for example, has been partially superseded by the growth of intra-firm trade in the office machine and electronics industries between the USA and South-east Asia.

Some sectors of the economy do, however, appear to have a relentless dynamic which continuously proliferates new products. Since the late nineteenth century, the machinery and chemical sectors have demonstrated this ability. As a result, intra-firm trade within these sectors tends to persist at relatively high levels. The primary sector, on the other hand, reveals very low levels of product innovation, for the obvious reason that there is little opportunity for differentiating naturally occurring products through human agency. There are exceptions, though, such as hybridisation of agricultural crops, and these exceptions may be increasing with the advent of biotechnology and genetic engineering. Likewise in the service sector, the opportunities for creating new forms of purely manual service are rather limited, but ample opportunity exists for new professional and information-based services. Advances in jet travel and telecommunications enable these services readily to enter trade, and the recent growth of output in this field has almost certainly led to higher levels of intra-firm trade, though reliable data on this are difficult to obtain.

The composition of exports from developing countries, which is weighted in favour of primary products and against manufactures and services, explains why intra-firm trade does not seem to be quite so important in these exports as in the exports of industrialised countries. The question remains, however, whether location-specific factors encourage firms within a given industry to prefer intra-firm trade to arm's length trade in developing countries more strongly than in industrialised countries. Data suggest that they do, but to only a limited extent.

Basic concepts and definitions relating to intra-firm trade are presented in the next section. The analytical framework is set out in detail in the following section, where key logical distinctions are drawn between different aspects of intra-firm trade. Three aspects are then examined more fully. They are, respectively, the role of intermediate products in the process of production, the extent to which intermediate products are traded, and the question of how far this trade is conducted within the same firm. Differences between US and Japanese attitudes to the control of intra-firm trade and differences between industrialised and developing countries in their pattern of dependence on intra-firm trade are then considered. These later sections of the paper report some new statistical evidence. The final section presents some concluding thoughts.

BASIC CONCEPTS AND DEFINITIONS

A *multinational enterprise* (MNE) is an enterprise that owns and controls value-adding activities in two or more countries. These activities can include production, marketing (or procurement) and R & D. Such activities are typically linked by flows of intermediate products. An *intermediate product* is any good or service flowing within or between industries; it therefore excludes final products supplied to households and factor services obtained from them. Intermediate products as well as final products enter into international trade; they do so whenever the plant generating the intermediate product and the plant utilising it are located in different countries.

It is important to distinguish between *final products* and *finished products*. Final products are products that are ready for consumption, whereas finished products are those that have completed manufacture and are ready for wholesale and retail distribution. Thus finished goods are typically intermediate rather than final products. Most goods entering into trade are, in fact, intermediate products in this sense, and it is one of the weaknesses of conventional trade theory that it ignores this.

The focus of this chapter is on *circulating intermediate products*. These are finished products and products that are transformed, used up or incorporated into some other product in the course of the production process. It is not principally concerned with *fixed intermediate products*, such as producer durables and other capital goods. These are usually held as stocks and utilised to generate productive services; they only enter into trade flows as part of a stock-adjustment process.

When an intermediate product is traded, it does not have to change ownership. The market for an intermediate product is said to be *internalised* when the transaction is between two different divisions of the same ownership unit. Internalisation of the market within a firm creates *intra-firm trade*. When an intermediate product does change ownership, the market is said to be *external* and the transaction at *arm's length*.

In fact, intra-firm trade and arm's length trade are just two extremes of a spectrum of possibilities. For example, firm A may own X_1 per cent of the equity of firm B and an X_2 per cent equity stake in firm C. If firm A then sells a product to firm B, the transaction is partly internal to firm A and partly external to it, the appropriate measure of the degree of internalisation being X_1. A more difficult case arises when firm B sells a product to firm C, for in this case, too, the transaction is partially internal to firm A. The appropriate measure of the degree of internalisation is more debatable: one possibility would be *min* $\{X_1, X_2\}$. Such arrangements may be referred to as *quasi internalisation*, leading to *quasi intra-firm trade*.

The major categories of products entering into intra-firm trade are the following:

1. foodstuffs and raw materials, grown on a plantation or mined by the extractive division of an MNE and exported to a processing or refining facility abroad;
2. components and semi-processed materials exported from one manufacturing facility to another;

3. finished goods ready for marketing and distribution by an overseas sales division;
4. second-hand capital equipment transferred for use in an overseas plant;
5. services of intangible assets such as technical know-how, proprietary product design and managerial expertise.

Most discussions of MNEs tend to focus on (5), but the issues relating to the transfer of technology are so complex that they require separate treatment in their own right. For reasons already noted, trade in capital equipment is also beyond the scope of this paper, so discussion of (4) is omitted too. The focus, therefore, is on categories (1)–(3) above.

EXPLAINING CHANGES IN INTRA-FIRM TRADE

Changes in intra-firm trade flows are most conveniently analysed in terms of four main factors. Changes in any one of these factors can affect the amount of intra-firm trade.

1. *The propensity to circulate* measures the tendency for production processes to create a large number of circulating intermediate products. It is defined as the ratio of the total value of circulating intermediate products to the value of final output within the production system. Since by definition intra-firm trade involves intermediate products, the propensity to circulate, when applied to the level of final output, sets an upper limit on the possible extent of such trade. The propensity may be regarded, loosely, as an industry-specific factor, for it reflects both the design of the final product and the nature of its production technology. Intuitively, it measures the extent to which products circulate between different parts of the production process before they emerge as final output. Strictly speaking, however, it is difficult to identify any 'propensity' with a specific industry, because many intermediate products enter into the final products of several industries. Changes in the propensity to circulate are governed, in part, by the life cycle of products, as explained in detail in the next section.

2. *The propensity to trade*, measured by the ratio of the total value of intermediate product trade to the total value of intermediate product output, indicates the tendency for intermediate products to enter into trade. The determinants of intermediate product trade are essentially the same as those of final product trade. However, some post-war changes in the world economy have tended to promote intermediate product trade at the expense of final product trade, while others have had the opposite effect. The net impact of these changes is considered on pp. 141–6.

3. *The propensity to internalise*, measured by the ratio of the value of intra-firm trade to the value of intermediate product trade, indicates the

TABLE 8.1 **Factors affecting the propensity to internalise intermediate product trade**

Factors	Positive or negative effect
Technical	
High fixed costs	+
Large non-recoverable investments	+
Perishable intermediate products	+
Quality variability, coupled with a natural asymmetry of information	+
Efficient scales at adjacent stages of production vary, and their lowest common multiple is large	−
Multiplicity of joint inputs and outputs	−
Economies of scope in the utilisation of assets	−
Market power	
Monopolist faces downstream substitution, or monopsonist faces upstream substitution	+
Multi-stage monopoly or monopsony	+
Entry-deterrence by dominant firm	+
Dynamic	
Novelty of product and its division of labour	+
Fiscal	
Incentives for transfer pricing: differential rates of profit taxation, *ad valorem* tariffs, or exchange controls	+
Statutory intervention in intermediate product markets, e.g. price regulation	+
Restrictions on foreign equity participation, and expropriation risk of foreign direct investment	−

Source: Casson *et al.* (1986), Table 1.3, p. 12.

tendency to internalise trade within the firm. Most theoretical and empirical work on intra-firm trade has tended to concentrate upon the internalisation issue. Internalisation theory, which is a branch of the modern institutional theory of the firm (Buckley and Casson, 1976, Casson, 1979, Williamson, 1975, 1985), has identified four groups of factors which either encourage or discourage profit-maximising firms from internalising intermediate product flows. The factors most relevant to international trade are listed in Table 8.1. The role of these factors is examined in detail on pp. 146–51.

4. *The composition of final output.* Because of the industry-specific nature of each of the three preceding factors, changes in the composition of output can affect the aggregate level of intra-firm trade. The post-war period has witnessed an increase in the output of manufactures and services, and a relative decline in the importance of primary products. The value of oil output has increased dramatically since the two OPEC price rises, but the volume of output has decreased since the second rise. Industry-specific

factors tend to promote relatively high levels of intra-firm trade in manufactures and relatively low levels for primary products. Changes in the composition of output have therefore tended to increase intra-firm trade. Composition effects have, however, been partly overshadowed by an industry-specific change in the propensity to internalise. The nationalisation of oil fields has significantly reduced levels of intra-firm trade in the oil industry, and, given the rise in value of oil output, this factor carries considerable weight in determining the overall value of intra-firm trade.

CHANGES IN THE PROPENSITY TO CIRCULATE

Intermediate products are created by the *vertical division of labour*. The vertical division of labour resolves production into a number of stages, with adjacent stages being linked by intermediate product flows. The horizontal division of labour, by contrast, creates different final products which appeal to individual consumers in varying degrees according to their personal tastes.

The stages of production created by the vertical division of labour are not always purely sequential. One stage may, for example, combine inputs from several earlier stages, or generate by-products which branch off into other processes. Successive combinations of inputs lead to a 'pyramid' structure, exemplified by manufacturing industries such as the motor industry, where the final product is assembled from components which are, in turn, subassemblies of other smaller components. The successive generation of by-products, on the other hand, leads to an 'inverted pyramid' structure, in which a single raw material is progressively refined to create new derivatives at every stage. In many industries both structures are present, leading to intricate networks of intermediate product flow.

Both the horizontal and vertical division of labour are dynamic. Changes in the horizontal division of labour occur when new products are developed or existing products go out of production, or when new varieties of an existing product proliferate. Changes in the vertical division of labour occur when production is resolved into a different sequence of stages. The usual tendency is to create a greater number of simpler stages, thereby splitting production into a multiplicity of trivial activities. This tendency was commented upon by Adam Smith in 1776 in the opening pages of *The Wealth of Nations*, when he discussed the famous pin-making example. It is, unfortunately, an aspect of industrial growth that economists, with one or two notable exceptions (such as Charles Babbage and Karl Marx) have neglected since then.

The development of a new variety of product often provides an opportunity to simplify its design, so that it can be fabricated from a hierarchy of components, each of which is simple to produce. In this case, a change in the horizontal division of labour alters the vertical division of labour, too. In other cases, the key to a new variety of final product may lie in the re-design of a component. Once relatively superficial forms of product differentiation are discounted, it is clear that in many cases differentiation of the final product is attributable to differentiation in the design of the components used. Thus differentiation of component design can provide the dynamic for differentiation of the final product.

In the early stages of an industry there are often several competing designs of product which are technologically quite distinct. As both producers and consumers gain experience, however, and the need to convert to mass-production methods makes itself felt, one technology is likely to emerge as superior to the others. It may be conjectured that this technology is typically the one that lends itself most readily to the vertical division of labour. Horizontal differentiation of the product is then effected by producing different variants on a basic formula. This makes it easier for different producers to draw upon a common pool of components and raw materials which they simply combine or configure in different ways. In this way the vertical division of labour reduces the marginal cost of superficial horizontal differentiation of the final product. Thus as the product matures, vertical division of labour and (superficial) horizontal differentiation go hand in hand.

These concepts are important in understanding the relation between intra-industry trade and intermediate product trade. It is well known that a growing proportion of trade, particularly trade among developed countries, is *intra-industry trade*, that is, two-way trade in products that are sufficiently similar to be classified to the same SITC industry (Greenaway and Milner, 1986b). Similarity can arise in both the horizontal and vertical dimensions. Until recently, most research on intra-industry trade assumed that it was horizontal differentiation that was the dominant factor. The SITC, however, does not usually distinguish different stages of manufacture at the three-digit level. These distinctions appear occasionally at the four-digit level, and more commonly at the five- and six-digit level. It is a consequence of this that at the three-digit level, at which most measures of intra-industry trade are constructed, intermediate product trade within the manufacturing sector appears predominantly as intra-industry trade (Kol and Rayment, 1986). The assumption that in all industries intra-industry trade is dominated by trade in horizontally differentiated products is therefore almost certainly false.

Direct evidence on post-war changes in the propensity to circulate is extremely difficult to obtain. However, some indirect evidence is available for certain types of product. Because reliable statistics of intermediate product output are so scarce, it is necessary to substitute statistics on intermediate product trade instead. Table 8.2 presents annual growth rates for the value of OECD export trade in various intermediate and final

TABLE 8.2 Comparative growth rates for the dollar value of OECD exports of fully assembled products and their components to the world

Commodity group	Rate of growth of exports (per cent)		
	1964–74	1974–84	1964–84
All commodities	17.1	8.6	12.8
Machinery and transport equipment	17.8	10.0	13.8
Motor vehicles			
Complete	18.3	11.5	14.8
Parts	19.4	11.4	15.3
Engines	14.1	11.6	12.8
Office machines and computers			
Complete	18.9	19.3	19.1
Parts	22.3	21.7	22.0

Note: figures for complete motor vehicles include motor cars, buses, lorries, trucks, vans, tractors and special-purpose vehicles; they relate to SITC groups 712.5 and 732.1–5 for 1964 and 1974, and to the revised SITC groups 722 and 781–7832 for 1984. Figures for parts of motor vehicles relate to SITC groups 732.6–8 for 1964 and 1974, and to 784 for 1984. Figures for engines relate to internal combustion piston engines, other than those for aircraft (SITC groups 711.5 for 1964 and 1974, and 713 for 1984). Figures for complete office machines and computers relate to SITC groups 714.1–714.91 for 1964 and 1974, and to 751–2 for 1984. Figures for parts are based upon 714.9 for 1964, 714.92 for 1974 and 759 for 1984; the 1964 figure pertains to a class which includes parts, but does not specifically distinguish them. The figure almost certainly overestimates trade in parts and, as a result, the corresponding growth rates shown for 1964–74 and 1964–84 are probably too low.

Source: Organisation for Economic Cooperation and Development, *Statistics of Foreign Trade, Series C. Trade by Commodities, Market Summaries* (Paris, OECD), various issues, 1964, 1974, 1984.

products for the period 1964–84. Table 8.3 presents some of this information in a more vivid form. It shows that in the machinery sector, trade in parts and components is quite significant compared to trade in final products. It indicates that in the relatively mature motor industry, trade in parts and components has grown roughly in the same proportion as trade in final products, whereas in the office machine and computer industry, where product innovation is much faster, trade in parts and components has been growing consistently relative to trade in final products. This is compatible with the view that in new-product industries the propensity to circulate increases as basic technology tends to standardise around certain common components. In view of the number of other factors which could conceivably have influenced the statistics, however, no definite conclusion can be drawn at this stage.

TABLE 8.3 An assessment of the importance of trade in parts and components in the motor vehicle and office machine industries

Commodity group	Ratio of the value of trade in parts to the value of trade in complete items		
	1964	1974	1984
Motor vehicles	0.35	0.39	0.39
Office machines and computers	0.35	0.46	0.56

Source and notes: see Table 8.2.

CHANGES IN THE PROPENSITY TO TRADE

This section discusses the propensity of intermediate products to enter into trade. It considers possible reasons why this propensity may have changed relative to the propensity for final products to enter into trade. Recall that in economic theory, international trade is explained principally by the tendency for each production activity to be concentrated upon a particular location. There are two main reasons for specialisation: economies of scale, which encourage a wide market to be supplied from a single source close to its centre, and comparative advantage, which, in its modern formulation, encourages processes which make intensive use of certain inputs to be located where these inputs are comparatively most abundant. It is economies of scale that tend to govern trade between countries with similar resource endowments, while the forces of comparative advantage are strongest between countries with dissimilar endowments. Thus trade in manufactures within Europe and North America tends to be driven by economies of scale, while trade between northern countries and the tropical and southern continents of Africa and Latin America tends to be driven by comparative advantage.

World trade has grown dramatically relative to world production since 1945, but most of this growth has been concentrated on the developed countries, with certain parts of the developing world becoming peripheral to the world trade system as a result. The main exceptions to this are the newly industrialising countries (NICs), particularly those in South-east Asia, namely Hong Kong, Singapore, the Republic of Korea, Taiwan, and so on.

The growth of world trade can be explained partly by post-war trade liberalisation among developed countries. This has been motivated by a complex of political and historical factors: US hegemony, the process of European political unification, and a policy response to the 'lessons of the 1930s'. Trade liberalisation has benefited trade in final products more than trade in intermediate products because it is final products that are normally subject to the highest *ad valorem* rates of duty. This discrepancy is reinforced by the high rate of effective protection that the discrepancy between these rates normally confers on the final stages of production. These stages convert products which are subject to low rates of duty into products which incur higher rates of duty – rates which apply to the entire value of the output and not just to the value-added in the final stages themselves. Effective protection encourages intermediate product trade to be substituted for final product trade. Thus tariff reductions which reduce effective protection tend to reverse this process.

Transport costs, too, have been reduced, and here the mechanisms have tended to favour intermediate product trade. The container revolution has reduced the risk of damage to cargoes, speeded up trans-shipment, and encouraged a proliferation of inter-modal routes which has made freight transportation much more competitive. Modern ships exploit economies of scale in vessel design and operation to an unprecedented degree; this applies not only to super-tankers and dry bulk-carriers, but also to cellular container ships and ro-ro vessels. Taken together, these developments have reduced the relative costs of moving products in bulk rather than in small consignments, and have therefore benefited trade in intermediate products, which move in bulk along trunk routes from one factory to another – more than trade in final products, which travel in small consignments to a wide variety of different destinations. They have also reduced the costs of long-distance haulage proportionately more than the costs of short-distance haulage, and therefore helped to promote inter-continental trade – this is one of the many factors that has benefited Japanese trade, and has also promoted off-shore processing, as explained below.

Changes in the pattern of comparative advantage have also tended to benefit intermediate product trade more than final product trade. Rural–urban migration in developing countries has created, in some cases, a relatively cheap, well-disciplined, non-unionised labour force, capable of performing semi-skilled work on production lines for relatively standardised products. At the same time, the emergence of the MNE as an institution for the transfer of technology and management practices has made it possible to relocate production to these countries from the industrialised countries. Only certain stages of production have been transferred, however, namely those stages making the most intensive use of unskilled and semi-skilled labour. Those stages involving the most valuable equipment and requiring the greatest skills in the maintenance and upgrading of equipment are normally retained at home. Key components are exported from the home country, and re-imported after processing and assembly overseas.

This pattern of 'export processing' has been promoted by two further developments. The first is the establishment of export-processing zones as a matter of government policy in certain developing countries. The second is the introduction of value-added tariffs by certain home countries, notably the USA, which levy tariffs on the value-added overseas and not on the total

TABLE 8.4   Average annual percentage growth of US imports under tariff provisions 806.30/807.00, 1969–81

	1969–74	1974–81	1969–81
Total value	24.0	16.9	19.8
Industrialised countries	16.0	16.6	16.3
Developing countries	42.8	17.5	25.2
Dutiable value	23.8	16.4	19.3
Industrialised countries	17.9	16.6	17.1
Developing countries	49.1	15.8	28.6

Source: calculated from data presented in Lee (1986).

value of a re-imported product. The tariff is designed specifically to reduce the effective protection of processing and assembly in the domestic market.

The growth of US imports under the provisions of the US value-added tariff is a widely used indicator of the growth of off-shore processing and of the volume of the intermediate product trade associated with it. Table 8.4 shows that in the period 1969–74, the total value of developing countries' exports to the US under the provisions of this tariff (i.e. in categories 806.30/807.00) grew at an annual rate of about 43 per cent. This compares with an annual rate of 16 per cent for the industrialised countries. For the 1974–81 period, however, the export growth from the developing countries decelerated sharply to 17 per cent, exactly the same rate of growth as the industrialised countries.

The dutiable value of the imports measures the value-added overseas on which the tariff is levied. Comparing the dutiable value with the total value allows inferences to be drawn about the proportion of total value that has been added overseas and, consequently, about the value of the intermediate products that were exported from the USA in the first place. Table 8.4 shows that in 1969–74 the dutiable value of imports originating in the developing countries grew even faster than their total value: at 49 per cent per annum compared to 43 per cent. Over the period 1969–81 as a whole, the dutiable value of imports originating from the developing countries grew at 29 per cent per annum, compared to 25 per cent for imports from industrialised countries.

These extraordinary growth rates appear much less impressive, however, when placed in the context of the initial structure of 806.30/807.00 trade. Table 8.5 shows that in 1969, developing countries accounted for only 21 per cent of this trade, 79 per cent being accounted for by exports from industrialised countries. The discrepancy was even greater where dutiable value is concerned. Industrialised countries accounted for 87 per cent of dutiable value and developing countries for only 13 per cent. Despite the discrepancy in the subsequent growth rates, the developing countries attained only 31 per cent of the dutiable value by 1981.

TABLE 8.5 Value and structure of US imports under tariff provisions 806.30/807.00, 1969–81

	1969	1974	1981
Total value ($US million)	1842	5393	16 145
Dutiable ($US million)	1399	4072	11 715
Share of total value (percentage)			
Industrialised countries	78.6	56.4	55.0
Developing countries	21.4	43.6	45.0
Share of dutiable value (percentage)			
Industrialised countries	87.3	68.0	69.0
Developing countries	12.7	32.0	31.0
Dutiable value as percentage of total			
Industrialised countries	84.4	91.0	91.0
Developing countries	44.9	55.4	49.9
All countries	76.0	75.5	72.6

Source: calculated from data presented in Lee (1986).

The proportion of value-added overseas has been consistently higher where the industrialised countries are concerned. Throughout the period 1969–81, it has been nearly double the proportion for the developing countries. The proportion for developing countries rose from 45 per cent to 55 per cent over the period 1969–74, but fell back to 50 per cent between 1974 and 1981. The simultaneous deceleration in the growth of the total value of exports from the developing countries, noted above, suggests that the opportunities for further expansion of off-shore processing in developing countries may be rather limited. It seems that the forms of off-shore processing introduced between 1974 and 81 may have afforded less opportunity for adding value overseas – for example, they may call for higher value components to be supplied from the industrialised countries. This suggests that, given the present level of world development, there may now be diminishing returns to this form of international production.

Other evidence corroborates the view that opportunities for profitable export processing may be more limited than at first appears. Table 8.6 shows that trade under 806.30/807.00 is dominated by a handful of countries. By 1983 Japan had wrested leadership in this trade from West Germany. The most important developing countries involved are Mexico (supplying 17 per cent of all imports under the tariff), Malaysia (5.5 per cent), Singapore (4.5 per cent), the Philippines (3.3 per cent), the Republic of Korea (2.6 per cent), Taiwan (2.6 per cent) and Hong Kong (2.1 per cent). Other countries have a relatively minor role. The major developing countries concerned are all characterised by relatively easy shipping access to the USA. They are also characterised by heavy involvement in one or more of a small number

TABLE 8.6   US imports under tariff provisions 806.30/807.00, 1969–83, analysed by country of export

Country	Share of total imports (per cent)		Share of overseas value-added (per cent)		Overseas value-added as a percentage of total value	
	1983	1969	1983	1969	1983	1969
Industrialised countries						
Japan	29.7	7.5	38.5	8.0	97.3	81.6
West Germany	12.5	34.1	16.3	44.0	97.8	98.2
Canada	6.5	18.5	5.8	15.8	67.2	65.1
Developing countries						
Mexico	17.0	8.1	11.0	3.7	48.6	34.7
Malaysia	5.5	*	3.1	*	42.2	75.0
Singapore	4.5	0.6	4.3	0.6	71.9	67.2
Philippines	3.3	0.3	1.6	0.1	37.2	32.7
Republic of Korea	2.6	1.3	1.4	0.6	40.9	33.2
Taiwan	2.6	3.7	2.9	3.2	82.3	65.4
Hong Kong	2.1	5.0	2.3	2.9	83.9	43.9
Haiti	0.9	0.2	0.4	0.1	29.4	40.0
Brazil	0.9	0.2	1.0	0.1	85.8	39.0
Dominican Republic	0.7	*	0.3	0.0	30.7	0.0
El Salvador	0.4	*	0.2	*	43.1	50.0
Columbia	0.1	*	0.1	*	32.9	50.0
15 countries	89.4	79.6	89.3	79.2	74.9	75.6
All countries	100.00	100.00	100.00	100.00	75.1	76.0

* indicates less than 0.05 per cent, but greater than 0.00 per cent.
Source: calculated from Grunwald and Flamm (1985), Table 2.1.

of industries which dominate 806.30/807.00 trade. Moxon (1984, Table 8) shows that in 1978 there were just five industries in which total US imports from developing countries exceeded $100 million and in which over 50 per cent of the imports were in categories 806.30/807.00. They are television receivers (where 806.30/807.00 trade accounts for 95.9 per cent of all US imports from developing countries), electronic components (93.6 per cent), parts of office and automatic data processing machines (81.2 per cent), electrical equipment, current carriers and resistors (63.3 per cent) and watches and clocks (53.1 per cent). These are all industries in which components requiring highly skilled labour are assembled by relatively unskilled labour, and in which components, and some final products, are miniaturised and are therefore relatively cheap to transport. Although Japanese and West German firms have extended off-shore processing to encompass textiles as well as electronics (see pp. 151–2), the fact remains that the industrial base for this form of trade is fairly narrow and that, as a result, the opportunities for other developing countries to join in may be quite small.

It remains true, however, that off-shore processing under 806.30/807.00 is of much greater significance to developing countries than to industrialised countries, simply because of the relatively poor performance of developing countries' exports to the industrialised countries outside of this category. Thus in 1980, imports from developing countries under 806.30/807.00 were 14.0 per cent of total US imports from these countries, compared to 7.7 per cent in 1970 (Lee, 1986, Table 1). By contrast, the corresponding imports from industrialised countries fell from 8.0 per cent to 7.6 per cent of total US imports from these countries over the same period. The recent export performance of developing countries under 806.30/807.00 therefore appears much better if it is compared with their own export performance as a whole, rather than with the export performance of industrialised countries within the same category of trade.

THE PROPENSITY TO INTERNALISE

When discussing the propensity to internalise, two points need to be made at the outset. First, internal trade within an MNE is, in principle, a two-way affair, involving both exports from the affiliate to the rest of the group, and imports by the affiliate from the rest of the group. Secondly, the propensity to internalise is product-specific. Together, these imply that a foreign subsidiary's propensity to internalise exports will normally differ from its propensity to internalise imports, because even within the same industry, different intermediate products will be involved in each case. They also imply that the propensities to internalise exports and imports will vary between industries.

These points are well illustrated in Tables 8.7 and 8.8. The proportion of intra-firm trade in the exports of US overseas affiliates in 1982 varied from 85.1 per cent in transportation equipment down to 15.4 per cent in the mining industry. The corresponding ratios for imports varied from 94.4 per cent in non-electrical machinery to 50.8 per cent in food and kindred products. Overall, the propensity to internalise affiliate exports was 52.2 per cent, and the propensity to internalise affiliate imports 84.7 per cent. These figures indicate that, at a global level, MNEs tend to be more important to their subsidiaries as a source of imports than as a market for their exports. In this context, the importance of the MNE is measured relative to that of the non-affiliated firms with which the subsidiary deals. The discrepancy is smaller, however, when attention is confined to the manufacturing sector alone, where in 1982 the respective ratios were 66.3 per cent and 83.1 per cent.

Turning first to subsidiary imports, most research has tended to focus on imports from the parent company, or at least from the country in which the parent company is based. Fortunately, there is evidence that subsidiary imports from other subsidiaries tend to follow the pattern of subsidiary imports from the parent, in some respects at least (Casson *et al.*, 1986, pp.

TABLE 8.7   Structure of sales of US foreign affiliates by industry, 1977–82

Industry	Export/sales ratio (percentage)		Intra-firm export ratios (percentage)					
			To world		To US		To rest of world	
	1977	1982	1977	1982	1977	1982	1977	1982
All industries	38.2	34.5	69.1	52.2	89.9	82.8	49.7	38.8
Mining	77.5	82.4	25.9	15.4	67.2	41.7	2.4	1.5
Petroleum	49.5	35.4	85.0	48.8	93.2	85.8	63.7	25.3
Manufacturing	30.8	33.9	64.6	66.3	81.4	86.1	57.5	58.4
Food & kindred products	14.8	15.6	50.6	42.7	81.8	70.2	44.2	39.3
Chemicals, etc.	26.1	31.7	57.7	56.8	82.5	77.7	55.5	54.1
Metals	26.8	25.7	33.1	38.6	39.6	63.5	29.6	32.7
Non-electrical machinery	36.8	40.6	66.9	69.7	91.4	90.2	63.6	64.9
Electrical & electronic	33.7	40.7	64.5	69.5	92.7	91.7	49.7	51.3
Transportation equipment	38.8	43.3	83.9	85.1	91.7	91.8	76.4	78.5
Other	28.6	30.7	44.4	54.8	48.5	64.2	42.7	52.3
Trade	34.6	36.9	32.5	32.2	75.4	58.7	28.6	28.8
Insurance, real-estate, etc.	12.0	37.8	59.6	65.0	69.4	76.6	50.1	47.2
Other industries	17.5	16.9	36.0	52.1	82.8	94.4	23.3	34.1

Notes: the data relate to non-bank majority-owned foreign affiliates of non-bank US parent companies. The export/sales ratios are the ratios of the total value of the exports of the foreign affiliates to the total value of their sales. The intra-firm export ratios are the ratios of the affiliates' exports to the parent company and other affiliates within the prescribed geographical area to the affiliates' total exports to the area.

Source: US Department of Commerce, Bureau of Economic Analysis, *US Direct Investment Abroad 1977*, Washington, DC, Tables III H.2–5 (pp. 319–22) for Table 8.7 and Tables III I.3, 7 (pp. 338, 342) for Table 8.8; and *US Direct Investment Abroad 1982*, Tables III E.2–5 (pp. 226–9) for Table 8.7 and Table III G.3, 7 (pp. 266, 270) for Table 8.8.

39–40). Table 8.8 presents data on the propensity to internalise subsidiary imports from the US. The data show that, unlike the case of subsidiary exports discussed below, there is little significant difference between subsidiaries in developing and in industrialised countries in the propensity to internalise imports.

The propensity of a subsidiary to internalise imports from the country of the parent company is related to the propensity of the parent to internalise its exports, though the two propensities by no means amount to the same thing. The parent's propensity to internalise exports has received some attention in its own right, and the results obtained suggest a reason for the similarities between the subsidiaries in industrialised and developing countries, noted above. The reason is that when the incentive to internalise the parent company's exports is present, it is normally very strong, and is therefore not traded off against location-specific factors. More specifically, in high-technology industries with novel products there is a strong incentive

TABLE 8.8   Structure of purchases of US foreign affiliates from the US, by industry, 1977–82

| | Intra-firm import ratios for affiliates based in | | | | | |
| | All countries | | Industrialised countries | | Developing countries | |
	1977	1982	1977	1982	1977	1982
All industries	81.7	84.0	82.1	84.7	80.3	81.9
Petroleum	82.9	64.3	77.2	77.0	n.a.	58.1
Manufacturing	81.6	83.1	80.5	82.0	87.4	87.4
Food & kindred products	46.6	50.8	47.3	50.9	44.1	50.2
Chemicals, etc.	88.3	81.7	89.2	84.4	84.8	72.7
Metals	74.8	76.9	74.3	82.6	78.2	57.7
Non-electrical machinery	92.6	94.4	92.6	94.6	91.7	93.3
Electrical & electronics	85.8	89.5	79.8	79.3	92.8	94.6
Transportation equipment	80.3	80.7	78.8	78.9	96.3	95.1
Other	78.8	88.0	78.8	89.7	78.4	78.2
Other industries	82.0	89.7	86.8	91.6	n.a.	82.2

Notes: the intra-firm import ratios are the ratios of the affiliates' imports from the parent company to the affiliates' total imports from the US, and are given separately for all affiliates, for affiliates based in industrialised countries, and for affiliates based in developing countries.
Source: as for Table 8.7.

for the parent company to produce the most sophisticated components itself and to supply them only to wholly-owned subsidiaries overseas. Buckley and Casson (1976) tested this hypothesis, by classifying fourteen industries according to research-intensity, using measures of R & D expenditure per unit sales for US firms as a whole. Using US Tariff Commission data (US Tariff Commission, 1973) they showed that in the six most research-intensive industries, the parent's intra-firm export ratio ranged between 50 and 62 per cent, while in the eight least research-intensive industries it ranged between 15 and 52 per cent.

Pearce (1982) has re-examined the issue using data on the ratio of the parent's intra-firm exports to its total sales derived from the Dunning and Pearce (1981) survey of the world's largest firms. Pearce shows that for research-intensive industries such as electronics and chemicals, the ratio is 5.5 per cent, while for medium research-intensive industries such as industrial and farm equipment, motor vehicles and metals, it is 7.8 per cent, and for low research-intensity industries, such as building materials, food and textiles, it is a mere 0.9 per cent.

Pearce then standardises the figures by the firm's degree of multinationality, as measured by the ratio of the sales of its overseas affiliates and associated companies to its total world-wide sales. When averaged across all industries, the ratio of parents' intra-firm exports to parents' total sales increases from 0.1 per cent for firms with a degree of multinationality less than 2.5 per cent, to 9.4 per cent for firms with a degree of multinationality between 22.5 and 32.5 per cent, and then tails off to 7.1 per cent for degrees of multinationality in excess of 52.5 per cent. The tailing off is explained by Pearce in terms of a transition from a set of bilateral internal trades centred on the parent company to an integrated network of multilateral trade in which cross-trade between subsidiaries begins to dominate trade between subsidiaries and the parent firm. For a given degree of multinationality, firms in relatively research-intensive industries tend, once again, to have the highest levels of intra-firm trade.

In high-technology industries, the parent firm may produce almost all of the products, and simply rely upon its overseas subsidiaries for marketing. Statistics confirm that in high-technology industries, a high proportion of intra-firm imports by subsidiaries include finished products awaiting distribution (Casson *et al.*, 1986). This phenomenon has been investigated in detail by Lall (1980, chapter 4). He argues that complex durable products requiring after-sales service are marketed through sales subsidiaries, while simple non-durable products are more likely to be advertised heavily to the public and distributed through small independent retailers. This is consistent with the view that intra-firm trade in finished products is stimulated by the need to control the quality of after-sales service. Lall therefore postulates that the parent's intra-firm exports will be positively associated with a dummy variable indicating the importance of after-sales servicing, and negatively associated with an index of advertising intensity. When the ratio of parents' intra-firm exports to the total sales of the foreign subsidiaries importing them is regressed upon these variables, and upon a dummy variable indicating the relevance of 'value-added' tariffs, then all variables are significant at the 10 per cent level and take the expected sign.

Turning now to exports from subsidiaries, the data in Table 8.7 show that, in all industries, internalisation is higher in exports to the parent country (i.e. the USA) than in exports to the rest of the world. For all industries, the respective internalisation propensities were 82.8 per cent and 38.8 per cent in 1982, and 89.9 per cent and 49.7 per cent in 1977. However, across industries, the pattern is fairly similar, in that industries with a relatively high propensity to internalise exports to the USA also have a relatively high propensity to internalise exports to other affiliates.

It is often convenient to study subsidiaries' exports indirectly by examining the internalisation of imports into the parent company's country. Helleiner (1981, chapter 2) has adopted this approach, and analysed data on US imports by related parties. The data aggregate intra-firm imports by US parent firms with exports by non-US parents to their US subsidiaries, and with exports by the non-US subsidiaries of non-US parents to US subsidiaries. He finds that in 1977, 48.4 per cent of all US imports were from related parties. The proportion increases from 23.5 per cent for primary products (excluding petroleum) to 37.6 per cent for semi-manufactures and 53.6 per cent for manufactures. This is in line with the other studies which suggest that the highest levels of intra-firm trade are found in the manufacturing sector, and that a high proportion of intra-firm trade is accounted for by finished manufactures consigned to sales and distribution subsidiaries.

The proportion of related-party imports of semi-manufactures and manufactures tends to be lower for imports originating in developing countries, as compared to developed countries (17.0 per cent and 37.0 per cent, compared to 43.4 per cent and 61.1 per cent). It is slightly higher, though, where primary products are concerned (49.1 per cent, compared to 41.3 per cent). The proportion of related-party imports in petroleum was 59.4 per cent, with no significant difference between imports from developing and developed countries.

Helleiner examines in detail a sample of 100 three-digit manufactured commodity groups. He postulates that intra-firm trade 'is most likely to be found in manufacturing industries in which firms possess certain advantages which are a potential source of quasi-rent: for example, scale economies, technology, skills, product differentiation and advertising, and other barriers to entry.'

Helleiner's single equation regression results explaining the proportion of related-party imports in US imports as a whole confirm the importance of research-intensity for intra-firm trade. The US wage rate also has a significant positive effect, though whether this reflects the appropriation of quasi-rents from skill-intensity, as Helleiner suggests, or the presence of a cost-saving incentive for off-shore production, must remain an open question. Size also has a significant positive effect, although because the variable is size of plant rather than size of firm, this may capture the importance of mass production in the industry rather than anything to do with quasi-rents. Both scale economies and concentration are insignificant, but since the measurement of scale economies is problematic, too much weight should not be given to this. Nevertheless, the fact that research intensity is important, while concentration is not, suggests that the novelty of the product rather than market structure is the more important factor governing intra-firm exports from the subsidiary. Since this same factor is also an important influence on the parent's intra-firm exports, the product cycle view of intra-firm trade receives considerable support from the data.

One of the most fruitful ways of analysing the propensity to internalise is through the industry case study. This makes it possible to consider the internalisation of exports and imports simultaneously, and also to do justice to the complexities created by quasi-internalisation. Using six case studies – motor vehicles, bearings, synthetic fibres, copper, tin and bananas – Casson *et al.* (1986) identify three main industry characteristics which stimulate internalisation of both exports and imports. They are, in order of importance, (a) the novelty of the products and their technological content – especially important with motor vehicles – (b) the need for quality control in overseas operations – important in motor vehicles, bearings and tropical banana exports – and (c) the existence of large non-recoverable investments – important in synthetic fibres, copper and tin. The two main factors which discourage internalisation, they suggest, are the existence in the industry of indivisible yet versatile assets, and diversity in the intermediate products coupled with complexity in the configuration of their flows. These two factors both significantly increase the costs of managing intra-firm trade. Opportunities for transfer pricing exist in many industries, but the case studies failed to pin-point any instances where trade was internalised purely for this reason. It should be noted, however, that one of the industries where transfer pricing is most strongly suspected, namely the oil industry, was not included in this study.

The case studies of the motor industry, synthetic fibres and copper highlight the importance of Japanese joint ventures in intermediate product trade. This factor is considered further below.

THE CONTROL OF INTERMEDIATE PRODUCT TRADE: A COMPARISON OF US AND JAPANESE STRATEGIES

The nationality of registration (source country) of an MNE appears to be a significant influence on its international investment strategy. In the past decade a major source of growth in intra-firm trade has been Japanese investments in South-east Asia (Kojima, 1978; Ozawa, 1985). Many of these investments are made by small and medium-sized firms and involve labour-intensive operations in the textile industry. Larger-scale Japanese investments include operations in the synthetic fibre and mineral industries (Read, 1986a, 1986b). Many Japanese operations are voluntarily organised as joint ventures with indigenous firms, whereas US firms have traditionally favoured outright ownership, where this is permitted by the host government.

US off-shore operations in South-east Asia have tended to focus much more on high-technology activities related to electronics. Samuelsson (1982) explains that the relatively low level of Japanese off-shore processing in electronics is attributable to Japanese concern with total quality control, and the consequent need to keep all precision activities in the hands of long-serving skilled employees working under the same factory roof.

In a sample of 153 subsidiaries of 111 MNEs in six light manufacturing industries operating in five ASEAN countries in 1978, Lecraw (1983, 1985) found that Japanese firms were particularly prone to utilise intra-firm trade.

The Japanese subsidiaries sent 79 per cent of their exports to related units of the MNE, compared to 68 per cent for US subsidiaries, 65 per cent for European subsidiaries, and 23 per cent for subsidiaries of MNEs from developing countries. The difference is even more pronounced for imports. Here the Japanese subsidiaries received 84 per cent of their imports from related units, compared to 53 per cent for US subsidiaries, 57 per cent for European subsidiaries, and 37 per cent for subsidiaries of MNEs from developing countries.

A study of Japanese participation in British industry by Dunning (1986) confirms this picture. It shows that 85 per cent of UK affiliate imports and about 80 per cent of exports are intra-firm. In the case of colour television manufacture, 90 per cent of both imports and exports are intra-firm.

The proportion of off-shore value-added in Japanese operations seems to vary considerably. MITI (Ministry of International Trade and Industry) survey evidence cited by Nakajo (1980) indicates that of 875 Asian subsidiaries, 320 carried out integrated processing from raw materials to final products and the remaining 555 carried out specialised processing or assembly, usually related to the final stages of the overall process of production; this comprised 319 processing final products, 92 processing 'near-final' products, 32 processing input materials, and 65 carrying out intermediate processing for parts and semi-finished products; 30 carried out processing unrelated to the production system of the parent company, and the remaining functions were unspecified.

European firms have, like the Japanese, made off-shore investments in the textile industry, but the scale has been much smaller and the locations have been more oriented to the Mediterranean and North Africa. West German firms have figured quite prominently in such operations, but British firms have tended to avoid them (Fröbel *et al.*, 1980; Toyne *et al.*, 1984).

The off-shore processing activities of Japanese firms constitute an elaborate and sophisticated network of interlocking ventures. These networks often involve indigenous partners for Japanese firms. Partnerships can involve not only joint equity stakes, but also production-sharing arrangements in which half the output is retained by the indigenous firm for independent use or resale, while the other half is repatriated to Japan. The networks also rely upon informal collaboration between Japanese firms themselves, which often seems to be co-ordinated by the Japanese general trading companies (*sogo shosha*) and even MITI itself. US operations, by contrast, are much less sophisticated. With one or two exceptions, European firms have only just begun to enter large-scale off-shore processing in a serious way.

THE INFLUENCE OF HOST COUNTRY FACTORS ON THE
EXTENT OF INTRA-FIRM TRADE

This section reports the provisional results of a pilot study of whether
subsidiaries of MNEs have a higher propensity to export their output, and to
internalise export flows, when producing in developing countries instead of
industrialised countries. Table 8.9 shows that in 1982 the ratio of total
exports to total sales was, on average, 45.8 per cent for affiliates in developing countries, compared to 31.2 per cent for affiliates in industrialised
countries. In 1977 the difference was even more marked, with the ratio for
developing countries being 59.9 per cent, more than double the corresponding figure for industrialised countries of 28.5 per cent.

The propensity to internalise these export flows is also greater, though
only marginally so, where subsidiaries in developing countries are concerned. Table 8.9 shows that in 1982 the ratio of intra-group exports to total
exports was 54.6 per cent for affiliates in developing countries, compared to
51.0 per cent for affiliates in industrialised countries; the discrepancy was
somewhat greater in 1977, with the respective figures being 84.0 per cent
compared to 54.7 per cent.

These figures suggest that something rather significant may have happened between 1977 and 1982 which caused both the export propensity and
the internalisation propensity of affiliates in developing countries to fall.
One such factor could be widespread US divestments of foreign affiliates in
industries characterised by both a high propensity to export and a high
propensity to internalise. These would have to be industries geographically
concentrated on the developing world. It is, however, extremely difficult to
disentangle industry effects from country effects because of the limitations of
the available data.

In general, it would be useful to know how far differences between
developing and industrialised countries can be attributed to differences in
the industrial composition of these countries, rather than to location-specific
differences within the industries themselves. The only way of doing this
using published statistics is, it seems, to utilise data on total exports and total
sales which is provided, on an industry basis, for developed and industrialised countries separately. These data make it possible to calculate, for a
given propensity, a hypothetical propensity for developing country affiliates
as a whole by applying to their industrial distribution of exports or sales the
industry propensities taken across all countries. The extent to which the
actual propensity for developing countries as a whole exceeds the hypothetical propensity measures the extent to which factors other than industrial
composition raise the propensity concerned.

When applied to the propensity to internalise, the results of this exercise
indicate that of the 14.9 per cent above-average internalisation observed in

TABLE 8.9 Structure of sales of US foreign affiliates by country, 1977–82

Country	Export/sales ratio (percentage)		Intra-firm exports/ total exports ratio (percentage)		Intra-firm exports/ total sales ratio (percentage)	
	1977	1982	1977	1982	1977	1982
All countries	38.2	34.5	69.1	52.2	26.4	18.0
Industrialised countries	28.5	31.2	54.7	51.0	15.6	15.9
Canada	21.6	23.3	65.7	72.9	14.2	17.0
Europe	33.9	37.3	52.5	47.1	17.8	17.6
Japan	7.2	8.7	83.8	72.6	6.1	6.3
Developing countries	59.9	45.8	84.0	54.6	50.3	25.0
Latin America	36.8	40.4	66.4	52.7	24.4	21.3
South America	10.8	10.2	63.9	59.6	6.9	6.1
Argentina	15.4	17.1	54.1	79.1	8.3	13.5
Brazil	7.1	8.9	66.6	63.0	4.7	5.6
Columbia	9.4	3.9	44.9	47.7	4.2	1.9
Peru	23.8	28.7	4.4	3.0	1.0	0.9
Venezuela	10.0	1.0	89.0	32.9	8.9	0.3
Central America	21.8	20.4	53.1	59.6	11.6	12.2
Mexico	10.0	10.3	71.9	80.6	7.2	8.3
Panama	55.9	54.6	31.4	37.3	17.5	20.4
Other	33.4	23.9	60.8	77.5	20.3	18.5
Other Western hemisphere	83.2	86.9	68.5	50.9	57.0	44.3
Bahamas	85.3	88.0	62.9	48.9	53.7	43.0
Bermuda	89.6	93.3	67.2	35.7	60.2	33.3
Africa (total developing)	52.0	63.1	69.9	72.9	36.4	46.0
Nigeria	54.7	n.a.	n.a.	n.a.	n.a.	n.a.
Middle East	82.7	25.0	95.9	88.8	79.3	22.2
Asia & Pacific (total developing)	60.9	58.7	71.8	46.2	43.8	27.1
Hong Kong	77.5	59.5	60.4	52.1	46.8	31.0
Indonesia	80.9	66.1	75.8	62.0	61.4	41.0
Malaysia	44.3	47.4	93.7	77.8	41.5	36.8
Philippines	17.2	n.a.	71.0	n.a.	12.2	n.a.
Singapore	67.3	82.0	78.2	18.6	52.7	15.3
South Korea	58.4	44.0	n.a.	99.2	n.a.	43.7
Taiwan	58.9	49.9	n.a.	86.3	n.a.	43.0
Thailand	11.4	17.5	76.9	89.4	8.7	15.6

Source: as Tables 8.7 and 8.8, but using Tables III.H.1 and III.E.1 respectively.

1977 among developing countries, 10.1 per cent is attributable to the industrial composition of developing countries, and 4.8 per cent to a higher location-specific propensity to internalise. There is similar evidence that industry composition explains much of the higher propensity to export in developing countries. The industry composition effects, however, seem to be dominated by the petroleum sector, and when estimated values are calculated excluding petroleum, the industry composition effect largely disappears from both propensities. The position may be summarised by saying that when petroleum is excluded, the developing countries' ratio of intra-firm exports to total sales of subsidiaries is only slightly above average, the remaining difference being attributable to location-specific factors. It seems likely that a location-specific increase in the propensity to internalise, rather than in the propensity to export, is the most important explanation, but data limitations make it difficult to be sure. If this were the explanation, it could reflect MNE concern over quality control in developing countries which, despite political risks of expropriation and the blocking of remittances, encourages them to seek outright control. In industrialised countries, where reputable subcontractors can be found more easily, this factor may not be so important.

Changes between 1977 and 1982 seem to be attributable chiefly to MNE withdrawal from the Middle Eastern oil industry, and in particular to the loss of oil operations in Iran. This eliminated a highly internalised, highly export-oriented activity which was specific to the developing world. Once this factor is discounted, the pattern of intra-firm trade appears much more stable for 1977–82 than the aggregate statistics suggest.

CONCLUSION

The main analytical contribution of this chapter has been to distinguish clearly between four separate factors which impact upon the level of intra-firm trade. These factors are often confused, and misleading conclusions may easily be drawn as a result. These factors are in turn related to other factors, such as the horizontal differentiation of products. For clarity of exposition, the factors have been examined as if the determinants of each were entirely independent of the determinants of the others, but this is not in fact the case. The management of an MNE may, for example, redesign a product in such a way that it simultaneously stimulates the horizontal differentiation of products through the adoption of standardised components, makes the components more easily tradeable through miniaturisation, and makes off-shore assembly easier by trivialising the labour content of the assembly process. Arguably Japanese production managers have already effected a partial breakthrough of this kind in one or two industries, and it is quite conceivable that the same approach can, in time, be applied to other industries. This could lead to a considerable extension in the range of intermediate products entering into intra-firm trade. Some developing countries would stand to gain from such a development, while others might lose. If it occurs, it will probably occur with a force that is difficult to resist, and developing countries would probably be well advised not to attempt to oppose it altogether, but rather to attempt to channel the forces in the direction that affords them the greatest potential benefit in the long run.

So far as the internalisation of trade is concerned, one of the major developments of the past decade has been the rising importance of quasi-internalisation, caused by the rapid growth of joint ventures and other collaborative ventures. Very little is known about whether quasi-internalisation is a complement to, or substitute for, conventional internalisation, although the latter seems the more likely possibility. Quasi-internalisation is now very significant in motor vehicle manufacture, synthetic fibre production, and certain mineral industries, but reliable statistics on it are practically non-existent.

Another recent development is intra-firm trade in information-related and professional services, and once again there is a serious paucity of data. For reasons indicated at the outset, there seems little reason to anticipate a dramatic global extension of intra-firm trade, but every reason to suppose that fast-growing sectors such as information services will be very susceptible to it. The internalisation of private international flows of information on a large scale gives legitimate cause for concern, especially in politically unstable countries, or where politically sensitive issues are concerned, and it is hoped that future research will address this issue.

9 Export Processing Zones in Developing Countries: Theory and Empirical Evidence

V. N. BALASUBRAMANYAM

INTRODUCTION

Export Processing Zones (EPZs), variously styled as free port zones, duty-free zones and free economic zones, are not a new phenomenon. The Rotterdam and Hamburg free port zones, for instance, date back to the latter half of the nineteenth century. Currently there are more than four hundred free port zones of differing description in various parts of the world, including the USA and the UK. Although they are a comparatively recent phenomenon in developing countries, they have steadily increased in number from seven at the end of 1970 to more than one hundred by the end of 1984. This chapter reviews the theory relating to EPZs and the available evidence on their benefits and costs to developing countries.

THE CONCEPT

An EPZ is defined as an enclave outside the customs territory of a country. Goods entering the zone can be processed, stored and manufactured without payment of customs duties and local taxes, and exported without payment of duties. Goods imported into and manufactured in the zones are liable to the payment of customs duties and local taxes only when sold on the domestic markets of the country. In addition, firms established in the zones are accorded freedom from various restrictions and regulations related to statistical reporting requirements and other legislation concerning consumer protection.

Freedom from trade taxes and bureaucratic regulations, however, are not the only characteristics of EPZs. The classic type of zones such as those in

157

the Far East also provide a wide range of fiscal and financial incentives to firms locating in them. Tax holidays of up to five or even ten years, generous depreciation allowances, and exemption from wage and welfare legislation are characteristic features of EPZs in several South-east Asian countries. For instance, firms in the Massan Zone in South Korea are given a number of fiscal and non-fiscal incentives, including exemption from corporate taxes during the first five years of operation and a 50 per cent exemption for the next three years; exemption from income taxation for foreign employees of firms operating in the zone; the provision of electricity at a subsidised rate; and an official guarantee that the workforce of firms in the zone will not be allowed to unionise. Although they differ in scope, such fiscal and non-fiscal incentives are a feature of most EPZs in developing countries.

Objectives

The avowed purpose of developing countries in establishing EPZs is the promotion of various development objectives. These include the promotion of manufacturing for export, the creation of employment opportunities, the importation and dissemination of foreign technology and know-how, and regional development. It is the hope of the developing countries that (a) foreign firms will be lured to the duty-free zones; (b) their production will be geared to export markets and they will be a source of foreign exchange; (c) they will be a source of technology and know-how to the economy in general; (d) they will establish links with locally owned firms through the purchase of locally produced inputs; and (e) they will generate employment opportunities.

Indeed, the demonstrated success of classic EPZs such as Singapore and Hong Kong in attracting foreign direct investment (FDI) and promoting exports has been a significant factor in the decision to establish EPZs on the part of other developing countries. In the case of countries such as South Korea, Taiwan and Mexico in recent years, EPZs are an additional instrument in their overall strategy of outward-looking development centered on export growth. In the case of countries such as India, Indonesia and the Philippines, for long wedded to an inward-looking strategy of development centred on import-substituting industrialisation, EPZs are in the nature of a grudging concession in favour of an outward-looking strategy of development. In other words, EPZs represent a compromise between the advocates of an inward-looking strategy of development, and those favouring an outward-looking strategy centred on a relatively liberal foreign trade regime and inflows of FDI.

These objectives and features of EPZs are central to an analysis of their benefits and costs to developing countries. Especially relevant in this context are two key features of EPZs, namely the wide presence of foreign private capital and technology in the zones, and the enclave nature of the zones.

The extent to which EPZs resemble an enclave depends on the nature of the foreign trade regime in place in the economy. In countries such as Hong Kong and Singapore, which operate liberal foreign trade regimes with little or no restrictions on foreign trade, the entire economy would be in the nature of an EPZ. But in countries such as India and Indonesia, which operate highly regulated foreign trade regimes with a panoply of tariff and non-tariff barriers to imports and exchange controls, EPZs are essentially enclaves, or small islands, practising free trade in the midst of an economy fraught with protectionist barriers to foreign trade.

Central to the analysis of the welfare implications of EPZs is the nature and extent of factor flows and other economic contacts between the economy and the enclaves.

THEORETICAL ANALYSIS

Theoretical analysis of EPZs is usually cast in terms of the standard two-factor, two-good, two-country Heckscher–Ohlin type of international trade model (Hamada, 1974; Hamilton and Svennson, 1982). The general conclusion of these models is that inflows of FDI into the zones, referred to as duty-free zones, reduce rather than increase economic welfare of the countries establishing the zones. This conclusion is based on a number of assumptions, some of which do not reflect the characteristics of duty-free zones in the real world. Nonetheless, the theoretical models provide a framework for analysing the benefits and costs of EPZs.

Assumptions of the models

The theoretical models incorporate the following assumptions:
1. There are two goods and two factors of production in the economy.
2. Good 1 is an importable good and good 2 is an exportable.
3. Good 1 uses more labour than capital per unit of output relative to good 2. In other words, good 1 is labour-intensive and good 2 is capital-intensive.
4. Both goods are produced in the post-tariff situation.
5. Both factors of production are fully employed.
6. When the country establishes a duty-free zone, labour, but not capital, is mobile between the domestic economy and the zone.

Case 1: FDI in the absence of a duty-free zone. The analysis of the welfare implications of duty-free zones builds on the by now familiar analysis of FDI in the presence of a tariff on the imported good (Hamada, 1974; Bhagwati, 1979; Brecher and Alejandro, 1980). In this case it is assumed that FDI is allowed into the economy and it is concentrated in the importable capital-intensive good. It flows into the importable good because of the tariff protection the good enjoys. This inflow of FDI accentuates the initial loss of economic welfare due to the production and consumption distortions caused by the imposition of the tariff.

The inflow of FDI into the capital-intensive good increases its production and reduces that of the exportable labour-intensive good. This conclusion follows from the Rybczynski theorem familiar to students of international trade.[1] This augments the production distortion to the extent that there is a further misallocation of resources in favour of the good in which the economy does not possess a comparative advantage. The profits repatriated abroad on account of FDI in the protected sector constitutes another source of welfare loss to the economy. The analysis implicitly assumes that the entire output of the economy is valued at international prices and not the tariff-inclusive domestic prices.

Case 2: FDI with a duty-free zone. The analysis in this case is analogous to that in Case 1. FDI is assumed to flow into the production of the relatively capital-intensive good located in the zone. In this case there will be an export of labour from the economy to the zone; the relatively labour-intensive good in the economy will experience a decline in production, and the production of the capital-intensive good in the zone will increase. This line of reasoning is again based on the Rybczynski theorem.

The price of the capital-intensive good in the zone will be the same as the international price for the good, as it does not enjoy tariff protection in the zone. When the output of the economy, including the production of the capital-intensive good in the zone, is valued at international prices, there is a loss of economic welfare.[2]

The assumption that FDI will be attracted to the relatively capital-intensive good in the zone, however, may be unrealistic. The zone, by definition, does not provide protection from international competition to the goods produced there. It is highly unlikely that FDI would be attracted into the unprotected capital-intensive good in the zone in the presence of an opportunity to invest in the protected sector of the economy.[3] In any case, the objective of developing countries in establishing EPZs is to promote the exports of labour-intensive manufacturers.

Case 3: FDI in the labour-intensive good in the duty-free zone. This is the most realistic case. Most duty-free zones in developing countries attract FDI into the production of labour-intensive goods destined for export.

What are the attractions of the labour-intensive exportable good for FDI? Obviously it is the availability of relatively cheap and easily trainable labour that attracts FDI to the labour-intensive goods in developing countries. But why is there a need for EPZs hived off from the economy? Why cannot the developing countries attract FDI into the labour-intensive goods located in the economy?

The answer to these questions is that the presence of a heavily protected sector producing importables, intensive in the use of capital, necessitates the establishment of EPZs. In the absence of EPZs, FDI is likely to be attracted into the relatively capital-intensive good, protected from international competition by tariffs, with highly profitable domestic markets in the host country. The relatively labour-intensive exportable good is unlikely to enjoy a high degree of protection, save in cases where it attracts an export subsidy. Indeed, if the imported inputs and components required for the production of exportables are subject to a tariff, the degree of effective protection afforded to them could be relatively low or even negative. Under these circumstances the inclination of profit-maximising foreign firms would be to invest in the importable capital-intensive good to take advantage of the relatively high rates of effective protection it enjoys.

Given this situation, countries pursuing inward-looking policies are driven to establish EPZs in their bid to promote exports of manufactured goods with the assistance of foreign private capital and technology. The EPZs they have established not only permit the importation of components and intermediates free of duties, but also provide various fiscal and non-fiscal incentives to foreign firms locating in the zone. In other words, EPZs are a second-best method of attracting FDI into the export industries for countries wedded to protecting their import-competing industries. The first-best method is the adoption of a liberal foreign trade regime bereft of tariffs and quotas on imports. In this case FDI would be attracted to the labour-intensive exportable industries to take advantage of the relatively cheap labour endowments of these countries.

What are the welfare implications of an influx of FDI into the relatively labour-intensive good located in the zone? The welfare gains to the economy from FDI in the zone consists of the wage payments it makes and the employment it creates for local labour, the payments it makes for inputs it purchases from the domestic sector of the economy, the technology and skills it transmits to the economy, and the income and profits taxes it pays.

The extent of these gains to the economy essentially depends on the opportunity cost of the locally owned resources that FDI attracts to the zone from the domestic economy, and the productivity of foreign firms relative to that of locally-owned firms.

The one major resource FDI attracts to the zone from the domestic economy is labour. In effect, FDI in the zone is equivalent to an export of labour from the domestic economy. Clearly, in this case the gain to the economy from the establishment of the EPZ would be positive only if the social opportunity cost of labour that moves to the zone from the economy is zero. In other words, if the wage paid to workers in the zone exceeds their contribution to the social product on the domestic sector of the economy, the zone would make a positive contribution. The net contribution of the zone in this case could be reckoned to be equal to the difference between the wage rate paid to workers in the zone and the shadow wage rate (equal to the social marginal product of workers), or the social opportunity cost of workers in the domestic economy. Under conditions of widespread unemployment or underemployment in the economy, the social opportunity cost of labour is likely to be negligible or zero. Even so, a properly designed analysis of the benefits and costs of EPZs has to take into account the possible contribution of labour to the social product if it were to be employed in the domestic economy: that is, the shadow wage rate of labour has to be estimated and the difference between the actual wage on the zone and the shadow wage rate in the economy would be the contribution of the zone per person employed.

The net foreign exchange contribution of the EPZ to the country establishing it would consist of all the payments the firms in the zone would make to the domestic economy, including the wage bill for domestic labour they employ, the payments to domestic inputs, and any income and corporation taxes they pay The assumption here is that the entire production of the zone would be exported, and hence all the earnings of the firms in the zone would be in foreign currency, which they would have to convert into local currency to make all the payments referred to above. Here again the analyst has to estimate the net social gains to the economy of obtaining foreign exchange from its links with the zone. To the extent that the official exchange rate of the country is overvalued, as is the case with most developing countries, the economy would be able to gain from its foreign exchange transactions with the zone. In other words, because of the overvalued official rate, the economy would be able to obtain foreign exchange at a rate lower than its true opportunity cost, i.e. the economy would be paying less units of local currency for a unit of foreign exchange than what it would have to pay on the free market in foreign exchange.

The extent of the other benefits to the economy from the presence of the zone, such as technology transfer, would obviously depend on the extent of the links between the economy and the zone. These include the sale of domestically produced inputs to foreign firms in the zone, the opportunities for training labour that the firms in the zone provide, and other externalities flowing from their presence in the zone.

In sum, the welfare effects of EPZs in developing countries turn on the extent and nature of the linkages between the zones and the domestic sector of the economy. In addition, the structure and stage of development of the domestic economy would also be relevant. These aspects are the subject of a number of empirical studies seeking to evaluate the social costs and benefits of EPZs to developing countries.

EMPIRICAL EVIDENCE

The pioneering empirical studies of EPZs in developing countries are by Peter Warr (1983a, 1983b). Warr has not only provided a framework for the evaluation of the benefits and costs of EPZs, but he has also estimated the returns to public investment in establishing EPZs in South Korea, Indonesia and the Philippines. We review here the main findings of these and other studies.

The objective of these studies is the estimation of the social gains to the economy from investments in establishing EPZs. The investment costs consist of the construction costs defrayed by the country for the buildings on the EPZ, the administration costs for personnel who administer the zone, and costs relating to other infrastructural facilities in the zones. The social benefits arising from the zones have been discussed in the previous section. In essence, the studies attempt to measure the benefits to the economy from the presence of the zone, as opposed to what it would have gained in the absence of the zone by deploying the resources committed to the zone elsewhere in the economy. In other words, as stated earlier, the social opportunity costs to the economy of the resources deployed in the zone form the crux of the analysis. The net benefits from the zone to the economy over the life-time of the zone are discounted back to the present at an appropriate discount rate to estimate the present value of the benefits.

Warr's studies show that while the Masan EPZ in South Korea conferred substantial benefits on the economy, the zones in Jakarta in Indonesia and the Bataan Zone in the Philippines have had little to offer to the economy. A study by Dean Spinnanger (1984) relating to EPZs in Malaysia, Singapore, Taiwan and the Philippines, concludes that while EPZs in the first three countries have been beneficial in varying degrees, the beneficial effects of the Philippines have been limited.

One of the important lessons for policy that these studies offer is that EPZs are unlikely to be potent tools of industrialisation and development in the absence of the requisite ingredients for development in the economies of the countries that establish them. Also, EPZs are unlikely to be successful in the presence of a highly protected sector producing importables in the domestic economy.

Both these propositions are borne out by the empirical studies. In the case of South Korea the economy has benefited from the wage and foreign exchange contribution of the Masan zone. Warr estimates the differential in wage rates between the zone and the domestic economy to be around 10 per cent in favour of the workers in the zone. The expertise and skills gained by Korean nationals employed in the zone have also been a source of gain to the economy. It is also to be noted that most of the exportables produced in this zone are relatively intensive in the use of labour, and the employees in the zone are mostly females. Warr estimates the internal rate of return to

Korean public investments in establishing the zone to be around 14 per cent, a substantially high figure for public projects.

Factors in the key to the success of South Korea's export zone are the resilient and easily trainable labour force Korea possesses, the orientation of the economy towards export-led growth, and the image which Korea has projected of a country sympathetic to private enterprise. South Korea, though, does possess a protected sector manufacturing importables. But the accent of economic policy is on utilising locally produced inputs for the promotion of exports. Moreover, South Korea does not harbour as much FDI as several other South-east Asian countries. It has relied more on technology licensing agreements than FDI for its requirement of foreign technology and know-how. In the absence of incentives to invest in the protected domestic sector of the economy, FDI has been attracted to the labour-intensive export industries in the zone.

The other success stories with EPZs relate to Hong Kong, Singapore and Taiwan. The success of the first two city states with EPZ is of little surprise, as the entire economy in the case of these countries could be regarded as a duty-free zone. In the case of Taiwan, the policy framework has established strong links between the zone and the domestic economy, and Taiwan's relatively liberal foreign trade regime has accounted for the success of its EPZs.

The relative lack of success of EPZs in Indonesia and the Philippines is to be attributed to the presence of various distortions in their domestic economy, including the highly protected sector producing importables. In the case of the Philippines the zone was established with regional development as one of the objectives. Setting up the zone in a relatively underdeveloped part of the country appears to have involved the economy in the expenditure of substantial amounts of scarce public funds. In addition, as Warr notes, foreign firms located on the zone were allowed to raise most of the capital in the Philippines capital market, where interest rates were deliberately held down below the social opportunity cost of capital. Warr estimates that whatever gains the zone conferred on the economy in terms of employment were offset by the heavy subsidies on capital afforded to foreign firms. Added to this were the heavy expenditures incurred in setting up the zone in a depressed region of the country. The lesson to be learned from the Philippines experience is that in the absence of the necessary ingredients of development, EPZs are likely to be a burden rather than an instrument of industrialisation and export promotion. The Philippines had to accord heavy subsidies on capital to foreign firms locating in the zone because of the political instability within the country at the time, the presence of a heavily protected domestic manufacturing sector, and its desire to promote regional development through the establishment of an EPZ.

One other finding of interest in the empirical studies relates to the factor proportions employed by firms located in the EPZs in various countries. In traditionally labour-intensive industries such as garments and electronics, the capital-intensity of firms located in the zones in Malaysia and the Philippines are found to be higher than that not only of comparable industries in Taiwan and South Korea, but also than that of firms located in the domestic economy (Spinnanger, 1984, Sahabdeen, 1985). This relatively high capital-intensity of firms located in the EPZs in Malaysia and the Philippines is attributed to the heavy subsidies on capital the firms enjoy. Such subsidies include not only relatively low rates of interest on domestic capital markets, but also generous depreciation allowances and other fiscal incentives. Such policies are self-defeating in so far as they militate against the objective of employment creation.

CONCLUSION

The theoretical and empirical literature on EPZs provides valuable lessons for policy. First, EPZs could be an adjunct to other instruments of development but cannot be expected to provide the basis for promoting exports and industrialisation. Second, they represent a move towards freer trade rather than free trade. They are, therefore, in the nature of a second-best policy measure, the consequences of which cannot always be expected to be beneficial. Third, the establishment of EPZs in the presence of a heavily protected sector in the economy is likely to impose costs rather than benefits on the economy. Fourth, the liberal incentive packages provided by several developing countries to entice FDI into the EPZs may have proved to be counter-productive. Finally, successive utilisation of EPZs as instruments of industrialisation and export promotion require the availability of the basic ingredients of development in the domestic economy. These include a resilient labour force, infrastructure facilities and ambitious entrepreneurs liberally endowed with animal spirits – an ingredient often dimmed by the protection from international competition afforded by the inward-looking development strategy pursued by several countries.

10 Trade and Aid

PAUL MOSLEY

INTRODUCTION

'Trade not aid', the slogan associated in particular with UNCTAD, is an attractive nostrum. Open up the economies of advanced countries to the free trade with all-comers which their governments preach, runs the underlying rationale, and Third World countries will be able to expand their exports to a point which makes the aid given by those same governments unnecessary. Development can then proceed on a basis of mutual self-respect, rather than on a basis which inflicts economic and technological dependence on Third World countries.

This rationale, however, may be supported by reference to any or all of three premises:

1. Taking into account the direct economic effects only, a dollar of aid is worth less than a dollar of foreign exchange earned by exporting.
2. Taking into account also the indirect effects on the recipient's public sector, on the supply of savings and, through the price mechanism, on the private sector, a dollar of aid is worth less than a dollar of foreign exchange earned by exporting.
3. A dollar of aid is inherently worth less than a dollar of foreign exchange earned by exporting, on account of the condition of economic dependence inescapably inflicted by the overseas aid relationship.

Debate on the relative merits of trade and aid has in the past been clouded by the fact that different protagonists in the debate have adopted different frames of reference, with some taking their stand on propositions (1) and (2), which are in principle capable of empirical refutation, some taking their stand on proposition (3), which is not, and some oscillating between the two modes of debate. In this chapter we shall examine the three approaches to the debate in sequence, although our survey of proposition (3), which does not yield to orthodox economic analysis, will be short. Our conclusion will be that whereas improbable assumptions have to be satisfied for it to be proved that the *direct* effects of a dollar earned by exporting exceed the direct effects of a dollar of aid, this conclusion no longer holds good once

166

one moves on to consider the side-effects of aid and trade gains and any inherent benefits which there may be in self-sufficiency.

DIRECT ECONOMIC EFFECTS

If aid is offered as a pure gift, without strings, it places additional resources for investment directly in the hands of the recipient government, and in so doing saves the recipient economy the excess cost of import substitution, i.e. the cost of making at home the things which aid makes it possible to import. The value of an amount of aid A to the economy is therefore $(1 + c) A$, where c is the excess cost of import substitution.

Exports do not provide additional resources for investment directly; they only do so indirectly, by offering the possibility of transforming domestic resources into goods and services more cheaply than domestic production is able to do – in other words by saving the excess cost of import substitution. The value of an amount X of exports to the economy is therefore cX, and the relative worth of exports by comparison with pure aid can be expressed, as Johnson (1967) has shown, as the ratio of these two values, i.e.

$$\frac{cX}{(1 + c) A} \quad \begin{array}{l} \text{(resources made available by an} \\ \text{amount } X \text{ of exports)} \\ \text{(resources made available by an} \\ \text{amount } A \text{ of pure aid)} \end{array} \qquad (10.1)$$

where X is the value of exports, A is the value of pure aid, and c is the proportional excess cost of import substitution. The relative value of exports will rise with the excess cost of import substitution, but the value of exports can never exceed the value of an equal amount of pure aid, since $c < 1 + c$.

Most aid, of course, is by no means pure. Firstly, a good part of *bilateral* aid is tied to the purchase of goods and services in the donor country, which may substantially exceed the value of those same goods and services on the free market. If r is the ratio of the price of goods supplied under tied aid to the minimum cost at which aid recipients could acquire those same goods on the free market, the relative worth of exports becomes:

$$\frac{cX}{(1 + c) A} \cdot r \qquad (10.2)$$

The value of exports will now exceed the value of aid if $cr > 1 + c$. This will only be true if both c and r are quite high, e.g. $c = 2$ and $r = 1\frac{1}{2}$. Secondly, however, much aid is not given on pure grant terms, but as a soft loan below the market rate, or as a mixture of grant and commercial loan. If F is the nominal amount of foreign assistance, g is the aid component as a proportion of nominal assistance, then A, the pure aid component of assistance, is equal to Fg. Then, as Thirlwall (1976) first demonstrated, substituting Fg for A in equation (10.2) will give the relative value of exports compared to the aid component of an equal amount of foreign assistance as:

$$\frac{cX}{(1 + c)\ Fg} \cdot r \qquad\qquad (10.3)$$

From (10.3) the value of exports will exceed the value of the aid component of an equal amount of foreign assistance if $cr > g\ (1 + c)$. The relative worth of exports is greater, the higher the excess cost of import substitution, the higher the excess cost of tied aid, and the lower the aid component of assistance. It is still the case, however, that c and r would have to be quite high and g relatively low for the worth of exports to exceed the worth of the aid component of an equal amount of foreign assistance. This is shown in Figure 10.1, which gives the approximate combinations of g and r for given values of c which would equate the worth of exports with an equal amount of assistance. For any combination of g and r above the 'boundary' lines, exports are more valuable. For example, suppose the excess cost of import substitution was 50 per cent ($c = 0.5$), and there was no aid-tying (or there was no excess cost attached to tied aid) so that $r = 1.0$, then exports would be worth more than the aid component of an equal amount of foreign assistance if the ratio of aid to assistance fell below 0.3. If the aid ratio exceeded 0.3, then exports would be worth less. If there was aid-tying which raised the cost of tied goods by 30 per cent above the free market price ($r = 1.3$), the aid ratio would have to be 0.4 for exports and the aid component of an equal amount of foreign assistance would have to be of equal worth.

INDIRECT ECONOMIC EFFECTS

The discussion so far has proceeded on the assumption that our measures of the direct economic gain from exports, cX, and the direct economic gain from aid, $\frac{1}{r}\ (1 + c)\ Fg$, are all that matters. Certainly both types of injections have side-effects which ramify deeply into the recipient economy, in particular:
1. their influence on the propensity to save, and thence on the growth rate, of the recipient country;
2. their influence on relative prices within the economy, and possibly also on the exchange rate of the recipient;
3. their influence on public sector spending patterns.

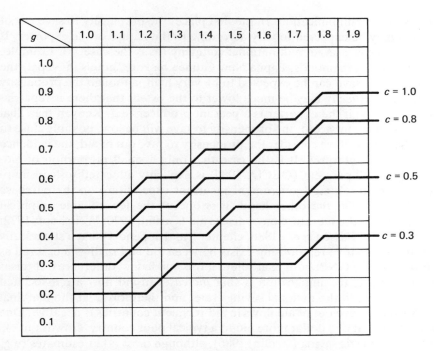

Note: Exports are worth less for given combinations of r and g above the 'boundary' lines, and more below the lines.
Source: Thirlwall (1976).

Figure 10.1 **Approximate combinations of *r* and *g* for given *c*, which will make exports worth more/less than the aid component of an equal amount of foreign assistance**

However, to draw attention to the existence of these side-effects is only relevant to the *comparison* between trade and aid if there is reason to believe that the nature of these side-effects will differ as between the two types of flow. Unfortunately there is. We consider the three categories of side-effects in sequence.

Savings

Thirlwall has written;

From the studies of Maizels [1968] and Lee [1971] the propensity to save out of exports would appear to be of the order of 0.6. On this basis, 40 per cent of foreign assistance would have to be 'consumed' for foreign assistance not to contribute as much to savings as exports. If anything, therefore, the economic secondary repercussions of exports and assistance favour assistance. (Thirlwall, 1976, p. 40)

This is an oversimplification. In the first place, the propensity to save out of exports may be expected to vary according to the nature of the exporter. If the exporter is a large multinational company (as is the case, for example, with Botswana diamonds, Papua New Guinea bauxite, hotels in Nepal) the propensity to save can be expected to be very high, although the propensity to save *domestically* may be much lower to the extent that there is repatriation of profits; if the exporter is a peasant producer (e.g. Kenyan tea, Thai rice, Malawian tobacco), the propensity to save will be low, possibly close to zero. Secondly, if we consider the propensity to save out of aid, the evidence is difficult to interpret. It is the case that only a small proportion of aid, possibly 20–30 per cent (OECD, 1986) is explicitly allocated to 'consumption expenditure', e.g. government recurrent expenditure on the purchase of foodstuffs. On the other hand, it is one of the few reliable empirical regularities of the literature on overseas aid (Griffin, 1970; Weisskopf, 1972; Mosley, 1980; Cassen *et al.*, 1986, chapter 2 and appendix) that a statistically significant negative relationship exists between aid and savings measured as a proportion of GNP, both in absolute terms and in first differences. If this is taken literally, the implication is that *increases* in aid flow are associated with *decreases* in the national savings rate, and therefore that the marginal propensity to save out of aid flows in aid-recipient countries is negative. One estimate is that one dollar more aid to a typical poor country 'crowds out' 48 cents of domestic saving (Griffin, 1986), although most other estimates (e.g. Mosley, 1980) are lower. The reasons for this negative correlation are much disputed, and it has been persuasively argued (see, for example, Papanek, 1973 and Cassen *et al.*, 1986) that the causation may run from economic crises in recipient countries to both high levels of aid and low levels of savings, rather than directly from aid to savings. But the mere existence of the correlation prohibits us from supporting aid inflows in preference to trade flows on the grounds that they promote a higher re-investable surplus.

Influence on relative prices

An injection of either aid or export finance naturally has effects on the prices of inputs and outputs throughout the recipient economy. In the case of aid the immediate effect is normally to lower the price of specific tradeable goods, for example fertilisers, food or industrial equipment. However, this fall in the price of tradeables may have undesirable knock-on effects: for example, inflows of food aid will reduce the price of food on the home market, and this in turn will depress the incentive to farmers in the recipient country to produce food which is in competition with foodstuffs being imported on concessionary terms. Aid may also provoke increases in the price of non-tradeables: for example, a large rural development project in a remote area, as is being seen in the Sudan at present, will push up the price of inputs such as cement, skilled labour and lorry transport, certainly in the locality of the project and possibly throughout the economy. Finally, large aid inflows may buoy up the exchange rate and, to the extent that this occurs, make exports less competitive. This special case of the 'Dutch disease' has recently been analysed by Van Wijnbergen (1985).

An inflow of export revenue has less complex, but potentially equally drastic, side-effects on the price system. An exhaustively documented case of such side-effects is the so-called 'Dutch disease' (Corden and Neary, 1982; Van Wijnbergen, 1984, in which discoveries in the natural resource sector provoke speculative upward pressure on the exchange rate which take it to a level far in excess of that which would be justified by existing levels of exports; this overvalued exchange rate then inflicts lasting damage on other exporting sectors, in particular manufacturing, where, the argument runs, the price elasticity of demand is likely to be greater than in the case of natural resource exports. This argument has obvious relevance, not only to oil-exporting less developed countries such as Indonesia and Ecuador, but also to others with a large, recently discovered mineral base such as Botswana and Papua New Guinea. Clearly, in the case of both aid and export inflows the likelihood of speculative 'Dutch disease' effects increases with the size of such inflows in relation to the size of the recipient economy. It is a classical 'small open economy' problem.

Impact on public spending patterns

This is the area in which the indirect impacts of trade and aid are likely to diverge most dramatically, for the benefits from export growth, in the normal case, will accrue to the *private* sector of the recipient economy, and the knock-on effect on public sector spending patterns is likely to be minor. Aid inflows, by contrast, go overwhelmingly to the *public* sector of the recipient country, and to the extent that what they finance is already budgeted for by the recipient government, may be switched into other uses. An aid inflow which finances a dam project, for example, can be used, to the extent that the dam project was already covered by domestic sources of finance, for further productive investment, for unproductive public investment such as sports stadiums and presidential palaces, for public consumption expenditure such as raising the wages of the army, or for reductions in public borrowing or taxation. Aid money, therefore, is potentially fungible into other uses, and ultimately finances only the marginal project. To the extent that a particular inflow leads to a fall in the average rate of return on capital by this route, it is possible to say that aid has had negative side-effects on the economy through its impact on the allocation of resources in the public sector. It must, however, be stressed that switching from productive to unproductive uses of aid money within the public sector, contrary to the speculations of, for example, Bauer (1981) and Griffin (1970), is by no means a necessary consequence of aid flows. Everything depends on the preferences of the recipient government between 'consumption' and 'investment' expenditures, and on the way in which aid flows impinge on those preferences.

If we now attempt to incorporate discussion of the side-effects of foreign inflows into the formal analysis of the previous section, we must first of all acknowledge that the side-effects of aid and exports on relative prices and spending patterns in the recipient economy materialise over a period of years (say n) and not at a point in time. Let us denote the propensity to save out of exports by s_1 and out of aid by s_2; the value of indirect effects of exports on the price system of the recipient economy by p_1, and the value of indirect effects of aid by p_2; and the impact of aid, if any, on the productivity of capital within the public sector of the recipient economy by π_2. With this notation, the formula for the relative worth of an amount of exports X and an amount of aid $A = Fg$ becomes:

$$\frac{\sum_{i=1}^{n} \{(rc\ X)\ s_1 + p_1\}}{\sum_{i=1}^{n} \{[(1+c)\ Fg]\ s_2 + p_2 + \pi_2\}} \tag{10.4}$$

By way of conclusion to this section let us consider the implications of attaching plausible values to the parameters of equation (10.4). If the excess cost of tying r is set at 50 per cent (Thirlwall, 1976), the aid component g of loans from the Development Assistance Committee of the OECD at 60 per cent (OECD, 1986) and the excess cost of import substitution c at 50 per cent (Little, Scitovsky and Scott, 1970), then even if the propensity to save out of aid turns out to equal the propensity to save out of exports at 0.6, which is probably charitable to aid, all that is needed for the effects of an export inflow X to match the effects of an aid inflow Fg of equivalent dollar value is that the combined side-effects of aid on the public and private sectors, $p_2 + \pi_2$, averaged over the period of analysis, exceed the side-effects of exports on the recipient private sector, p_1, by 0.39 per cent of the nominal dollar inflow. As yet, the available methodology for estimating side-effects such as p_1, p_2 and δ_2 is primitive. But it is certainly no longer possible, once side-effects are taken into account, to support Thirlwall's contention that aid is likely to be superior to exports on any plausible parameter values. Recent quantitative analysis of the macro-effects of aid (for example, Cassen *et al.*, 1986, appendix to chapter 2; Mosley, Hudson and Horrell, 1987) suggests that aid inflows, in spite of having high *ex post* rates of return, have a negligible macro-impact on the growth of GNP worldwide. If these results are reliable, then the side-effects of aid, i.e. macro-effects which are not picked up by project rates of return, must be large indeed, and the case for aid rather than export gains of equivalent value is *pro tanto* weakened.

'Intrinsic worth of self-sufficiency'

The analysis so far has proceeded on the assumption that self-sufficiency has no intrinsic value, and that a dollar received as a direct or indirect consequence of aid has equivalent value to a dollar received as a direct or indirect consequence of exporting. This may be plausible in terms of standard accounting conventions, but less so in terms of psychology: many of us would value a dollar earned from gainful employment more highly than the same dollar handed over as a gift, and by the same token the governments of recipient nations may consider that the intrinsic value of a dollar earned from exporting is greater than the intrinsic worth of a dollar transferred as aid. If the recipient attaches a weight w ($w \neq 1$) to the value of a dollar earned by exporting in relation to the value of a dollar earned as overseas aid, then (10.4) becomes:

$$\frac{\sum_{i=1}^{n} \{(r \, c \, w \, X) \, s_1 + p_1\}}{\sum_{i=1}^{n} \{[(1 + c) \, Fg] \, s_2 + p_2 + \pi_2\}} \tag{10.5}$$

and in proportion as w exceeds 1, the value of aid in relation to trade for that recipient government is diminished.

CONCLUSION

It will be apparent from the above discussion that an evaluation of the relative merits of expanding export earnings and aid inflows, even assuming these to be realistic alternatives for each developing country, is no straightforward matter. If only the direct economic effects of trade and aid are taken into account, then it is indeed true, as Thirlwall and others have shown, that 'gains from aid' outclass trade gains of equivalent value on any plausible estimate of the excess costs of tying and import substitution. Unfortunately from the point of view of a clean and simple assessment, however, the indirect effects of exports, and even more of aid, are likely to ramify very deeply into a recipient country's economy, which restricts the value of comparisons which limit themselves to the direct effects. Beyond this, it is the case that considerations of national pride and self-sufficiency, which may have small or zero value in the calculations of analytical economists, may bulk very large in the political decision-making process of less developed countries, and hence in any assessment which ministers of finance in those countries make. And it is only for those people, of course, that the assessment of the relative merits of trade and aid is something more than a matter of academic discussion.

11 Revenue Implications of Trade Taxes

G. K. SHAW

INTRODUCTION

Trade taxes, by which we mean taxes levied both upon imports and exports, and also the profits of import and export marketing boards, form an important source of revenue for many of the less advanced economies. Moreover, they appear to be relatively more important in the structure of government receipts, in those countries with lower per capita income on the one hand, and in those countries with lower ratios of fiscal receipts to GDP on the other. There is a clear negative relationship between the importance of trade taxes as a percentage of all government revenues and the level of economic development where the latter is proxied by estimates of per capita income (Hitiris and Weekes, 1986). Moreover, for many less advanced economies in the early stages of development, the degree of openness of the economy (where openness may be defined as exports plus imports as a percentage of GDP) serves as a much superior indicator of taxable capacity than per capita income (Hinrichs, 1965). The salient facts are summarised with the aid of Table 11.1. Compare also Lewis (1963) and Greenaway (1980, 1984).

This chapter attempts first to explain the reasons for these stylised facts, and second to examine some of the consequences and implications of this dependency upon trade taxes. Reliance upon trade taxes as a means of generating fiscal revenues is very much a second-best solution reflecting the immense difficulties of raising revenues from alternative and generally preferred sources of finance. Trade taxes as a primary source of finance typically decline in importance as development proceeds and per capita income rises, and improved administration permits the adoption and extension of other forms of taxation. Nonetheless, during the period that trade taxes are in the ascendancy, they can exert extremely important impacts upon resource allocation, income distribution and attitudes to fiscal compliance.

TABLE 11.1 Trade taxes, openness and income per capita

Country	TT	XM	GNP
Gambia	62.56[d]	91.7	378
Yemen	60.51	50.8	442
Swaziland	59.44	127.5	903
Rwanda	53.52	28.0	233
Chad	52.43[d]	56.4	125
Sierra Leone	47.80	52.3	320
Sri Lanka	46.22	40.5	269
Mauritius	44.76	93.2	116
Sudan	44.60	28.2	436
Ethiopia	40.54[d]	21.5	132
Honduras	40.22	73.0	649
El Salvador	39.63	64.1	791
Ghana	38.28	30.4	389
Botswana	35.79	109.0	848
Zaire	35.10	43.3	194
Dominican Republic	34.76	42.5	1 236
Liberia	33.71	129.4	530
Pakistan	33.46	27.3	327
Bolivia	33.42	40.3	630
Fiji	27.61	66.5	1 856
Peru	26.94	29.1	1 192
Tunisia	25.20	54.3	1 210
Philippines	24.58	37.5	733
Thailand	24.03	40.4	686
Paraguay	23.02	25.7	1 333
Gabon	22.95[d]	128.1	4 919
Costa Rica	22.20	60.9	1 438
Kenya	21.13	51.6	365
Cyprus	21.10	78.4	3 164
Colombia	21.02	22.1	1 329
Nicaragua	20.01	59.5	1 010
India	19.85	12.0	204
Barbados	19.84	79.5	2 800
Morocco	19.46	125.8	787
Mexico	19.34	10.8	2 016
Tanzania	18.31	42.0	284
Nigeria	17.38[d]	85.2	842
Malawi	15.89	53.1	203
Korea	15.47	59.7	1 544
Burma	15.46	11.0	158
Syria	14.43	45.3	1 419
Ireland	13.22	85.7	4 931
Turkey	11.84	16.3	1 273
Uruguay	11.02	32.9	2 640
Spain	8.50	20.9	5 043
Indonesia	8.32	43.5	490
Zambia	7.42	90.0	614
Venezuela	7.21	54.3	3 365

continued on p. 176

Table 11.1 continued

Country	TT	XM	GNP
Singapore	6.89	272.8	4 064
Canada	6.75	43.5	11 017
Israel	5.99	68.0	5 140
Chile	5.52	24.5	2 266
Australia	5.43	27.5	10 600
South Africa	5.28	44.1	2 474
Greece	4.81	36.2	4 031
Brazil	4.15	15.7	2 144
New Zealand	3.40	42.0	7 313
Austria	1.76	48.3	8 849
Finland	1.70	48.6	9 496
USA	1.54	14.7	12 451
Sweden	1.15	45.0	13 132
Denmark	0.95	51.0	11 415
Norway	0.80	59.7	12 835
Italy	0.30	41.9	6 250
United Kingdom	0.17	46.1	8 954
France	0.04	32.5	10 684
Belgium	0.02	99.5	9 994
Germany	0.02	41.4	11 398
Netherlands	0.01	84.6	10 508
World	4.98		2 481
Industrial countries	1.61		10 201
Non-oil developing countries	16.96		593
Asia	21.61		300
Africa[d]	23.56		625

[a] Trade taxes as a percentage of total government revenues – average of seven-year period 1976–82; compiled from *Government Finance Statistics Yearbook*, IMF, 1984, pp. 42–3.
[b] Exports plus imports as a percentage of GDP culled from Greenaway (1984) and Hitiris and Weekes (1986).
[c] GNP per capita of mid-year population in $ US 1980 market prices: average of seven-year period 1976–82; Compiled from *International Financial Statistics, Supplement No. 8*, IMF, 1984.
[d] Data incomplete for seven-year period.

REASONS FOR TRADE TAXES

Conventional economic theory would conclude that trade taxes are very much an inferior form of tax to alternatives (on *ceteris paribus* assumptions) since they impose excess burdens by distorting comparative internal and external prices, thus promoting production effects in addition to consumption effects. This conclusion may be questioned under conditions where trade taxes are resorted to in order to effect an improvement in the terms of trade confronting a country, and the literature on the 'optimal tariff' under such conditions is now well known. However, for the most part, trade taxes tend to dominate in those economies with the least ability to influence world prices; in many cases it is the small African country with no ability to influence either the price it pays for its importables or the prices it receives for its exports where trade taxes dominate. Why, then, if this is the case, do trade taxes so dominate?

The explanation lies in the difficulty and cost of levying alternative taxes upon the domestic economy. Thus, for example, income taxes are extremely limited in economies where incomes cannot be readily assessed or where income in kind often dominates. Resorting to presumptive income taxes tends to generate inflexible revenues as they are invariably imposed at the lowest rate – that which the marginal taxpayer can bear – and may paradoxically serve to impede the growth of income taxes at a later stage of development. The existence of substantial subsistence or non-monetarised sectors limits the ability to adopt general sales taxes. Company taxation may be curtailed by the decision to grant tax holidays to foreign investors, and even when these privileges have expired the foreign multinational may exercise considerable discretion over the actual amount of tax it pays.[1] In like manner, it may be impossible to tax foreign contractors engaged in aid projects financed by donor countries or international agencies.[2] The inability to impose general forms of taxation tends to stimulate the search for specific taxes upon certain activities, whether production or consumption activities. Thus we encounter taxes in the form of licence fees, upon producer activities (birds' nest tax, for example) or bicycle taxes, radio taxes and similar nuisance taxes. Such taxes of necessity are specific and suffer the drawback of declining real yields in conditions of inflation. Moreover, they are difficult to administer and costly to collect, and in some cases it is probable that their yields are highly interdependent.

High cost–yield ratios are a feature of many taxes in less advanced economies. This results from tax evasion on the one hand, which reduces yields well below potential, and administrative difficulties on the other, which generate high collection costs. In many cases, the virtual impossibility of correctly determining incomes and turnover reduces the tax assessment/collection process to a bargaining situation between potential taxpayer and tax official. The scope for collusion between the two is not inconsiderable, especially when the activities of assessor and collector are undertaken by the same individual, and in this situation it becomes imperative to provide incentives in the interest of promoting revenues. In certain developing countries incentive payments equal to 10 per cent of the revenue yield characterise a wide range of taxes where audit capacity is lacking and where the tax levy depends upon information not readily available to the tax official.[3]

In view of these difficulties, the appeal of trade taxes must appear irresistible. Both import duties and export taxes are levied upon a comparatively few taxpayers (in reality fiscal agents of government, since the duties will be passed either forwards to consumers or backwards to producers) who can be controlled relatively easily by the granting of import/export licences and by the medium of foreign exchange controls. Import values and the world prices of primary exports are readily available, and duties can be levied on an *ad valorem* basis, thus overcoming problems arising from inflation. Since the effective assessment and collection of revenue duties is concentrated in a few key locations of entry and exit, the demand on administrative resources is minimised. Finally, the process of economic growth generates an automatic raising of revenues – in particular, with respect to import tariffs, rising internal demand leads to a raising of tariff revenue with no change in domestic prices (see Greenaway, 1981).

As a corollary of the above, there is an inherent tendency for the fiscal importance of trade taxes to decline progressively with economic development. Numerous explanations are offered to account for this universal phenomenon (Musgrave, 1969; Corden, 1974). First and foremost, in the course of development and in particular with the promotion of import-substitution activities, the purpose of trade taxes alters from that of raising revenue to providing the requisite degree of protection for small-scale infant industries. In some cases, tariffs will be superseded by strict quotas or even outright prohibition. In a similar vein, economic development is accompanied by a tendency for importables to become capital and intermediate inputs as opposed to final finished products. It then becomes desirable to reduce the average rate of tariff to provide incentives to domestic production[4] and also to reduce the distortion effects of taxes '*a la* cascade'. Also in the wake of economic development, the gradual raising of incomes and the adoption of commercial practices serve to reduce the collection costs associated with non-trade tax revenues. This leads to the general conclusion that there is a 'threshold level of economic development, proxied by a certain level of income per head, below which trade taxes are fiscally important and above which they are not' (Hitiris and Weekes, 1986).

The concern in the present chapter is with trade taxes as an important revenue device. The question which we raise is whether we can reach any conclusion about the most appropriate rate of tariff duty to aid the revenue-raising process. As we shall see, the issue is decidedly more complex than might appear at first sight; when dynamic considerations are taken into account, the interdependence between trade and non-trade taxes becomes of paramount importance.

THE OPTIMAL RATE OF REVENUE TARIFF

It is perhaps as well to begin by reviewing the standard theoretical argument concerning the welfare implications of tariffs. Stated simply, tariffs restrict imports, thus contradicting the doctrine of comparative advantage, and in so doing they reduce the international division of labour and sacrifice world output. The real income of the world economy is reduced, and this includes, *ceteris paribus*, the income of the country imposing the tariff barriers. There is, however, one very important exception to this general proposition. In the case of a country which is large enough in its involvement in international trade to be able to influence world prices, the adoption of tariffs may lead to an improvement in its terms of trade. Assuming the absence of retaliation, it is then possible for a country's *real* income to increase and more than compensate for the distortion costs involved in the tariff imposition. If this is the case, there will be one unique rate of tariff consistent with maximising national income, which is determined solely by the foreign elasticity of demand for importables. More formally, the rate of tariff consistent with maximising national income is given by

$$t = \frac{1}{ef-1} \tag{11.1}$$

where *ef* indicates the foreigners' elasticity of demand for importables.[5] A rate of tariff in excess or below this rate implies a level of national income below that theoretically attainable.

The corollary of this argument is that where a country is unable to influence world prices, which is the case for most small developing economies, then the rate of tariff consistent with maximising national income is zero. Since a zero rate of tariff duty is consistent with zero tariff revenue, it follows that the rate of tariff which maximises revenue must exceed that which maximises national income. Indeed, this is a perfectly general proposition, even in cases where the country can influence world prices. In short, the revenue-maximising rate of tariff must exceed the optimum tariff which maximises national income. This is the situation we illustrate in Figure 11.1. The tariff revenue curve is drawn on the assumption that at a zero tariff rate, tariff revenue will be zero, and likewise that at the prohibitive rate of duty t_1, when all imports cease, revenue is again zero. Accordingly, t_2 is the tariff rate which maximises tariff revenue, whereas t_0 is the rate consistent with

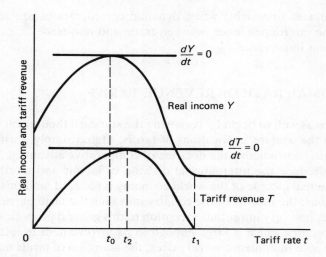

Figure 11.1   Maximising tariff revenue and maximising real income

maximising real income. It may also be noted that the level of real income at the prohibitive tariff rate t_1 falls below that at the zero tariff rate. This is because even with zero imports, there are nonetheless distortion costs in production generated by the prohibitive tariff. This point is important for our subsequent analysis. For a formal proof of this proposition see, for example, Caves and Jones (1977, p. 444f.) The implication of this analysis is clear. Tariffs adopted purely for revenue purposes are in conflict with optimal strategy in terms of maximising national income and economic welfare. Such rates of duty must then be regarded as a second-best situation arising from the need for revenue on the one hand, and the difficulties of generating non-trade revenue on the other. This is the accepted conventional wisdom in international trade theory to which we will return.

TWO CAVEATS TO THE CONVENTIONAL WISDOM

Tariff revenues for investment

The preceding analysis rests on the proposition that the government transfers the revenues so obtained to the public at large either in the form of cash transfers or as payments and services provided in kind. Such an assumption has the virtue of greatly simplifying the analysis, but it is clearly untenable as a description of reality. It is precisely because of the difficulties involved in generating revenues that the government is forced to rely upon trade taxes, and it is hardly likely to dissipate the proceeds so obtained in such a cavalier manner. Once this fact is admitted, two implications follow. First, where the revenues are utilised to finance investment projects, attention may be given to the discounted values of the returns stemming from such investment. In this case our concern would be not with the rate of tariff duty which maximises tariff revenue, but rather with that rate of duty which will maximise the net present value of the income generated by the investment resulting from the tariff revenue. This is the question posed by Vanek (1971), and his general conclusion is that the optimum tariff rate will fall below, although not significantly below, the rate which will maximise tariff revenue.

Revenue interdependency

The second qualification turns on the fiscal interdependency of trade and non-trade taxes. If the proceeds of tariffs are not returned to the public at large, then clearly private sector disposable income is reduced. It follows, *ceteris paribus*, that sales tax revenues and arguably other tax revenues will fall in consequence. In other words, the rate of tariff duty which is consistent with maximising tariff revenue need not be consistent with maximising total government revenues as a whole. Clearly, it is the latter issue which is the relevant one for the less advanced economy. The question of fiscal inter-dependency is an obvious one, but one which is commonly ignored, particularly in discussions comparing the differential effects of different types of taxes. The traditional appraisal of competing tax regimes has always been made under the assumption of equal yield; that is to say, the comparison of an income tax *vis-à-vis* a sales tax has always been undertaken on the assumption that one is comparing an income tax which generates revenue of X with a sales tax which also yields precisely the same amount (Musgrave and Musgrave, 1976). In a multi-tax world this is at best a dubious exercise. The effect of a given change in the sales tax will depend upon the prevailing rate of income taxation; conversely, the effect of a given change in the income tax will depend upon the sales tax rate (Peston, 1971).

Precisely the same argument applies to the interdependency between trade and non-trade taxes. Trade taxes will deplete non-trade tax revenues, and vice versa. Moreover, the existence of trade taxes may serve to inhibit the development of non-trade taxes over time. To consider initially the comparative statics of the argument, consider Figure 11.2, which illustrates the yield of both trade taxes *and* non-trade taxes as a function of the tariff rate.[6] Clearly, assuming the existence of non-trade taxes, there will no longer be any *unique* rate of tariff duty which will maximise the trade tax yield. This follows because now the trade tax yield will itself be dependent upon the *strictness* of the non-trade tax regime. In Figure 11.2, we illustrate three distinct non-trade tax regimes. In the strictest regime, regime 1, tariff revenue peaks with the tariff rate t_1; in the most lenient regime, regime 3,

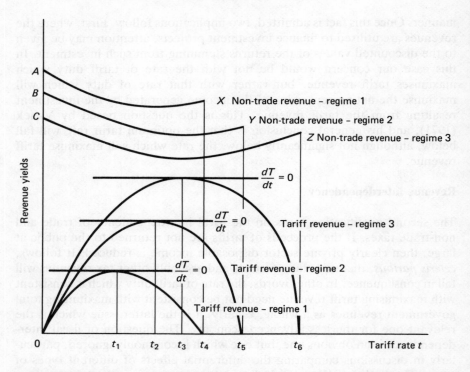

Figure 11.2 Tariff revenue yields and non-trade tax yields as a function of tariff rates

tariff revenue peaks at the tariff rate t_3. Regime 2 provides the intermediate case, with tariff rate t_2 maximising the trade tax yield. In principle, there is an infinite number of tariff rates consistent with maximising the trade tax yield, depending upon the nature of the non-trade tax regime. *A priori*, do we have any means of choosing between them, assuming our objective is to maximise total government revenue?

To deal with this issue we need to consider how non-trade tax revenue responds to the rate of tariff duty. Clearly, the most favourable rate of tariff duty for non-trade tax revenues is a zero rate. Points A, B and C indicate the maximum non-trade revenue positions corresponding to the strictness of the fiscal regime; point A corresponds to fiscal regime 1 with a zero tariff rate, B to the intermediate regime at a zero tariff rate, and so forth. Regardless of the regime, non-trade taxes will begin to decline with the imposition of a positive tariff rate as the tariff rate depletes private sector disposable income. The decline will continue until that rate of tariff is attained which maximises tariff revenue for the regime in question. Thereafter, further increases in the rate of tariff duty will deplete tariff revenues, and non-trade taxes may start to increase in consequence. Ultimately, a rate of duty will be attained which becomes prohibitive and chokes off all imports so that tariff revenues again become zero. However, it is important to appreciate that in such a situation, with a prohibitive rate of duty and zero tariff revenues, non-trade taxes will not regain their maximum. This follows from the distortion costs implicit in the prohibitive rate of tariff duty on the production side of the economy. National income is lower with a prohibitive rate of tariff duty than with a zero rate on account of these costs. Thus, for example, to consider fiscal regime 1, point X, corresponding to the prohibitive rate of tariff duty t_4, falls below point A, while equally for fiscal regime 3, point Z, corresponding to the prohibitive rate of tariff duty, t_6, falls below point C.

The foregoing analysis can be summarised very simply: a partial equilibrium approach is unsatisfactory as a means of answering questions in general equilibrium theory. For a government seeking revenue maximisation, the optimal rate of tariff and the non-trade tax regime must be determined together. However, from all practical policy considerations, the existing fiscal regime may be considered as a datum. This permits us to concentrate on just one tariff revenue possibility curve, but it does not allow us to ignore the fact of fiscal interdependency. What can we say about the optimal rate of tariff in these circumstances? First and foremost, it is clear that we would no longer be indifferent between two rates of tariff duty which yielded the same tariff revenue. In Figure 11.3, for example, the same tariff revenue is obtained by tariff rates t_1 and t_2, but t_1 must be judged superior, since regardless of the fiscal regime it is consistent with higher non-trade tax revenues.

Secondly, for any given regime, the optimum rate of tariff which will maximise total government revenues must fall below that consistent with the maximisation of tariff revenue alone. This may be demonstrated quite simply in the following way. Total government revenues R are equal to trade tax revenues T plus non-trade tax revenues N. Thus the total change in government revenues arising from a change in the rate of tariff is given by;

$$\frac{dR}{dt} = \frac{dT}{dt} + \frac{dN}{dt} \qquad (11.2)$$

where t is the rate of tariff duty. First-order conditions for a maximum require $\frac{dR}{dt}$ to equal 0, which implies that $\frac{dT}{dt} = -\frac{dN}{dt}$. Since, under present assumptions, the non-trade tax revenue curve must have a negative slope, at least until the tariff revenue maximising rate of duty is attained, then clearly this equation implies that total government revenues will be maximised at a rate of tariff duty which falls upon the positive portion of the tariff revenue curve. This situation we portray with the aid of Figure 11.4, where tariff rate

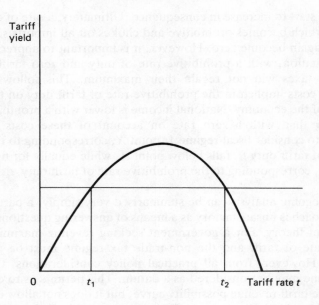

Figure 11.3 Tariff rates with equal yields

t_1 maximises total revenues and falls below t_2, which maximises tariff revenue.

Finally, once fiscal interdependency is allowed for, there is no guarantee that the tariff revenue rate will change in line with the needs of total revenue as non-trade taxes evolve over time. This is especially the case when we distinguish between nominal and effective rates of duty, to which we now turn.

PRACTICAL POLICY CONSIDERATIONS

The foregoing has dealt with the theoretical issues concerning optimal rates of tariff duty consistent with maximising government revenue. However, knowledge of the theoretical rate may be irrelevant for all practical policy purposes if it falls outside the range which is both politically and administratively feasible. The political difficulties of unduly high tariff rates, particularly on finished consumer goods, are obvious enough and may limit the room for manoeuvre of democratically elected governments. The administrative difficulties are, however, arguably more serious, particularly when high rates of duty induce evasion and smuggling activities.

Theoretical work on optimal revenue tariffs has suggested the necessity of rates in excess of 200 per cent (see Greenaway, 1982), and certain countries

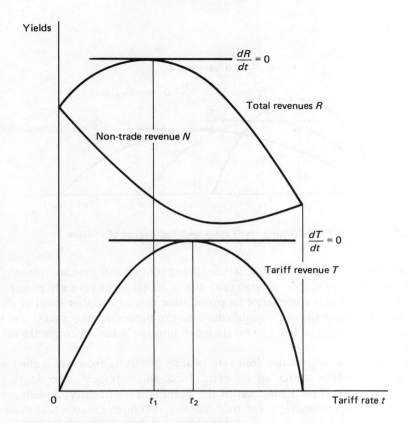

Figure 11.4 The maximisation of total revenue

have adopted nominal rates well in excess of this for certain products. Even casual empirical observation, however, readily confirms that in practice such rates are hardly ever effective because of the profitability of smuggling. Most smuggling, it may be noted, is generally via 'official' channels, often with the connivance of custom officers and officials. Thus, for example, items may be deliberately underinvoiced or falsely described; crates of Scotch whisky carrying a 600 per cent nominal tariff may be described as 'nuts and bolts' and subject to a 2 per cent levy.[7]

Now in principle, of course, this modification does not materially affect the preceding argument. All that it does is to alter the position and slope of the tariff revenue possibility curve. That is to say, we may distinguish between what the tariff revenue would have been in the absence of evasion, namely the nominal tariff revenue possibility curve, and what it is in fact – the effective tariff revenue possibility curve. Clearly, the nominal rate of tariff which will maximise tariff revenues in the light of evasion must be

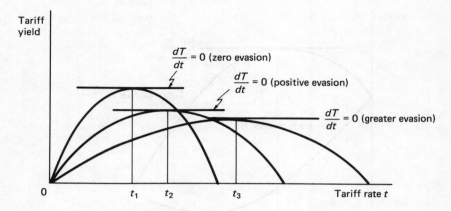

Figure 11.5   Yield-maximising tariff rates and the degree of evasion

higher than that in its absence, since the effective tariff revenue possibility curve will be less steeply sloped than the nominal tariff revenue possibility curve, and will also experience its prohibitive rate at a higher level of duty. Essentially, this is the only modification to the preceding argument, and the same qualifications as before pertain when non-trade tax revenues are taken into account.

However, the higher nominal rate of duty resulting from smuggling and evasion is itself a source of concern. First and foremost, the degree of evasion may itself be a function of the nominal rate of duty, and thus the need for higher nominal rates to maximise revenues creates a climate of evasion. When nominal rates of duty become absurdly high, then evasion becomes almost a socially acceptable form of behaviour, generating greater evasion which then necessitates even higher nominal rates. We illustrate this situation with the aid of Figure 11.5. There t_1 is the optimal rate of duty which would maximise tariff revenue in the absence of evasion, whereas t_2 is the revenue-maximising rate once we posit evasion. If the existence of the higher nominal rate t_2 is conducive to further evasion, then the effective tariff possibility curve is progressively moved outwards, and t_3 becomes the revenue-maximising rate of tariff.

Secondly, the existence of extremely high nominal rates generates a climate of uncertainty because one can never be fully sure that the legally endorsed nominal rate will not be applied on any particular occasion. What this means, of course, is that the effective rate of duty is not known with any degree of precision.

Moreover, it implies, *inter alia*, that the normal conventions of equity are being flouted because now the effective rate of tariff imposition will contain an element of chance or will be related to the ease or difficulty involved with the 'smuggling' of any particular commodity and not with the income of the trader *per se*. When the avoidance or evasion of the nominal tariff revenues becomes a commonplace, it is non-conducive to the development of attitudes of fiscal compliance towards other forms of taxation. Arguably, an excessive dependency on overly high nominal rates of duty serves to impede the development of a tax-paying consciousness in the population at large.

CONCLUSION

This chapter has focused on the role of trade taxes as a means of generating revenues for the government. It is clear that such taxes are essentially of the nature of a necessary evil in the face of the difficulties in generating alternative non-trade tax revenues, and experience indicates that such taxes decline in relative importance as development proceeds. However, in the early stages of development such is the reliance placed upon trade taxes that it becomes relatively easy to pursue the goal of maximising tariff revenues regardless of the costs imposed on other sectors of the economy. This is particularly the case when the officials charged with levying such duties are judged solely in the light of their own performance, with interdependencies ignored. In contrast, the viewpoint adopted here is that the revenue-maximising rate of trade taxes will generally exceed that which is optimal, not only because of the distortion costs involved but also because it serves to deplete non-trade tax revenues and generate attitudes which are non-conducive to fiscal compliance.

End-Notes

CHAPTER 2

* The author acknowledges the helpful comments of Helmut Forstner and Tracy Murray, but is himself responsible for any errors and omissions. The views expressed in this article are personal and not necessarily those of UNIDO.

CHAPTER 3

* This chapter is a slightly revised version of Chapters 2 and 3 of Thames Essay No. 47, *Myth and Reality of External Constraints on Development*, by James Reidel, published by the Trade Policy Research Centre, London. It also contains material published in 'Trade as an Engine of Growth in Developing Countries, Revisited', *Economic Journal*, March, 1984, pp. 56–73. Thanks are due to Cambridge University Press and the Trade Policy Research Centre for permission to republish in this volume.

1. The opening of an economy to trade leads to changes in relative prices and shifts in the distribution of income, both of which may also affect growth. A detailed analysis of the effects on growth of efficiency gains and resulting shifts in relative prices and income distribution is contained in Corden (1971).
2. For reference to, and a critique of, the Nurkse–Prebisch–Myrdal thesis, see Irving B. Kravis (1970).
3. This model, which is characteristic of the traditional colonial economy, is described and analysed empirically in Thomas Birnberg and Stephen Resnick (1975).
4. A typical expression of the view that exports of developing countries in general are tied to growth in developed countries is contained in the *World Development Report* produced by the World Bank in 1978: 'Since the industrial countries' demand for imports depends on their income, their growth is very important to the export prospects of developing countries' (p. 13).
5. The failure to take account of the 'price factor' in explaining increased substitution for exports of primary commodities from developing countries was one of several telling criticisms of Professor Nurkse's thesis detailed by Cairncross (1960).
6. As Ian Little notes in his *Economic Development: Theory, Policy and International Relations* (New York: Basic Books, 1982), trade between countries at different wage levels is also alleged to be unfair by trade unionists in developed

countries when seeking protection from successful exporters from developing countries.

7. See Lewis and more modern 'trade engine' theorists, such as Findlay (1980). Nurkse did not have a model, nor did Singer and Prebisch reach their view of declining terms of trade for developing countries by theoretical reasoning.

8. Simon Kuznets (1980) puts the population growth of developing countries at 0.6 per cent a year from 1850 to 1900.

9. Evidence is provided by estimating a regression equation which includes population (POP), the rate of investment (I/GDP) and per capita income (GDP/POP) as explanatory variables of the import-GDP ratio (M/GDP). The results for a sample of 117 countries including 18 developed and 99 developing countries, using data for 1980, are

$(M/GDP) = 1.19 + 1.61 (I/GDP) - 0.05 (POP) + 0.00 (GDP/POP)$
    (0.14)   (4.76)   (−2.62)   (0.20)
$\bar{R}^2 = .237; F = 9.64$

where t- statistics are in parenthesis. (Source of data: World Bank, *World Development Report*, 1983.)

10. The World Bank, judging from the *World Development Report*, 1980, set it in 1978 at $3500, though apparently other factors are involved, since Ireland with per capita income of $3470 is considered developed, while Israel with $3500 is not.

11. A trade weighted average for the eleven would put the share of manufactures above 50 per cent.

12. Because of the unavailability of disaggregated data on exports from developing countries for the entire period covered in Table 3.4, it was necessary to use data on imports into developed countries. Since about two-thirds of the exports of primary commodities from developing countries go to the markets of developed countries, the figures in Table 3.4 reflect the structure of total exports of primary commodities (excluding fuel) from developing countries fairly well.

CHAPTER 4

1. Chapter 5 does in fact devote some attention to the wider issue of the impact of the incentive structure of relative prices in the discussion on 'true' tariffs and subsidies, but the aim there is to identify the 'incidence' or burden of protection between sectors.

2. Given the difference in elasticity conditions in international markets and differences in the composition of imports and exports in many developing countries, the divergences from unity are likely to be absolutely greater in the case of *IS* than *EP* regimes.

3. These concern the choice of weights (w_i and w_j) and of the criterion for categorising products as importables (m) and exportables (x). For a discussion of these problems see Krueger *et al.* (1981).

4. South Korea can be identified as having reversed trade strategies from IS to EP in the early 1960s.

5. This approach tends to capture only the 'direct' effects of trade policy interventions on value-added.

6. The motivation for a particular trade strategy on the part of national policy-makers has, in any case, varied between countries and over time.

7. Countries that rely on administrative control of imports are unlikely to allow

goods in duty-free. Tariff revenue is frequently an important source of government income in developing countries (see Greenaway, 1980, 1984).

8. There was no uniform pattern of planning. It was formal and explicit in the case of countries such as India, but equally pervasive and informal in the case of somewhere like Mexico.

9. For a more detailed description of typical IS policies and processes see Little, Scitovsky and Scott (1970).

10. The 'model' is set out in World Bank (1983). Some commentators would argue that the 'model' has been imposed on developing countries by the World Bank in return for (structural adjustment) loans.

11. These estimates are for Balassa et al. (1982). Beverages and tobacco are excluded from both of these estimates.

12. This argument is developed by Myint (1958 and 1977).

13. In some modern representations of 'vent for surplus' arguments a case against excessive dependence on external markets in made.

14. For a formal Ricardian model of trade and growth see Findlay (1974) or Findlay (1984). Baldwin (1987) draws attention to its value as a model of economic change.

15. There is a case for a non-zero optimal tariff where a large country enjoys international market power, and is able to influence the terms of trade. This is not likely to apply across a wide range of products or LDCs, and therefore is not likely to be a major consideration in the formulation of an LDC's trade strategy.

16. Trade interventions may be better than nothing in the absence of first-best domestic policy interventions.

17. The standard theory of optimal intervention is based on the assumption that lump sum (non-distorting) taxes are available to finance subsidies and costlessly redistribute income. Trade taxes can in fact be first-best instruments to deal with some domestic distortions if subsidy disbursement costs are sufficiently high. Moreover, the financing of subsidies may have undesirable income distributional effects. These complications do not make a general case, however, for the use of trade interventions.

18. This is not usually based on formal economic modelling, although there are formal 'North–South' models which generate 'uneven development' (e.g. Krugman, 1982) or asymmetrical gains (discussed in Findlay, 1984).

19. Not all Marxists subscribe to dependency theory. Indeed, they are not likely to subscribe to the pursuit of 'independent capitalism' by the Third World.

20. Some commentators, in describing the experience of the NICs during the 1960s and 1970s, have coined the phrase 'debt-led growth' (e.g. Griffith-Jones and Rodriguez, 1984).

CHAPTER 5

1. The role of interest groups in the formation of policy has been extensively discussed in the context of the political economy of protection. Essentially this involves the application of public choice ideas to the domain of trade policy. A useful introduction to the subject is provided by Frey (1985).

2. See Corden (1974) for a thorough appraisal of the theory of optimal intervention, and Greenaway (1983) for a terser review.

3. Domestic resource cost (DRC) analysis is a related concept to effective protection. The technique essentially attempts to evaluate the domestic resources

required to earn or save a unit of foreign exchange in a particular activity. The essence of the technique is the valuation of inputs at social opportunity costs. By so doing it attempts to adjust not only for trade distortions but also for non-trade distortions, be they policy-induced or not (e.g. monopoly pricing, minimum wages, and so on). The relationship between DRC analysis and effective protection analysis is discussed in Bruno (1972) and Krueger (1972). Applications of the principle are many; good examples are the classic work of Little, Scitovsky and Scott (1970) and Krueger *et al.* (1981). Bias estimation attempts to estimate the bias in relative prices induced by the protective structure. As we shall see shortly there are some similarities between this technique and incidence analysis, although the theoretical foundations of the latter are much more fully developed. Estimates of bias in several countries are provided in Krueger (1978).

4. For a brief history of thought on the concept see Corden (1971), Appendix 1.
5. Against this, it is often the case that the technology used in simple manufacturing processes is relatively unsophisticated, making the basic data more readily obtainable from survey information.
6. There is an important technical point to be made here. Bhagwati and Srinivasan (1973), among others, have argued that there is a fundamental problem in using a partial equilibrium technique (effective protection analysis) to make general equilibrium inferences (relative resource pulls). Logically, their position is correct (if somewhat nihilistic). If one is using effective rates to try and predict *exact* resource movements between *specific* industries, the logic of the argument is compelling. If, however, one is adopting the weaker position and focusing on potential resource pulls, then the argument is somewhat weaker.
7. Complementarity would generate a positively sloped *HH*. This possibility is explored in Dornbusch (1974). Further comment will be made on the slope of *HH* below.
8. Formal derivations of the shift parameter can be found in Sjaastad (1980), Sjaastad and Clements (1981) or Greenaway and Milner (1987a), (1987b).
9. There is potentially some scope for confusion here. When $w=0$ the incidence of protection is equally shared by the non-tradeable and exportable sectors. In effect, then, w measures the share of the remaining 50 per cent which is shifted to the export sector. In other words, the incidence on the export sector is $0.5 + 0.5.w$ or $.5(1+w)$.
10. Greenaway and Milner (1986) provide a discussion of the potential policy conflict between import protection under the Development Certificate scheme, and export promotion under the Export Processing Zone provisions in the context of Mauritius. See also Chapter 9 of this volume.

CHAPTER 6

* This chapter draws in part upon MacBean, 'Export Instability and Economic Growth', published in METU, *Studies in Development*, 77 (1–2), 1984, and MacBean and Nguyen, *Commodity Problems: Policies and Prospects* (Croom Helm, 1987). The authors are grateful to the Overseas Development Administration for a research grant which aided this work. The Overseas Development Administration bears no responsibility for any of the opinions expressed here.

1. See Kubuta (1969), Moran (1983, pp. 198–202), Lawson (1974, p. 59), Stein (1978, pp. 279–82); Leith (1970, pp. 268–9).
2. See MacBean (1966, pp. 28–30, 108–10, 114, 116, 121, 124–7); Lim (1976, pp. 311–22).

3. See MacBean (1966, pp. 32, 113), Caine (1954), Knudsen and Parnes (1975), and Yotopoulos and Nugent (1976, ch. 18).
4. The most recent are Moran (1983) and Adams and Behrman (1982). See the references there.
5. MacBean (1966) was concerned with whether export instability was a general problem for LDCs, and availability of data was the only criterion for inclusion in the sample studied. Several later studies used a sample of countries which *prima facie* were more likely to be affected by export instability, e.g. Glezakos (1973). Most subsequent studies have followed suit.
6. Asymmetrical expectation on the part of investors considering the upswings (as permanent) and downswings (as temporary) is really not rational. However, as long as the expansion of the industry is profitable, this expectation will appear to be justified *ex-post*.
7. See Obidegwu and Nziramasanga (1981). From the results of simulations of an econometric model of copper in Zambia, the authors concluded that stabilising the copper price has no impact on the Zambian economy, since the rest of the economy is insulated by net international reserves changes and the foreign share of net exports. Unstable copper price had no adverse effect on economic growth (p. 109).
8. Even where the ratchet effects are in fact present, insufficient sample variance in instability in time-series studies can cause failure to detect them. Therefore, one cannot even say that Adams and Behrman have shown that one route-ratchet effects – were not present, unless, over the period investigated, there was sufficient variation in instability for the individual countries involved.

CHAPTER 7

* The work reported in this chapter was completed while the author was employed in the Commodities Division of the Research Department of the International Monetary Fund in Washington DC. The author is indebted to Ke-Young Chu, Nihad Kaibni and Tom Morrison (IMF) and to Alan Winters (World Bank and University College of North Wales, Bangor) and Hans Singer (University of Sussex) for their comments on earlier versions. Especial thanks are due to Ximena Cheetham for her outstanding research assistance. All views expressed in this paper, and any remaining errors, are the responsibility of the author alone.
1. Although attention throughout this chapter is focused on the NBTT (real price of commodities), it is useful to note that in his seminal work on long waves, Kondratieff (1935) viewed *nominal* commodity price movements as one of the major components of the long-run *cyclical* behaviour of the world economy and found evidence in their behaviour of three great cycles during the period since the end of the 1780s, with duration between forty-seven and sixty years (p. 107). For further discussion see Lewis (1978, pp. 69–93) and Sapsford (1985a, p. 6).
2. The series analysed by Prebisch (1950) referred to the net barter terms of trade of the United Kingdom for its complete merchandise trade from 1876 to 1947. As the UK was, for much of this period, the major exporter of manufactures and importer of primary commodities, Prebisch interpreted the secular increases in the UK's terms of trade as implying a secular deterioration in the net barter terms of trade of primary products traded world-wide. However, Singer (1950) based his case on arguably more direct statistical evidence taken from his earlier unsigned United Nations (1949) study.
3. Autocorrelation is a common problem in time-series analysis. It arises when

successive values of the disturbance term are related, for instance due to the fact that shocks have a prolonged influence. When autocorrelation exists, failure to treat the problem in some way can result in the usual confidence tests which econometricians use being invalid. The Durbin–Watson statistic is a diagnostic statistic used to test for the presence of autocorrelation. Its value ranges between 0 and 4. Values of around 2 are consistent with an absence of autocorrelation. Values tending towards 0 are consistent with positive autocorrelation, while those tending towards 4 are consistent with negative autocorrelation. The precise values at which it will be deduced that autocorrelation is present depends upon the sample size and the number of variables in the model.

4. The Cochrane–Orcutt estimation procedure is a statistical method of correcting for autocorrelation.

5. Because of data availability problems it was not possible to adjust the UN series (which also formed the first element of Spraos's hybrid series) for petroleum movements as far back as 1900. However, some calculations reported in Sapsford (1984) suggest that the adopted procedure (involving the linking of more recent petroleum-exclusive data to earlier petroleum-inclusive data) might not be too unreasonable.

6. As already noted, it is not possible to properly appraise Spraos's own reported equations because of the absence of reported D–W statistics. However, replication of his OLS estimation procedure and re-estimation by the Cochrane–Orcutt iterative procedure confirms the significance of each of the sub-period trends (see Sapsford 1985a, table 1, equations 1.3–1.5). Notice also that Spraos's equation (10) relates to the World Bank (petroleum inclusive) series rather than the hybrid series; where the latter is made up of the UN series for the period 1950 to 1956 and the World Bank (petroleum inclusive) series thereafter. However, a negative and significant trend is also clearly evident from a 1950–1970 sub-period regression of the hybrid series (Sapsford, 1985a, table 1, equation 1.4).

7. For a formal proof, see Sapsford (1981, pp. 506–7).

CHAPTER 9

1. The Rybczynski theorem postulates that, in the case of the standard $2 \times 2 \times 2$ model, if one of the factors of production increases autonomously, there will be an absolute expansion in production of the commodity intensive in the use of the increasing factor and a reduction in the production of the commodity relatively less intensive in the use of the factor. This analysis is based on the assumptions that both goods are subject to linear homogeneous production functions, and the price ratio of the two commodities remains the same after factor accumulation.

2. Hamada (1974) notes that the misallocation of factors in this case would be of a lower magnitude than in Case 1. This is because the price of capital in the zone would be given by the international price of capital and would be lower than that prevailing in the protected domestic economy. Hence the capital-intensity of the capital-intensive good produced by the foreign firms in the zone would be higher than that of the same good produced in the domestic economy. As a result, less labour would be drawn from the production of the labour-intensive good in the domestic economy to the zone.

3. In the context of the $2 \times 2 \times 2$ model, Hamilton and Svenson (1982) demonstrate that foreign firms in the zone are likely to specialise totally in the production of the labour-intensive good. This is because the wage rate facing the foreign firms in the zone is likely to be relatively low for two reasons. First, the protection

afforded to the capital-intensive good in the domestic sector artificially lowers the wage rate, and, second, the wage rate tends to be low in terms of world prices for the good facing the firms in the zone compared to the wage in terms of domestic prices in the domestic sector. The theoretical analysis of this issue in the context of the $2 \times 2 \times 2$ model incorporating all the assumptions stated earlier, comes to the conclusion that welfare necessarily decreases more in this case than in the case where FDI flows into the domestic sector. This is based on the argument that foreign firms totally specialise in the production of the labour-intensive good in the zone, and they pay labour employed in the zone, at least partly, in the form of the capital-intensive good. Labour would prefer to be paid in the capital-intensive good because of its relatively high price in the domestic economy. Foreign firms do not produce the capital-intensive good but are able to buy it at world market prices. Further, they repatriate profits in the form of the relatively cheap labour-intensive good. In the domestic sector, however, foreign capitalists cannot buy the capital-intensive good at world market prices because of the presence of a tariff on the good. Hence they are forced to pay a relatively high wage in terms of the capital-intensive good in the domestic zone. Hence welfare decreases more if FDI flows into the zone than in the case were it flows into the domestic sector.

CHAPTER 11

1. This is because for accounting purposes it may price imported intermediate inputs from the parent company at virtually anywhere between marginal cost and final price, depending upon the prevailing rates of company taxation within the two economies.
2. This might be on the insistence of the donors that foreign aid should not substitute for domestic tax effort.
3. The payment is not necessarily retained by the tax official. Village headsmen and other local dignitaries may be compensated for providing information on their villagers, their ownership of land, cattle, and so forth.
4. Tariffs on intermediate inputs effectively reduce the degree of protection afforded to final goods. For this reason it is necessary to distinguish between 'nominal' and 'effective' rates of protection, and it is worth noting that the latter may be negative in certain cases (see chapter 5).
5. The intuitive explanation for this result is that if a country is successful in changing the terms of trade in its favour by the adoption of tariffs, it effectively increases the price of its exports. The precise consequences then depend upon the foreigners' demand for importables. For this and related arguments see Johnson (1950–1).
6. For purposes of exposition in what follows, we will consider tariff revenues as being representative of trade tax revenues as a whole.
7. This example is culled from the writer's own experience.

References

Adams, F. G., Behrman, J. R. and Roldan, R. A. (1979) 'Measuring the Impact of Primary Commodity Fluctuations on Economic Development: Coffee and Brazil', *American Economic Review*, 69, pp. 164–8.

Adams, F. G. and Behrman, J. (1982) *Commodity Exports and Economic Development: The Commodity Problem, Goal Attainment and Policy in Developing Countries* (Lexington, Mass., Lexington Books, D. C. Heath).

Adams, F. G. and Privolos, T. (1981) 'Commodity Exports, Economic Development and Policy: Coffee and Brazil', unpublished report to USAID (Philadelphia, Wharton Econometric Forecasting Associates Inc).

Anderson, K. and Baldwin, R. E. (1981) *The Political Market for Protection in Industrial Countries; Empirical Evidence*, Staff Working Paper No. 492 (Washington, World Bank).

Ariff, M. and Hill, H. (1985) *Export-Oriented Industrialisation: The ASEAN Experience* (London, Allen & Unwin).

Arndt, H. W. (1985) 'The Origins of Structuralism', *World Development*, 13, pp. 151–9.

Bacha, E. (1978) 'An Interpretation of Unequal Exchange from Prebisch–Singer to Emmanuel', *Journal of Development Economics*, 5, pp. 319–30.

Balassa, B. (1965) 'Trade Liberalisation and 'Revealed' Comparative Advantage', *The Manchester School of Economic and Social Studies*, 33, pp. 99–123.

Balassa, B. (1971) *The Structure of Protection in Developing Countries* (Baltimore, Johns Hopkins University Press).

Balassa, B. (1977a) '"Revealed" Comparative Advantage Revisited: An Analysis of Relative Export Shares of the Industrial Countries, 1953–1971', *The Manchester School of Economic and Social Studies*, 45, pp. 327–44.

Balassa, B. (1977b) 'A Stages Approach to Comparative Advantage', paper presented to the Fifth World Congress of the International Economic Association, Tokyo.

Balassa, B. (1978) 'Exports and Economic Growth: Further Evidence', *Journal of Development Economics*, 5, pp. 181–9.

Balassa, B. (1979) 'The Changing Pattern of Comparative Advantage in Manufactured Goods', *The Review of Economics and Statistics*, 61, pp. 259–66.

Balassa, B. *et al.* (1982) *Development Strategies in Semi-Industrial Economies* (Baltimore, Johns Hopkins University Press).

Balasubramanyam, V. N. (1984) *The Economy of India* (London, Weidenfeld & Nicolson).

Baldwin, R. E. (1987) 'Structural Change and Patterns of International Exchange', in J. Black and A. MacBean (eds), *The Changing Structure of World Trade* (forthcoming).

Ballance, R. (1987) *Industry and Business: Structural Change, Industrial Policy and Industry Strategies* (London, Allen & Unwin).

Ballance, R., Ansari, J. and Singer, H. (1982) *The International Economy and Industrial Development* (Totowa, NJ, Allanheld, Osmun).

Ballance, R., Forstner, H. and Murray, T. (1985) 'On Measuring Comparative Advantage: A Note on Bowen's Indices', *Weltwirtschaftliches Archiv*, 121, pp. 346–50.

Ballance, R., Forstner, H. and Murray, T. (1986) 'Consistency Tests of Alternative Measures of Comparative Advantage', *Review of Economics and Statistics*, 86.

Bauer, P. T. (1981) *Equality, the Third World and Economic Delusion* (London, Methuen).

Bhagwati, J. N. (1978) *Anatomy and Consequences of Trade Control Regimes* (New York, Ballinger).

Bhagwati, J. N. (1979) 'International Factor Movements and National Advantage', *Indian Economic Review*, October.

Bhagwati, J. N. and Srinivasan, T. (1973) 'General Equilibrium, The Theory of Effective Protection and Resource Allocation', *Journal of International Economics*, 3, pp. 259–81.

Bhagwati, J. N. and Srinivasan, T. (1975) *Foreign Trade Regimes and Economic Development: India* (New York, National Bureau of Economic Research).

Bienefeld, M. (1982) 'The International Context for National Development Strategies: Constraints and Opportunities in a Changing World', in M. Bienefeld and M. Godfrey (eds) *The Struggle for Development: National Strategies in an International Context* (Wiley, Chichester).

Birnberg, T. and Resnick, S. (1975) *Colonial Development: An Econometric Study* (New Haven, Yale University Press).

Blackhurst, R., Marian, N., and Tumlir, J. (1977) *Trade Liberalization, Protectionism and Interdependence*. GATT Studies in International Trade No. 5 (Geneva, GATT).

Blackhurst, R., Marian, N. and Tumlir, J. (1978) *Adjustment, Trade and Growth in Developed and Developing Countries*. GATT Studies in International Trade No. 6 (Geneva, GATT).

Bowden, R. (1983) The Conceptual Basis of Empirical Studies of Trade in Manufactured Commodities. *Manchester School*, 51, pp. 209–34.

Bowen, H. (1983) 'On the Theoretical Interpretation of Indices of Trade Intensity and Revealed Comparative Advantage', *Weltwirtschaftliches Archiv*, 119, pp. 464–72.

Brecher, R. A. (1974) 'Optimal Commercial Policy for a Minimum-Wage Economy', *Journal of International Economics*, 4, pp. 139–49.

Bruno, M. (1972) 'Domestic Resource Costs and Effective Protection: Clarification and Synthesis', *Journal of Political Economy*, 80, pp. 16–33.

Buckley, P. J. and Casson, M. C. (1976) *The Future of the Multinational Enterprise* (London, Macmillan).

Caine, S. (1958) 'Comment', *Kyklos*, 11.

Cairncross, A. K. (1960) 'International Trade and Economic Development', *Kyklos*, 13, pp. 545–58.

Cassen, R. *et al.* (1986) *Does Aid Work?* (Oxford, Oxford University Press).

Casson, M. C. (1979) *Alternatives to the Multinational Enterprise* (London, Macmillan).

Casson, M. C. *et al.* (1986) *Multinationals and World Trade: Vertical Integration and the Division of Labour in World Industries* (London, Allen & Unwin).

Caves, R. E. and Jones, R. W. (1977) *World Trade and Payments: An Introduction*

(Boston, Little, Brown and Company) (2nd edition).

Chenery, H. B. (1980) 'Interactions between Industrialization and Exports', *American Economic Review*, 70, pp. 281–7.

Chenery, H. B. and Bruno, M. (1962) 'Development Alternatives in an Open Economy: The Case of Israel', *Economic Journal*, 72, pp. 79–103.

Chow, G. C. (1960) 'Test of Equality between Sets of Coefficients in Two Linear Regressions', *Econometrica*, 28, pp. 591–605.

Chu, K. Y. and Morrison, T. K. (1984) 'The 1981–82 Recession and Non-oil Primary Commodity Prices', *International Monetary Fund Staff Papers*, 31, pp. 93–140.

Clements, K. W. and Sjaastad, L. A. (1985) *How Protection Taxes Exporters*, Thames Essay, 39 (London, Trade Policy Research Centre).

Cochrane, D. and Orcutt, G. H. (1949) 'Application of Least Square Regressions to Relationships Containing Autocorrelated Error Terms', *Journal of the American Statistical Association*, 44, pp. 32–61.

Coppock, J. D. (1962) *International Economic Instability* (London, McGraw Hill).

Corden, W. M. (1971a) 'The Effects of Trade on the Rate of Growth', in J. N. Bhagwati *et al.* (eds) *Trade, Balance of Payments and Growth* (Amsterdam, North-Holland).

Corden, W. M. (1971b) *The Theory of Protection* (Oxford, Oxford University Press).

Corden, W. M. (1974) *Trade Policy and Economic Welfare* (Oxford, Oxford University Press).

Corden, W. M. (1984) 'The Normative Theory of International Trade', in R. W. Jones and P. B. Kenen (eds).

Corden, M. and Neary, P. (1982) Booming Sector and Deindustrialisation in a Small Open Economy, *Economic Journal*, 92, pp. 825–48.

Deardorff, A. (1980) 'The General Validity of the Law of Comparative Advantage', *Journal of Political Economy*, 88, pp. 941–57.

Deardorff, A. (1984) 'Testing Trade Theories and Predicting Trade Flows', in R. W. Jones and P. B. Kenen (eds).

DeVries, J. (1980) 'The World Sugar Economy: An Econometric Analysis of Long Term Development', unpublished mimeo, BK9047 (World Bank, Washington, DC).

DeVries, J. (1982) 'Analysis of the World Coffee Market', unpublished mimeo, BK9049 (World Bank, Washington, DC).

Diaz, C. (1980) 'The Effects of Commercial Policy in El Salvador', unpublished thesis, Graduate Institute of International Studies, Geneva.

Diaz-Alejandro, C. F. (1975) 'Trade Policies and Economic Development', in P.B. Kenen (ed.) *International Trade and Finance: Frontiers for Research* (Cambridge, Cambridge University Press).

Donges, J. and Riedel, J. (1977) 'The Expansion of Manufactured Exports in Developing Countries: An Empirical Assessment of Supply and Demand Issues', *Weltwirtschaftliches Archiv*, 113, pp. 58–87.

Dornbusch, R. (1974) 'Tariffs and Non Traded Goods', *Journal of International Economics*, 4, pp. 177–85.

Drabicki, J. and Takayama, A. (1979) 'An Antimony in the Theory of Comparative Advantage', *Journal of International Economics*, 9, pp. 211–23.

Dunning, J. H. and Pearce, R. D. (1981) *The World's Largest Industrial Enterprises*, (Farnborough, Hants, Gower Press).

Dunning, J. H. (1986) *Japanese Participation in British Industry* (London, Croom Helm).

Ellsworth, P. T. (1956) 'The Terms of Trade between Primary Producing and

Industrial Countries', *Inter-American Economic Affairs*, 10, pp. 47–65.

Emmanuel, A. (1972) *Unequal Exchange* (New York, Monthly Review Press).

Fendt, R. (1981) 'Brazilian Trade Liberalisation: A Reassessment', in L. A. Sjaastad (1981).

Findlay, R. (1971) 'The "Foreign Exchange Gap" and Growth in Developing Countries', in J. Bhagwati *et al.* (eds) *Trade, Balance of Payments and Growth* (Amsterdam, North-Holland).

Findlay, R. (1974) 'Relative Prices, Growth and Trade in a Simple Ricardian System', *Economica*, 41, pp. 1–13.

Findlay, R. (1980) 'The Terms of Trade and Equilibrium Growth in the World Economy', *American Economic Review*, 70, pp. 291–9.

Findlay, R. (1984) 'Growth and Development in Trade Models', in R. W. Jones and P. B. Kenen (eds).

Finger, M. (1975) 'A New View of the Product Cycle', *Weltwirtschaftliches Archiv*, 3, pp. 80–99.

Ford, D. (1978) *An Econometric Model of the World Coffee Economy: Version 2* (Philadelphia, Wharton Econometric Forecasting Associates Inc.).

Forstner, H. (1984) 'The Changing Patterns of International Trade in Manufactures: A Logit Analysis', *Weltwirtschaftliches Archiv*, 120, pp. 1–17.

Frank, A. G. (1967) *Capitalism and Underdevelopment in Latin America* (New York, Monthly Review Press).

Frey, B. (1985) 'The Political Economy of Protection', in D. Greenaway (1985).

Fröbel, F., Heinrichs, J. and Kreye, O. (1980) *The New International Division of Labour* (Cambridge, Cambridge University Press).

Garcia, R. (1981) *The Effects of Exchange Rates and Commercial Policy on Agricultural Incentives in Colombia, 1953–78* (Washington, International Food Policy Research Institute).

Glezakos, C. (1973) 'Export Instability and Economic Growth: A Statistical Verification', *Economic Development and Cultural Change*, 21, pp. 670–8.

Glezakos, C. (1983) 'Instability and the Growth of Exports', *Journal of Development Economics*, 12, pp. 229–36.

Glezakos, C. (1984) 'Export Instability and Economic Growth: Reply', *Economic Development and Cultural Change*, 32, 615–23.

Goldfeld, S. M. and Quandt, R. E. (1973) 'The Estimation of Structural Shifts by Switching Regressions', *Annals of Economic and Social Measurement*, 2, pp. 475–85.

Greenaway, D. (1980) 'Trade Taxes as a Source of Government Revenue: An International Comparison', *Scottish Journal of Political Economy*, 27, pp. 175–82.

Greenaway, D. (1981) 'Taxes on International Trade and Economic Development', in Peacock, A. T. and Forte, F. (eds) *The Political Economy of Taxation* (Oxford, Blackwell).

Greenaway, D. (1982) 'Maximum Revenue Tariffs and Optimal Revenue Tariffs: Concepts and Policy Issues', *Public Finance*, 37, pp. 67–79.

Greenaway, D. (1983) *International Trade Policy: From Tariffs to the New Protectionism* (London, Macmillan).

Greenaway, D. (1984) 'A Statistical Analysis of Fiscal Dependence on Trade Taxes and Economic Development', *Public Finance*, 39, pp. 70–89.

Greenaway, D. (ed.) (1985) *Current Issues in International Trade: Theory and Policy* (London, Macmillan).

Greenaway, D. (1986a) 'Estimates of the Incidence of Protection in a Non Industrialised Economy', mimeo.

Greenaway, D. (1986b) 'Characteristics of Industrialization and Economic Performance under Alternative Development Strategies, background paper to, *World Development Report 1987* (Oxford, Oxford University Press).

Greenaway, D. and Milner, C. R. (1986a) 'Estimating the Shifting of Protection Across Sectors: An Application to Mauritius', *Industry and Development*, 16, pp. 1–22.

Greenaway, D. and Milner, C. (1986b) *Economics of Intra-Industry Trade* (Oxford, Blackwell).

Greenaway, D. and Milner, C. R. (1987) 'Trade Theory and Less-Developed Countries', in N. Gemmell (ed.) *Surveys in Development Economics* (Oxford, Blackwell).

Greenaway, D. and Milner, C. R. (1987a) 'True Protection Concepts and their Role in Evaluating Trade Policies in LDCs', *Journal of Development Studies*, 23, pp. 200–19.

Griffin, K. (1970) 'Foreign Capital, Domestic Savings and Economic Development', *Oxford Bulletin of Economics and Statistics*, 32, pp. 99–112.

Griffin, K. (1986) 'Doubts about Aid', *Institute of Development Studies Bulletin*, 17, pp. 36–45.

Griffith-Jones, S. and Rodriguez, E. (1984) 'Private International Finance and Industrialization of LDCs', *Journal of Development Studies*, 21, pp. 47–74.

Grubel, H. G. and Johnson, H. G. (1971) *Effective Tariff Protection* (Geneva, GATT).

Grunwald, J. and Flamm, K. (1985) *The Global Factory: Foreign Assembly in International Trade* (Washington, DC, Brookings Institution). ·

Haberler, G. (1961) 'Terms of Trade and Economic Development', in Ellis, H. S. (ed.) *Economic Development for Latin America* (London, Macmillan).

Hamada, K. (1974) 'An Economic Analysis of the Duty-Free Zone', *Journal of International Economics*, 4, pp. 225–41.

Hamilton, C. and Svennson, L. E. O. (1982) 'On the Welfare Effects of a Duty-Free Zone', *Journal of International Economics*, 2, pp. 45–64.

Hartigan, J. (1985) 'What Can We Learn from the Effective Rate of Protection', *Weltwirtschaftliches Archiv*, 121, pp. 53–60.

Harrylyshyn, D. and Wolf, M. (1983) Recent Trends in Trade Among Developing Countries, *European Economic Review*, 21, pp. 333–62.

Helleiner, G. K. (1972) International Trade and Economic Development (Harmondsworth, Penguin).

Helleiner, G. K. (1979) 'Structural Aspects of Third World Trade: Some Trends and Prospects', *Journal of Development Studies*, 15, pp. 70–88.

Helleiner, G. K. (1981) *Intra-firm Trade and the Developing Countries* (London, Macmillan).

Higgins, B. (1968) *Economic Development: Problems, Principles and Policies* (New York, Norton).

Hillman, A. (1980) 'Observations on the Relation between 'Revealed Comparative Advantage' and Comparative Advantage as Indicated by Pre-trade Relative Prices', *Weltwirtschaftliches Archiv*, 116, pp. 315–21.

Hinrichs, H. H. (1965) 'Determinants of Government Revenue Shares among Less-Developed Countries', *Economics Journal*, 75, pp. 546–56.

Hirschman, A. D. (1968) 'The Political Economy of Import-substituting Industrialization in Latin America', *Quarterly Journal of Economics*, 82, pp. 1–12.

Hirschmann, A. (1981) *Essays in Trespassing: Economics to Politics and Beyond* (Cambridge, Cambridge University Press).

Hitiris, T. and Weekes, A. J. (1986) 'Trade Taxes and Economic Development', Discussion Paper No. 112, University of York.

Hughes, H. and Waelbroeck, J. (1981) 'Can Developing Country Exports Keep Growing in the 1980s?', *The World Economy*, pp. 127–47.

Johnson, H. G. (1950–1) 'Optimum Welfare and Maximum Revenue Tariffs', *Review of Economic Studies*, 19, pp. 28–35.

Johnson, H. G. (1967) *Economic Policies towards Less Developed Countries* (London, Allen & Unwin).

Johnston, J. (1972) *Econometric Methods* (London, McGraw-Hill) (2nd edition).

Jones, R. W. and Kenen, P. B. (1984) *Handbook of International Economics*, vol. I (Amsterdam, North-Holland).

Kaldor, N. (1983) 'The Role of Commodity Prices in Economic Recovery', *Lloyds Bank Review*, July, pp. 21–34.

Keesing, D. B. (1967) 'Outward Looking Policies and Economic Development', *Economic Journal*, 77, pp. 303–20.

Kenen, P. B. and Voivodas, C. (1972) 'Export Instability and Economic Growth', *Kyklos*, 25, pp. 791–804.

Kirkpatrick, C. (1987) 'Trade Policy and Industrialization in Developing Countries', in N. Gemmell (ed.) *Surveys in Development Economics* (Oxford, Blackwell).

Kirkpatrick, C. and Nixson, F. (1976) 'UNCTAD IV and the New International Economic Order', *Three Banks Review*, 12, pp. 30–49.

Kitchin, P. D. (1976) 'Effective Rates of Protection in UK Manufacturing for 1963 and 1968', in M. J. Artis and A. R. Nobay (eds) *Essays in Economic Analysis* (Cambridge, Cambridge University Press).

Knudsen, O. and Parnes, A. (1975) *Trade Instability and Economic Development*.

Kojima, K. (1978) *Direct Foreign Investment* (London, Croom Helm).

Kol, J. and Rayment, P. (1986) 'Specialisation, Intermediates and Trade', paper presented at the symposium on intra-industry trade held at the European Institute for Advanced Studies in Management, Brussels, May 29–30.

Kondratieff, N. D. (1935) 'The Long Waves in Economic Life', *Review of Economics and Statistics*, 17, pp. 105–15.

Krause, L. (1982) *US Economic Policy Towards the Association of Southeast Asian Nations: Meeting the Japanese Challenge* (Washington DC, Brookings Institution).

Kravis, I. B. (1970) 'Trade as the Handmaiden of Growth: Similarities between the Nineteenth and Twentieth Centuries', *Economic Journal*, 80, pp. 850–72.

Krueger, A. O. (1972) 'Evaluating Restrictionist Trade Regimes: Theory and Measurement', *Journal of Political Economy*, 80, pp. 48–62.

Krueger, A. O. (1978) *Liberalisation Attempts and Consequences* (New York, Ballinger).

Krueger, A. O. (1980) 'Trade Policy as an Input to Development', *American Economic Review*, 70, pp. 288–92.

Krueger, A. O. (1984) 'Trade Policies in Developing Countries', in R. W. Jones and P. B. Kenen (eds).

Krueger, A. O. *et al.* (1981) *Trade and Employment in Developing Countries* (Chicago, University of Chicago Press).

Krugman, P. (1982) 'Trade, Accumulation and Uneven Development', *Journal of Development Economics*, 8, pp. 149–61.

Kubuta, K. (1969) 'A Note on Instability Indexes', *Research Memorandum* (New York, UNCTAD).

Kunimoto, K. (1977) 'Typology of Trade Intensity Indices', *Hitotsubashi Journal of Economics*, 17, pp. 15–32.

Kuznets, S. (1980) 'Recent Population Trends in Less Developed Countries, and Implications for International Income Inequality', in R. Easterlin (ed.) *Population and Economic Change in Developing Countries* (Chicago, University of Chicago Press).

Lall, D. (1975) 'Is Dependence a Useful Concept in Analysing Underdevelopment?', *World Development*, 2, pp. 799–810.

Lall, D. (1983) *The Poverty of 'Development Economics'*, Hobart Paperback 16 (London, Institute of Economic Affairs).

Lall, S. (1980) *The Multinational Corporation: Nine Essays* (London, Macmillan).

Lam, N. V. (1980a) 'Export Instability, Expansion and Market Concentration: A Methodological Interpretation', *Journal of Development Economics*, 7, pp. 99–115.

Lam, N. V. (1980b) 'Export Instability, Growth and Primary Commodity Concentration', *Economia Internazionale*.

Lancieri, E. (1978) 'Export Instability and Economic Development: A Reappraisal', *Banca Nazionale del Lavoro Quarterly Review*, 125, pp. 135–56.

Lancieri, E. (1979) 'Instability of Agricultural Exports', *Banca Nazionale del Lavoro Quarterly Review*, 130.

Lasaga, M. (1981) *The Copper Industry in the Chilean Economy, An Econometric Analysis* (Lexington, Mass., Lexington Books).

Lawson, C. (1974) 'The Decline in World Export Instability, A Re-Appraisal', *Oxford Bulletin of Economics and Statistics*, 36.

Lecraw, D. J. (1983) 'Performance of Transnational Corporations in Less Developed Countries', *Journal of International Business Studies*, 14, pp. 15–33.

Lecraw, D. J. (1985) 'Some Evidence on Transfer Pricing by Multinational Corporations', in A. M. Rugman and L. Eden (eds) *Multinationals and Transfer Pricing* (London, Croom Helm) pp. 223–40.

Lee, J. K. (1971) Exports and the Propensity to Save in Less Developed Countries', *Economic Journal*, 81, pp. 341–51.

Lee, J. (1986) 'Determinants of Offshore Production in Developing Countries', *Journal of Development Economics*, 20, pp. 1–13.

Leith, J. C. (1970) 'The Decline in World Export Justability: A Comment', *Oxford Bulletin of Economics and Statistics*, 32, no. 3.

Lewis, S. R. Jr. (1963) 'Government Revenue from Foreign Trade: An International Comparison', *Manchester School*, 31, pp. 39–46.

Lewis, W. A. (1969) *Aspects of Tropical Trade 1883–1965* (Stockholm: Almqvist and Wicksell).

Lewis, W. A. (1978) *Growth and Fluctuations* (London, Allen & Unwin).

Lewis, W. A. (1980) 'The Slowing Down of the Engine of Growth', *American Economic Review*, 70, pp. 555–64.

Lim, D. (1974) 'Export Instability and Economic Development: The Example of West Malaysia', *Oxford Economic Papers*, 26, pp. 78–92.

Lim, D. (1976) 'Export Instability and Economic Growth: A Return to Fundamentals', *Oxford Bulletin of Economics and Statistics*, 38.

Lim, D. (1980) 'Income Distribution, Export Instability and Savings Behaviour', *Economic Development and Cultural Change*, 28, pp. 359–64.

Lindbeck, A. (1981) 'Industrial Policy as an Issue in the Economic Environment', *The World Economy*, 4, pp. 391–406.

Little, I. (1981) 'The Experience and Causes of Rapid Labour-Intensive Development in Korea, Taiwan Province, Hong Kong and Singapore: and the possibilities of emulation', in E. Lee (ed.) *Export-Led Industrialization and Development* (Geneva, ILO).

Little, I. (1982) *Economic Development: Theory, Policy and International Relations* (New York, Basic Books).

Little, I., Scitovsky, T. and Scott, M. (1970) *Industry and Trade in Some Developing Countries* (Oxford, Oxford University Press, for the Organisation of Economic Cooperation and Development).

MacBean, A. I. (1966) *Export Instability and Economic Development* (London, Allen & Unwin and Harvard University Press).

McKinnon, R. (1964) 'Foreign Exchange Constraints in Economic Development and Efficient Aid Allocation', *Economic Journal*, 74, pp. 388–409.

Maizels, A. (1968) *Exports and Economic Growth of Developing Countries* (Cambridge, Cambridge University Press).

Maizels, A. (1968a) 'Review of Export Instability and Economic Development', *American Economic Review*, 58, pp. 575–80.

Michaely, M. (1977) 'Exports and Growth: An Empirical Investigation', *Journal of Development Economics*, Amsterdam, 4, pp. 49–53.

Moran, C. (1983) 'Export Fluctuations and Economic Growth', *Journal of Development Economics*, 12, pp. 195–218.

Morgan, T. (1957) 'The Long-Run Terms of Trade between Agriculture and Manufacturing', *Econometrica*, 25, p. 360.

Mosley, P. (1980) 'Aid, Savings and Growth Revisited', *Oxford Bulletin of Economics and Statistics*, 42, pp. 79–97.

Mosley, P., Hudson, J., and Horrell, S. (1987) 'Aid, the Public Sector and the Market in Less Developed Countries', Bath University Papers in Political Economy, 23; forthcoming *Economic Journal*, 97.

Moxon, R. W. (1984) 'Export Platform Foreign Investments in the Asia-Pacific Region', in R. W. Moxon, T. W. Roehl and J. F. Truitt (eds) *International Business Strategies in the Asia-Pacific Region: Environmental Changes and Corporate Responses*, Research in International Business and Finance, vol 4, part A (Greenwich and London, Jai Press).

Murray, D. (1978) 'Export Earning Instability: Price, Quantity, Supply, Demand?', *Economic Development and Cultural Change*, 37, p. 68.

Murray, R. (ed.) (1981) *Multinationals Beyond the Market* (Brighton, Harvester).

Musgrave, R. A. (1969) *Fiscal Systems* (New Haven, Yale University Press).

Musgrave, R. A. and Musgrave, P. B. (1976) *Public Finance in Theory and Practice* (New York, McGraw Hill) (second edition).

Myint, H. (1958) 'The Classical Theory of International Trade and the Underdeveloped Countries', *Economic Journal*, 68, pp. 317–37.

Myint, H. (1971) *Economic Theory and the Under-developed Countries* (Oxford, Oxford University Press).

Myint, H. (1977) 'Adam Smith's Theory of International Trade in the Perspective of Economic Development', *Economica*, 44, pp. 231–48.

Naqvi, S. N. H., Kemal, A. R. and Heston, A. (1983) *The Structure of Protection in Pakistan 1980–81* (Islamabad, Pakistan Institute of Development Economics).

Nakajo, S. (1980) 'Japanese Direct Investment in Asian Newly Industrialising Countries and Intra-firm Division of Labour', *The Developing Economies*, 18, pp. 463–83.

Nurkse, R. (1959) *Patterns of Trade and Development* (Stockholm: Almquist and Wicksell).

Obidegwu, C. F. and Nziramasanga, M. (1981) *Copper and Zambia: An Econometric Analysis* (Lexington, Mass., Lexington Books, D. C. Heath).

OECD (1986) *Twenty-five Years of Development Co-operation: A Review* (Paris, OECD).

Ozawa, T. (1985) 'Japan', in J. H. Dunning (ed.) *Multinational Enterprises, Economic Structure and International Competitiveness* (Chichester, Sussex: Wiley for IRM).

Palma, G. (1978) 'Dependency: A Formal Theory of Underdevelopment or a Methodology for the Analysis of Concrete Situations of Under-development?', *World Development*, 6, pp. 881–924.

Pearce, R. D. (1982) *Overseas Production and Exporting Performance: An Empiri-*

cal Note, University of Reading Discussion Papers in International Investment and Business Studies, 64.

Peston, M. H. (1971) 'The Tax Mix and Effective Demand', *Public Finance*, 3, pp. 493–96.

Pobukadee, J. (1980) 'An Econometric Analysis of World Copper Market', mimeo (Philadelphia, Wharton Econometric Forecasting Associates Inc.).

Prebisch, R. (1950) 'The Economic Development of Latin America and its Principal Problems' (New York, UN ECLA); also published in *Economic Bulletin for Latin America*, 7, 1962, pp. 1–22.

Priovolos, T. (1981) *Coffee and the Ivory Coast: An Econometric Study* (Lexington, Mass, Lexington Books, D. C. Heath).

Rangarajan, C. and Sundarajan, V. (1976) 'Impact of Export Fluctuations on Income' – a Cross Country Analysis', *Review of Economics and Statistics*, 58.

Ray, G. (1977) 'The "Real" Price of Primary Products', *National Institute Economic Review*, 81, pp. 72–6.

Read, R. A. (1986a) 'The Synthetic Fibre Industry: Innovation, Integration and Market Structure', in M. C. Casson *et al.* (1986).

Read, R. A. (1986b) 'The Copper Industry', in M. C. Casson *et al.* (1986).

Reynolds, L. D. (1963) 'Domestic Consequences of Export Instability', *American Economic Review*, 53, pp. 93–102.

Reynolds, L. G. (1983) 'The Spread of Economic Growth to the Third World: 1850–1980', *Journal of Economic Literature*, 21, pp. 941–80.

Ricardo, D. (1971) *Principles of Political Economy and Taxation* (London, Penguin), Ch. 1.

Sahabdeen, M. R. (1985) 'Export Processing Zones In Less Developed Countries: A Case Study of the Katrinayaki Investment Promotion Zone in Sri Lanka', unpublished MSc. thesis, University of Lancaster.

Samuelson, H-F. (1982) 'Transnational Corporations in the Export-Processing Zones of Developing Countries', mimeo (New York, United Nations Centre on Transnational Corporations).

Samuelson, P. A. (1948) 'International Trade and Equalisation of Factor Prices', *Economic Journal*, 58, pp. 163–84.

Samuelson, P. A. (1976) in D. A. Belsey *et al.* (eds) *Inflation, Trade and Taxes* (Columbus, Ohio, Ohio State University Press).

Sapsford, D. (1981) 'Productivity Growth in the UK: A Reconsideration', *Applied Economics*, 13, pp. 499–511.

Sapsford, D. (1984) 'Long-run Trends in Real Commodity Prices: Some Statistical Evidence', International Monetary Fund Research Department Paper, September (Washington, DC, IMF).

Sapsford, D. (1985a) 'Real Primary Commodity Prices: An Analysis of Long-run Movements', International Monetary Fund D.M. Series, No. 85/31 (Washington DC, IMF).

Sapsford, D. (1985b) 'The Statistical Debate on the Net Barter Terms of Trade between Primary Commodities and Manufactures: A Comment and Some Additional Evidence', *Economic Journal*, 95, pp. 781–8.

Sapsford, D. (1985c) 'The Prebisch–Singer Terms of Trade Hypothesis: Some New Evidence', *Economics Letters*, 18, pp. 229–32.

Sapsford, D. (1987) 'Primary Commodities in International Trade: An Analysis of Real Prices', *Applied Economics*, 19, pp. 317–22.

Sarkar, P. (1985) 'The Terms of Trade Experience of Britain since the Nineteenth Century', mimeo (Calcutta, Bangabasi College).

Savvides, A. (1984) 'Export Instability and Economic Growth: Some New Evidence', *Economic Development and Cultural Change*, 32, pp. 607–14.

Schmitz, H. (1984) 'Industrialization Strategies in Less Developed Countries: Some Lessons of Historical Experience', *Journal of Development Studies*, 21, pp. 1–21.

Sen, A. K. (1983) 'Development: Which Way Now?', *Economic Journal*, 93, pp. 745–62.

Singer, H. W. (1950) 'The Distribution of Gains between Investing and Borrowing Countries', *American Economic Review*, 40, pp. 473–5.

Singer, H. (1984) 'The Terms of Trade Controversy and the Evolution of Soft Financing: Early Years at the UN', in G. Meier and D. Seers (ed.) *Pioneers in Development* (New York, Oxford University Press).

Singer, H. W. (1986) 'Terms of Trade and Economic Development', *New Palgrave Dictionary*.

Siri, G. (1980) 'World Coffee Prices and the Economic Activity of the Central American Countries', unpublished report to USAID (Philadelphia, Wharton Econometric Forecasting Associates Inc.).

Sjaastad, L. A. (1980a) 'Commercial Policy Reform in Argentina: Implications and Consequences', mimeo (University of Chicago).

Sjaastad, L. A. (1980b) 'Commercial Policy, True Tariffs and Relative Prices', in J. Black and B. Hindley (eds) *Current Issues in Commercial Policy and Diplomacy* (London, Macmillan).

Sjaastad, L. A. (1980c) 'The Incidence of a Uniform Tariff in Uruguay', mimeo (University of Chicago).

Sjaastad, L. A. (ed.) (1981) *The Free Trade Movement in Latin America* (London, Macmillan).

Sjaastad, L. A. and Clements, K. W. (1981) 'The Incidence of Protection: Theory and Measurement', in Sjaastad (1981).

Smith, Adam (1904) *An Inquiry into the Nature and Causes of the Wealth of Nations*, ed. Edwin Cannan (London, Methuen) (first published 1776).

Spraos, J. (1980) 'The Statistical Debate on the Net Barter Terms of Trade between Primary Products and Manufactures', *Economic Journal*, 90, pp. 107–28.

Spraos, J. (1983) *Inequalising Trade?* (Oxford, Oxford University Press).

Spraos, J. (1985) 'Response to Sapsford', *Economic Journal*, 95, p. 789.

Spinnanger, D. (1984) 'Objectives and Impact of Economic Activity Zones – Some Evidence from Asia', *Weltwirtschaftliches Archiv*, 120, pp. 64–89.

Staelin, C. B. (1976) 'A General Equilibrium Model of Tariffs in a Non-Competitive Economy', *Journal of International Economics*, 6, pp. 39–63.

Stein, L. (1978) 'Export Instability and Development: A Review of Some Recent Findings', *Banca Nazionale del Lavoro*, 30, pp. 279–90.

Stewart, F. (1977) *Technology and Underdevelopment* (London, Macmillan).

Tan, G. (1983) 'Export Instability, Export Growth and GDP Growth', *Journal of Development Economics*, 12.

Teitel, S. and Thoumi, F. E. (1986) 'From Import Substitution to Exports: The Manufacturing Exports Experience of Argentina and Brazil', *Economic Development and Cultural Change*, 34, pp. 455–90.

Thirlwall, A. P. (1976) 'When is Trade More Valuable than Aid?', *Journal of Development Studies*, 13, pp. 35–41.

Toyne, B., Arpan, J. S., Barnett, A. H., Ricks, D. A. and Shrimp, T. A. (1984) *The Global Textile Industry* (London, Allen & Unwin).

Tumlir, J. and Till, T. (1971) 'Tariff Averaging in International Comparisons', in H. G. Grubel and H. G. Johnson (1971).

Tyler, W. G. (1976) 'Manufactured Exports and Employment Creation in Developing Countries: Some Empirical Evidence', *Economic Development and Cultural Change*, 24, pp. 355–73.

Tyler, W. G. (1981) 'Growth and Export Expansion in Developing Countries', *Journal of Development Economics*, 9, pp. 121–30.

Tyler, W. G. (1985) 'Effective Incentives for Domestic Market Sales and Exports: A View of Anti Export Biases and Commercial Policy in Brazil 1980–81', *Journal of Development Economics*, 18, pp. 219–42.

UNCTAD (1983) *Protectionism and Structural Adjustment: An Overview* (Geneva, United Nations).

UNIDO (1981) *World Industry in 1980* (New York, United Nations).

UNIDO (1982) *Changing Patterns of Trade in World Industry* (New York, United Nations).

UNIDO (1985) *Industry in the 1980s: Structural Change and Interdependence* (New York, United Nations).

UNIDO (1986) *International Comparative Advantage in Manufacturing* (Vienna, UNIDO).

United Nations (1949) *Relative Prices of Exports and Imports of Underdeveloped Countries* (New York, United Nations Department of Economic Affairs).

US Tariff Commission (1973) *Implications of Multinational Firms for World Trade and Investment and for US Trade and Labour* (Washington, DC, US Government Printing Office).

Vanek, J. (1971) 'Tariffs, Economic Welfare and Development Potential', *Economic Journal*, 81, pp. 904–13.

Van Wijnbergen, S. (1984) 'Inflation, Employment and the Dutch Disease in Oil Exporting Countries: A Short Run Disequilibrium Analysis', *Quarterly Journal of Economics*, 84, pp. 233–50.

Van Wijnbergen, S. (1985) 'Aid, Export Promotion and the Real Exchange Rate: An African Dilemma?', Country Policy Department Discussion Paper No. 1985–14 (Washington DC, World Bank).

Vernon, R. (1966) 'International Investment and International Trade in the Product Life Cycle', *Quarterly Journal of Economics*, 80, pp. 190–207.

Vernon, R. (1979) 'The Product Cycle Hypothesis in a New International Environment', *Oxford Bulletin of Economics and Statistics*, 41, pp. 255–67.

Viner, J. (1953) *International Trade and Economic Development* (Oxford, Clarendon Press).

Voivodas, C. (1974) 'The Effect of Foreign Exchange Instability on Growth', *The Review of Economics and Statistics*, 56, pp. 410–12.

Warr, P. (1983) 'The Jakarta Export Processing Zone, Benefits and Costs', *Bulletin of Indonesian Economic Studies*, 19.

Warr, P. (1984) Export Processing Zones in the Philippines. *ASEAN Economic Papers*, No. 20 (School of Pacific Studies, Australian National University).

Weisskopf, T. (1972) 'The Impact of Foreign Capital Inflow on Domestic Savings in Underdeveloped Countries', *Journal of International Economics*, 2, pp. 21–38.

Williamson, O. E. (1975) *Markets and Hierarchies: Analysis and Anti-trust Implications* (New York, Free Press).

Williamson, O. E. (1985) *The Economic Institutions of Capitalism: Firms, Markets, Relational Contracting* (New York, Free Press).

World Bank (1978) *World Development Report* (Washington, DC, World Bank).

World Bank (1983) *World Development Report* (New York and Oxford, Oxford University Press for the World Bank).

Yeats, A. (1985) 'On the Appropriate Interpretation of the Revealed Comparative Advantage Index: Implications of a Methodology Based on Industry Sector Analysis', *Weltwirtschaftliches Archiv*, 121, pp. 61–73.

Yotopoulos, P. A. and Nugent, J. B. (1977) *Economic Development: Empirical Investigations* (New York, Harper & Row).

Author Index

Adams, F. G.   96, 109, 110, 111, 112, 192
Alejandro, D.   159
Anderson, K.   48
Ansari, J.   19, 20
Arndt, H. W.   68

Bacha, E.   70
Balassa, B.   6, 10, 11, 12, 18, 32, 57, 74, 84, 190
Balasubramanyam, V. N.   77
Baldwin, R. E.   48, 190
Ballance, R.   13, 14, 19, 20, 59
Bauer, P. T.   171
Behrman, J. R.   96, 109, 110, 111, 112, 192
Bhagwati, J. N.   36, 159, 191
Bienefeld, M.   73
Birnberg, T.   188
Blackhurst, R.   1
Bowen, H.   13
Brecher, R. A.   68, 159
Bruno, M.   68, 191
Buckley, P. J.   137, 148

Caine, S.   101, 192
Cairncross, A. K.   188
Cassen, R.   170, 172
Casson, M. C.   137, 146, 148, 149, 150
Caves, R. E.   180
Chenery, H. B.   68, 74
Chow, G. C.   127
Chu, K. Y.   125
Clements, K. W.   92, 191
Cochrane, D.   123
Corden, W. M.   67, 171, 178, 181, 190, 191

Deardorff, A.   7, 8
DeVries, J.   50
Diaz, C.   92
Diaz-Alejandro, C. F.   63, 70
Donges, J.   10, 12
Dornbusch, R.   191
Drabicki, J.   8
Dunning, J. H.   148, 152

Ellsworth, P. T.   118
Emmanuel, A.   68

Fendt, R.   92
Findlay, R.   31, 32, 34, 64, 68, 189, 190
Finger, M.   19
Ford, D.   112
Forstner, H.   8, 13, 14
Frank, A. G.   32
Frey, B.   190
Frödel, F.   152

Garcia, R.   92
Glezakos, C.   105, 108, 109, 192
Goldfeld, S. M.   127
Greenaway, D.   64, 74, 84, 90, 92, 139, 174, 178, 184, 190, 191
Griffin, K.   170, 171
Griffith-Jones, S.   190

Haberler, G.   118
Hamada, K.   159, 193
Hamilton, C.   159, 193
Havrylyshyn, O.   43
Helleiner, G. K.   60, 69, 149
Higgins, B.   120
Hillman, A.   8
Hinrichs, J.   174
Hirschman, A. D.   34, 59
Hitiris, T.   174, 178
Horrell, S.   172
Hudson, J.   172
Hughes, H.   46, 48

Jones, R. W.   180
Johnson, H. G.   167, 194

Kaldor, N.   118
Keesing, D. B.   65
Kenen, P. B.   104, 105
Kirkpatrick, C.   64, 69, 73
Kitchin, P. D.   81
Knudsen, O.   101, 106, 192
Kojima, K.   151
Kol, J.   139
Kondratieff, N. D.   192

206

Kravis, I. B.   188
Krueger, A. O.   64, 65, 74, 189, 191
Krugman, P.   190
Kubuta, K.   191
Kunimoto, K.   12
Kuznets, S.   189

Lall, D.   70, 149
Lam, N. V.   108
Lancieri, E.   107
Lasaga, M.   112
Lawson, C.   191
Lecraw, D. J.   151
Lee, J.   146
Lee, J. K.   169
Leith, J. C.   191
Lewis, S. R. Jr.   174
Lewis, W. A.   28, 30, 31, 32, 48, 192
Lim, D.   106, 107, 191
Little, I.   36, 64, 70, 73, 172, 188, 190

MacBean, A. I.   104, 127, 191, 192
McKinnon, R.   68
Maizels, A.   104, 169
Meier,   120
Michaely, M.   32, 74
Milner, C. R.   64, 90, 92, 139, 191
Moran, C.   108, 191, 192
Morgan, T.   118
Morrison, T. K.   125
Mosley, P.   170, 172
Murray, D.   13, 14, 51
Murray, R.   133
Musgrave, P.   181
Musgrave, R. A.   178, 181
Myint, H.   64, 190

Nakajo, S.   152
Neary, P.   171
Nixson, F.   69
Nugent, J. B.   192
Nurkse, R.   30
Nziramasanga, M.   112, 192

Obideewu, C. F.   112, 192
OECD   170, 172
Orcutt, G. H.   123
Ozawa, T.   151

Palma, G.   69
Papanek   170
Parnes, A.   101, 106, 192

Pearce, R. D.   148
Peston, M. H.   181
Pobukadee, J.   112
Prebisch, R.   69, 118, 121, 192
Priovolos, T.   112

Quandt, R. E.   127

Rangarajan, C.   96, 111
Ray, G.   117
Rayment, P.   139
Read, R. A.   151
Resnick, S.   188
Reynolds, L. G.   32, 33, 36, 75, 100
Ricardo, D.   26, 64
Riedel, J.   10, 12
Rodriguez, E.   190

Sahabdeen, M. R.   165
Samuelson, H. F.   151
Samuelson, P. A.   32, 65
Sapsford, D.   119, 123, 126, 127, 128, 129, 192, 193
Sarkar, P.   121
Savvides, A.   109
Schmitz, H.   59, 72
Scitovsky, T.   36, 70, 172, 190
Scott, M.   36, 70, 172, 190, 191
Sen, A. K.   73
Singer, H.   4, 19, 20, 69, 117, 118, 119, 120, 121, 192
Siri, G.   112
Sjaastad, L. A.   92, 191
Smith, A.   26, 64, 138
Spinnanger, D.   163, 165
Spraos, J.   4, 118, 120, 121, 122, 123, 128
Srinivasan, T.   191
Stein, L.   191
Stewart, F.   69
Sundarajan   96, 111
Svennson, L. E. O.   159, 193

Takayama, A.   8
Tan, G.   108
Teitel, S.   75, 86
Thirlwall, A. P.   168, 169, 172
Thoumi, F. E.   75, 86
Till, T.   81
Toyne, B.   152
Tumlir, J.   81
Tyler, W. E.   32, 73

UNCTAD   11, 84
UNIDO   12, 15, 16, 17
United Nations   109, 192

Vanek, J.   181
Van Wijnbergen, S.   171
Vernon, R.   133
Viner, J.   118
Voivodas, C.   104, 105, 106

Waelbroeck, J.   46, 48
Warr, P.   163
Weekes, A. J.   174, 178
Weisskopf, T.   170
Williamson, O.   137
Wolf, M.   43
World Bank   37, 43, 188, 189, 190

Yeats, A.   11
Yotopoulos, P. A.   192

Subject Index

aid *see* trade and aid
arms-length trade   133
ASEAN   151
asymmetrical expectations   192
autarky   9, 65

bias in trade regime   56–9, 72–3
by-product distortions   67

classical theories of trade   26, 27, 64–5
Common Fund   97
community indifference curve   66
comparative advantage
  Balassa measure   12
  cardinal measures   11
  and country size   8–9
  Donges–Riedel measure   12
  empirical studies   15–21
  net export measure   12
  normalised net export measure   12
  patterns of   15–21
  revealed   7–15
  stages approach   2, 18–19
  and trade performance   2, 21
  and trade restrictions   8–9
Compensatory Financing Facility   97
competing and non competing
  imports   45–6
COMECON   132

demand for precautionary balances
  101
domestic resource costs   70, 78, 190–1
dualism   34
Dutch disease   171
duty drawback   62

economies of scale   27, 65, 150
Engel's Law   119
effective protection
  effective tariffs   3, 62, 70–1
  empirical evidence   82–6
  interpretation of   81–2
  inter-country comparisons   84–6
  inter-temporal comparisons   86
  and intra-firm trade   142–3

  measurement of   81–2
  negative   79–80, 84–5
  theory of   78–80
  variance of   83–6
effective subsidy   57, 58
elasticities
  demand elasticity   31
  income elasticity   49–51, 118
  supply elasticity   31
excess costs of import substitution   167
exchange controls   56
exchange-rate overvaluation   70, 71
export instability
  cross-country studies   102–3, 104–11
  empirical research on   102–16
  and growth   3, 95–116
  hypotheses of   98–101
  and investment   98–101
  time-series studies   103, 111–13
export-oriented strategies   *see* export
  promotion
export pessimism   3, 32
export-processing zones   157–65
  definition of   165–6
  evidence on   163–5
  and FDI   158, 162
  incentives   157–8
  objectives of   158–9
  and protection   93
  welfare effects   4
export promotion   3, 55–7, 61–3
  evidence on   72–4

factor endowments   18, 27, 102, 160
  see also Heckscher–Ohlin theorem
fiscal importance of trade taxes
  see revenue effects of trade taxes

gains from trade   26, 66, 69
Group of   77, 95

Heckscher–Ohlin theorem   7, 14, 27,
  65–6
hierarchy of policies   67

IMF   128

import substitution
  and industrialisation   2, 3, 55–7,
    59–61
  evidence on   70–2, 77
incidence analysis   3, 87–94, 189
  empirical evidence on   92–4
  interpretation of   91–2
  measurement of   90–1
  theory of   87–90
industrialisation in LDCs   36–7
inward orientation   *see* import
  substitution
infant-industry protection   67–8
instability indexes   104–9
intermediate goods   15–17, 79–80,
  138–41
  see also multinational enterprises
internalisation   135
intra-firm trade   69
  control of   151–2
  and LDCs   132–56
intra-industry trade   9, 139
ISIC   46, 48

linkages   98

marginal rate of substitution   66
marginal rate of transformation   66
maximum revenue tariff   179–80
mixed strategies   55, 57, 75
multinational enterprises
  and intermediate goods   4
  and intra-firm trade   69, 132–56
  and technology   4
  and transfer pricing   4, 69, 133
MITI   132, 152

net barter terms of trade   *see* terms of
  trade
New International Economic Order
  69
NICs   16–17, 57, 61–2, 141
non-tradeables and protection   87–9
non-traded inputs   80–1
non-traditional exportables   90–3

OECD   139
openness   1
optimal intervention   67, 190
optimal rate of revenue tariff   179–80
outward processing   16

Prebisch–Singer thesis   *see* terms of
  trade decline
product-cycle model   19–20, 133
propensity
  to circulate   136, 138–40
  to internalise   136–7, 146–151
  to trade   136, 141–6
protection
  structure of in DMEs   48–9, 132
  structure of in LDCs   79–94, 134

quotas   56, 93

revenue effects of trade taxes
  economic effects of   177–9
  evidence   174–6
  and revenue interdependency   181–4
Ryczynski theorem   160, 193

saving ratios   27, 101, 106, 169–70
shift parameter   89, 91–2, 191
SITC   139
STABEX   97
structural adjustment loan   190
structuralism   31–4, 59–61, 68–70
structure of exports in LDCs   39–48,
  97

tariff averaging   81
taxable capacity   174
terms of trade
  empirical evidence on   121–31
  secular decline   2, 3, 31–2, 69,
    117–31
  and structural instability   126–7
trade performance
  and comparative advantage   2, 6–24
  measures of   2, 6
trade and aid   4, 166–73
  comparative effects of   167–8
  and public expenditure   171–2
  and relative prices   170–1
  and savings   169–70
trade strategies
  characteristics of   56–63
  and development   55–76
trade taxes, fiscal importance of   5
  see also tariff averaging, effective
    protection
traditional exportables of   90–3
transportation costs   142

true subsidy   89, 91–2, 189
true tariff   89, 91–2, 189
two-gap models   68

UNCTAD   4, 121, 128, 166
unequal exchange   69–70

value added   79–80
   negative   79–80, 84–86

World Bank   61, 84, 122–3, 125–6,
      188, 189, 190, 193
world trade
   as an engine of growth   3, 25–54
   expansion   1
   and output   1, 2
   volume   1, 2

X-efficiency   76